MW00749403

Understanding Pascal:
Turbo Version

Understanding Pascal:
Turbo Version

Susan K. Baumann
B.A., Computer Educator, Computer Programmer.

Steven L. Mandell
B.A., B.S.Ch.E., M.B.A., D.B.A., J.D.
Software Developer; Computer Lawyer;
Associate Professor of Computer Systems,
Bowling Green University.

West Publishing Company
St. Paul   New York   Los Angeles   San Francisco

Copy Editors: Pat Lewis, Cheryl Drivdahl
Composition: Rolin Graphics
Artwork: Rolin Graphics
Cover Artwork: Sinfel 1977. 99¼ x 49⅝" by Victor Vasarely

COPYRIGHT © 1990 By WEST PUBLISHING COMPANY
610 Opperman Drive
P.O. Box 64526
St. Paul, MN 55164-0526

Printed in the United States of America

96 95 94 93 92   8 7 6 5 4 3 2

Library of Congress Cataloging-in-Publication Data

Baumann, Susan.
    Understanding Pascal : Turbo version / Susan Baumann, Steven L.
Mandell.
        p.   cm.
    Includes index.
    ISBN 0-314-49897-4
    1. Turbo Pascal (Computer program)   I. Mandell, Steven L.
II. Title.
QA76.73.P2B38   1990
005.26—dc19   88-34659
                                                                          CIP

Photo Credits
3 (*left*) Courtesy of International Business Machines Corporation; **3** (*right*) Courtesy of Blythe Software; **4** (*top left*) Photograph courtesy of BASF Systems Corporation; **4** (*bottom left*) Courtesy of the Perkin-Elmer Corporation; **4** (*top right*) Photograph Courtesy of BASF Systems Corporation; **4** (*bottom right*) Photo courtesy of COMSHARE, Inc. © COMSHARE, Inc. 1987; **5** Courtesy of AT&T Bell Laboratories; **6** Courtesy of AT&T Bell Laboratories; **7** Courtesy of International Business Machines Corporation; **8** Courtesy of International Business Machines Corporation; **11** Courtesy of International Business Machines Corporation.

∞

Contents in Brief

Contents

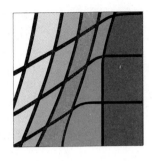

CHAPTER 3
The Parts of a Program   39

CHAPTER 11
Arrays   237

CHAPTER 12
Records and Sets   266

CHAPTER 13
Files   291

CHAPTER 14
Graphics   313

APPENDIX A
Rules for Creating Identifiers   A-1

APPENDIX B
Syntax Diagrams   A-2

APPENDIX C
Turbo Pascal Reserved Words   A-13

APPENDIX D
Turbo Pascal Operators   A-14

Preface

In recent years, Pascal has become widely accepted as an effective language for teaching structured problem-solving and programming skills. The increasing popularity of Borland's Turbo Pascal has been a driving force behind its success. Therefore, this textbook teaches the student to use the computer as a problem-solving tool with the language implementation being Turbo Pascal, Version 4.0. Turbo Pascal is an easy-to-learn structured programming language that includes many useful extensions to standard Pascal. Its screen-driven menu provides a convenient means of typing in, executing, and saving programs. The text is written to allow the student to begin using the system early in the course and to gradually build on these skills.

Because many schools continue to use Version 3, boxes indicating differences between Version 3 and Version 4 are placed throughout the text. Difference boxes for Turbo Pascal for the Macintosh are also included. Appendix I explains Borland's newest version of Turbo Pascal, Version 5. Fortunately, at the level of this textbook there are few differences between Version 4 and Version 5. Therefore, the textbook can easily be used with Version 5, using Appendix I to inform the student of significant differences.

Each chapter contains standard pedagogical devices: A chapter outline, objectives, and an introduction provide a framework for permitting the student to focus on the material being presented. Numerous sample programs are included to help the student make a smooth transition from the abstraction of language rules to the concrete design of program instructions. Learning checks with answers in Appendix K are included as a means of self-testing before proceeding to the next section. Summary points and a vocabulary list are used to reinforce the most important concepts presented in the chapter. Finally, a chapter test and programming problems allow the teacher and students to evaluate the level of mastery of the material.

The teacher's manual to support this textbook is divided into three parts: Classroom Administration, Test Bank, and Additional Teacher Materials. In the administration section a standard format is used for each chapter: Summary, Objectives, Vocabulary, Outline, Learning Activities, Answers to Chapter Test, Solutions to Programming Problems in Text, and Additional Programming Problems with Solutions. The test bank section is divided by chapter and includes over six hundred multiple choice questions with answer key. The final section of the teacher's manual includes a resource list and expanded glossary. Blackline masters for use as transparencies, tests, or student study sheets are also available.

▬▬▬ TO THE STUDENT

In writing and editing *Understanding Pascal: Turbo Version*, the authors and editors had two goals in mind: To help you learn the Turbo Pascal language and the problem solving skills needed to create well designed programs using that language. This text includes a number of features to help you recognize important ideas and to make remembering the material easier.

Chapter Outline

Each chapter begins with an outline that gives you an overall picture of what is covered in the chapter and prepares you to read more effectively.

Objectives

This list which follows the chapter outline tells you specifically what you will achieve by studying and understanding the chapter.

Learning Checks

Short-answer questions are interspersed throughout the chapter. Answers are given in Appendix K. You will be able to check your progress if you stop to answer these questions as you study. If you are able to correctly answer the Learning Check questions, you are ready to go on to the next section.

Sample Computer Programs

The many sample computer programs will help you understand the chapter and learn how to write well-designed programs.

Summary Points

A point-by-point summary at the end of each chapter restates the important ideas covered to make studying and remembering easier.

Vocabulary List

A list of the important new terms and concepts is included at the end of each chapter as another study aid. A complete glossary appears at the end of the book.

Chapter Test

End of chapter tests with vocabulary and word problems will help you in determining how much of the chapter material you remember and understand.

Programming Problems

Programming problems are included at the end of Chapters 3 through 14 to help you build good programming skills. These problems have been divided into levels to provide a variety of difficulty.

Color Coding

Color coding has been used in programming examples throughout the text to assist the reader. The legend for this coding is shown below:

Highlighted Statements

Computer Output

User Response

■■■■ REVIEWERS

A special thanks to Dr. James R. Aman, Wilmington College, Wilmington, Ohio for his contributions as a technical reviewer of this text. Additionally, we thank the following:

Kit Janes
Cedar High School
Cedar City, Utah

Joseph M. Klimaszewski
Stratford High School
Stratford, Connecticut

Otis McNaught
East Troy High School
East Troy, Wisconsin

Gary Ross
Hoisington High School
Hoisington, Kansas

Roger A. Smith
Jefferson High School
Monroe, Michigan

■■■■ ACKNOWLEDGMENTS

Many individuals have added their professional expertise to the development of this textbook. Many thanks are owed to Shannan Christy on Instructor Manual preparation and Linda Cupp and Cheryl Drivdahl on manuscript preparation. The design of this text is a credit to the talents and energy of Terry Casey. A final thanks to Carole Grumney for her continual support and encouragement.

CHAPTER 1

Introduction to Computer Programming and Pascal

OBJECTIVES

After studying this chapter, you should be able to:

- Explain the three types of tasks that computers are able to perform.
- Explain what a computer system is and list its three basic components.
- Name the two parts of the central processing unit and explain what each part does.
- Describe various peripheral devices and their purposes.
- Describe the process of compiling and executing a program.
- Give a brief history of the Pascal language.

OUTLINE

▬▬▬ INTRODUCTION

A computer is an electronic machine with many different parts that work together to perform a specific job. Like any machine, the computer will only do what it is told to do. The list of instructions that work together to allow the computer to solve a specific problem is called a **program** (or **software**).

Programs must be written in a language that the computer can understand. Such languages are called **programming languages**. A person who writes programs is called a **computer programmer** (or a **programmer** for short). Programmers have a great deal of power and can make a computer do many interesting things. However, because the computer cannot think for itself, an exact list of instructions must be written. If a single step is left out of a program, the results may be completely different from what was expected. If the right words and punctuation aren't used, the computer won't understand the instructions.

This book will teach you the programming language Pascal. You will also learn how to write programs in a clear, logical way.

▬▬▬ WHAT CAN COMPUTERS DO?

Computers like the ones shown in Figure 1–1 can be very useful to humans. Basically, however, they can only perform three types of tasks:

1. They can perform arithmetic (addition, subtraction, and so forth).
2. They can make comparisons (determining whether a given value is greater than, equal to, or less than another value).

The IBM PS/2   The Macintosh Plus

FIGURE 1–1 TWO POPULAR MICROCOMPUTERS

3. They can perform storage and retrieval operations (such as saving a program on a disk so that it can be used later).

If there are so few things computers can actually do, what makes them so useful? Computers are useful for three basic reasons:

1. They are fast.
2. They are accurate.
3. They can store and retrieve information.

With care, a person can add 100 numbers together and get the correct result. But the chances of making an error somewhere along the way are considerable. It is also a boring job. This is the kind of task that is ideal for the computer. The computer can do the work very quickly. It will not get bored or add four and four and get seven. Also, it can store the information away to be used again.

PARTS OF A COMPUTER SYSTEM

The physical parts of the computer system are called **hardware**. Regardless of the type of system, the three basic components of a computer system are the same; they are the central processing unit, the primary storage unit or main memory, and peripheral devices. Figure 1–2 illustrates how these three components are related.

The Central Processing Unit

The part of the computer system that does the processing is called the **central processing unit (CPU)**. In a microcomputer, the CPU is

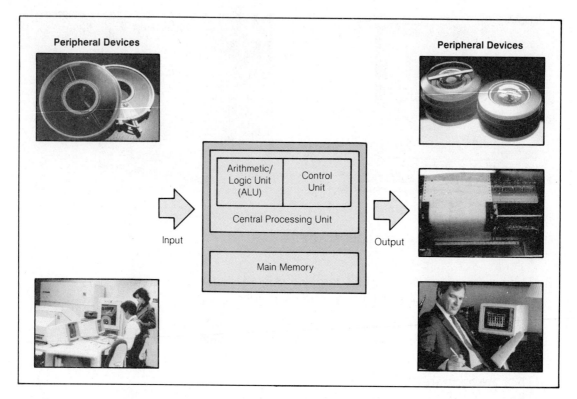

FIGURE 1–2 THE BASIC PARTS OF A COMPUTER SYSTEM

contained on a single silicon chip. This silicon chip is called the micro-processor. A microprocessor is shown in Figure 1–3. The CPU is the "brain" of the computer and is composed of two major parts: the control unit and the arithmetic/logic unit.

The Control Unit.   The **control unit** is in charge of the activities of the CPU. It does not process or store data itself, but instructs various parts of the computer to perform these jobs. The instructions that the user gives the computer are interpreted by the control unit, which sends out signals to electrical circuits to execute the instructions. The appropriate input devices are directed to send the necessary data to the computer. The control unit also keeps track of which parts of the program have al-ready been executed and which ones remain. Finally, it controls the ex-ecution of specific instructions, collects the output, and sends it to the designated output device, for example, a display screen.

The Arithmetic/Logic Unit.   The **arithmetic/logic unit (ALU)** is the computer's own personal mathematician. It performs arithmetic com-putations and logic operations. A logic operation makes a comparison

FIGURE 1-3 A MICROPROCESSOR
In a microcomputer, the CPU is on a single chip called a microprocessor.

and then takes action based on the result. For example, consider the instruction, "If today is Friday, then pick up your paycheck and go to the bank; if not, don't." This is not exactly the type of logic statement a computer would work with, but the idea is the same. The computer would work with a logic statement more like this: "If this is the end of the input data, then make the calculations and print the results; if not, read the rest of the input data." Arithmetic and logic statements are the only type of instructions that the ALU can execute.

1. What is a computer program?
2. Name the three basic types of tasks that computers can perform.
3. What are the three parts of the computer system?
4. What two types of operations can an arithmetic/logic unit perform?

LEARNING CHECK 1-1

Main Memory

Main memory is the storage area where the computer keeps information that is given to it. This storage area holds instructions, data, and the intermediate and final results of processing. Main memory is made up of a large number of storage locations, each of which can hold a small amount of information. These storage locations may be thought of as mailboxes lined up in a row.

Peripheral Devices

Peripheral devices are those devices attached to the computer itself. The computer and all of its peripheral devices are referred to as the computer system. Printers and disk drives are common peripheral devices. These devices can be divided into three categories: input devices, output devices, and secondary storage devices. Programs and data that are entered into a computer to be processed are called **input**. The word **data** refers to facts that have been collected but not organized in any meaningful way. When data is processed, or converted to some meaningful form, the result is **information**. For example, in a national election, the records of all the votes cast for a candidate for the office of president are data. When these votes are tabulated and the final totals are determined, the result is information.

Input devices are used to enter programs or data into the computer so that it can be processed. There are many input devices; some examples are a keyboard (shown in Figure 1–4), a mouse, and an optical scanning device (often used to read price codes at grocery stores). A given computer system can have many different input devices.

FIGURE 1–4 A MONITOR KEYBOARD
The keyboard is a commonly used input device.

Output devices, such as monitor screens and printers, allow the user to read the computer's **output**, or processing results. Displaying output on the screen, as shown in Figure 1–5, gives the user the results in a convenient, readable form; this output is referred to as **soft copy**. These results are lost as soon as something else replaces them on the screen. Printing the results on paper, on the other hand, gives the user a way of permanently saving this information so that he or she can refer to it at a later time. This output is called **hard copy**. A printer that can be used to obtain hard copy is shown in Figure 1–6. As with input devices, a particular computer system can have many different output devices.

Computers have only a limited amount of storage space in main memory. Programs, information, and data that need to be saved for later use can be transferred to **secondary storage** (also called **auxiliary storage**). Secondary storage devices allow programs, data, and results to be saved on secondary storage such as magnetic tape or floppy diskettes. Disk and tape drives are commonly used secondary storage devices. When the computer needs to process something on secondary storage, it can be transferred back into the computer's main memory. Although it takes more time to access items in secondary storage than those in main memory, secondary storage can store enormous quantities of data at reasonable cost.

FIGURE 1–5 A DISPLAY SCREEN
A display screen can be used to temporarily display output.

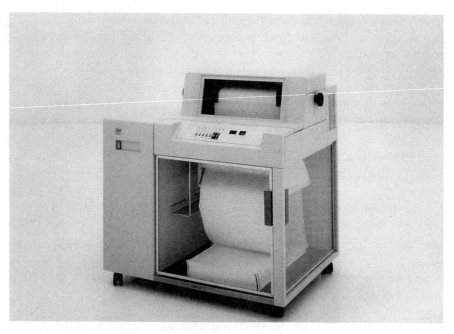

FIGURE 1-6 A PRINTER
Hard copy output can be obtained by using a printer.

LEARNING CHECK 1-2

1. Give a definition for peripheral devices.
2. Another name for secondary storage is _____.
3. Explain the difference between hard copy and soft copy. Give an advantage of each.
4. How is main memory different from secondary storage?

COMPILING AND EXECUTING A PROGRAM

Machine language is the only language that the computer can execute directly. Programs written in any other language (such as Pascal or BASIC) must be translated into machine language before they can be executed. Machine language statements consist of series of 1s and 0s (called binary code) that represent "high" and "low" states of electronic devices. Usually a 1 represents the "high" state and a 0 the "low" state. Every operation that the computer is capable of performing (such as addition or storing a value in a memory location) is indicated by a specific binary code. The programmer must use the proper code for each operation. Here is an example of a few machine language statements:

```
1010    0000    0000    0000    0000    1101
1010    1101    0000    1110    0000    1101
```

Because these series of 1s and 0s have no meaning to humans, writing machine language programs is very error-prone. In addition, machine language is different for each type of computer. To simplify programming, **high-level languages** such as Pascal have been developed. These high-level languages use English-like words in their instructions. Consider the following Pascal statement:

```
C := A + B;
```

Even a nonprogrammer would have little difficulty in understanding that this statement adds two values together (A and B) and assigns the sum to C.

One of the advantages of using high-level languages is that the same program can generally be run on different types of computers. For example, a Turbo Pascal program that runs on an IBM Personal Computer can also be run on an Apple Macintosh SE. This is a distinct advantage over machine language, which is very different for each type of central processing unit.

However, as previously mentioned, all high-level language programs must be translated into machine language before execution. The program to be translated is referred to as the **source program** because it is the source of the translation. This translation can be accomplished by a program referred to as a **compiler**. The compiler translates the entire source program into machine language, creating an **object program** that consists of a machine language version of the source program. Once this object program is loaded into the computer's memory, the computer can execute it. When a program is executed, the computer reads the object program from beginning to end and does what the program statements instruct it to do. Figure 1–7 illustrates this process.

▬▬▬ BACKGROUND ON PASCAL

Pascal is considered to be one of the best general-purpose computer programming languages. A general-purpose language is one that can be used to write many different types of programs.

Pascal was designed by Professor Niklaus Wirth of Switzerland in 1969 and 1970. He created it for his students to use while learning to write programs. Professor Wirth named the language after Blaise Pascal, a seventeenth-century mathematician and philosopher. Pascal was

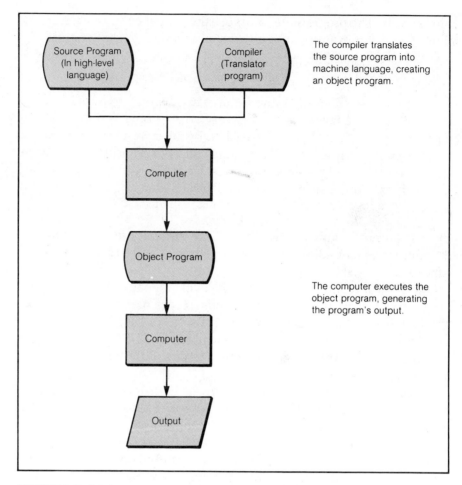

FIGURE 1-7 COMPILING AND EXECUTING A PROGRAM

only 19 when he invented a mechanical adding machine to help his father perform his job as a tax collector, which involved doing a great deal of arithmetic. Pascal and his adding machine are shown in Figure 1–8.

**LEARNING
CHECK
1-3**

1. The only language that a computer can execute directly is _____ language.
2. What are some characteristics of high-level languages?
3. How does a compiler work?
4. Who was Pascal?

 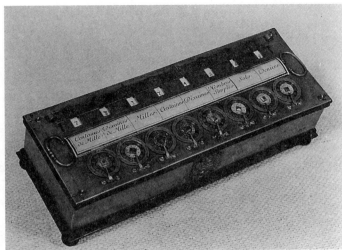

FIGURE 1–8 PASCAL AND HIS ADDING MACHINE

The version of Pascal taught in this textbook is Turbo Pascal for the IBM Personal Computer. Turbo Pascal is similar to the Pascal developed by Niklaus Wirth, but contains some additional features. It was developed by Borland International, Inc.

▐▬▬▬ SUMMARY POINTS

- This chapter has discussed some basic facts about computers. Computers are electronic machines that can be used to solve problems. A program is a series of instructions that a computer uses to solve a problem. It must be written in a programming language.
- Computers can only perform three types of tasks: arithmetic operations, comparisons, and storage and retrieval operations.
- Computers are useful to us because they are fast and accurate and can store information.
- A computer system has three basic components: the central processing unit (CPU), the main memory, and the peripheral devices.
- The CPU is composed of the control unit, which controls the order in which computer operations are performed, and the arithmetic/logic unit, which performs arithmetic and makes comparisons.
- The computer stores information in its main memory.
- Peripheral devices allow programs and data to be entered into the computer and program results to be output.
- Output devices such as monitor screens display soft copy whereas printers provide hard copy.

- Secondary storage such as magnetic tapes or disks allows programs and data to be stored permanently. When these items need to be processed again, they can be copied into the computer's main memory.
- The only statements that a computer can execute directly are machine language statements. These statements consist of series of 1s and 0s.
- High-level languages, such as Pascal, contain English-like statements that are much easier for people to understand than machine language. However, before these statements can be executed, they must be translated into machine language. A program called a compiler can be used to perform this translation.
- Pascal is the programming language taught in this book. It is a high-level programming language developed by Professor Niklaus Wirth in 1969 and 1970.

▄▄ VOCABULARY LIST

Arithmetic/logic unit (ALU)	Machine language
Auxiliary storage	Main memory
Central processing unit (CPU)	Object program
Compiler	Output
Computer programmer	Peripheral device
Control unit	Program
Data	Programmer
Hard copy	Programming language
Hardware	Secondary storage
High-level language	Soft copy
Information	Software
Input	Source program

▄▄ CHAPTER TEST

Vocabulary

Match a term from the numbered column with the description from the lettered column that best fits the term.

1. Compiler

2. Machine language

a. The physical components of the computer system.

b. Facts that the computer uses to obtain results.

3. Arithmetic/logic unit

c. The part of the computer that performs the processing.

4. Central processing unit

d. A person who writes instructions for the computer to use to solve a problem.

5. Software

e. A program that translates an entire source program into machine language. The resulting program is the object program.

6. Main memory

f. The part of the CPU that performs arithmetic and logic operations.

7. Output

g. The part of the CPU that determines the order in which computer operations will be performed.

8. Data

h. Output that is printed on paper.

9. Control unit

i. Any programming language using English-like statements that must be translated into machine language before execution.

10. High-level language

j. Data that is processed so that it is meaningful to the user.

11. Program

k. Data that is submitted to the computer so that the computer can process it.

12. Input

l. The only type of instructions that the computer can execute directly.

13. Object program

m. The storage area where the computer keeps programs, data, and processing results.

14. Information

n. The program that results when a compiler translates a source program into machine language.

15. Soft copy

o. Results the computer obtains after processing input.

16. Hard copy

p. A device, such as a monitor screen or a printer, that is attached to the computer.

17. Peripheral device

q. A list of instructions written by a programmer that the computer can use to solve a specific problem.

18. Hardware

r. A language that can be used to give instructions to a computer.

19. Programming language

s. Storage such as floppy diskettes or magnetic tape that is not a part of the main memory.

20. Computer programmer   t. Output displayed on the monitor screen.
21. Secondary storage   u. A computer program.
22. Source program   v. The program that is submitted to a compiler to be translated into machine language so that the computer is able to execute it.

Questions

1. Computers are actually very limited in the types of tasks they can do. Name several reasons why they are still useful to people.
2. Into which of the three categories of computer functions can each of the following be placed?

   a. Finding the square of a number.
   b. Storing a program so that it can be run later.
   c. Determining which of two letters comes first alphabetically.
   d. Calculating a grade point average by adding all the grades together and dividing by the number of classes.

3. Explain the difference between computer software and computer hardware.
4. Give an example of an arithmetic operation a computer could perform. Give an example of a comparison (or logic) operation that a computer could perform.
5. Define hard copy and soft copy. Give an advantage of each.
6. Name the peripheral devices used by the computer system you will be using for this class. If you are not certain, check with your instructor. What is the purpose of each of these devices?
7. Name an advantage that main memory has over secondary storage. Name an advantage that secondary storage has over main memory.
8. Why is it difficult to write programs in machine language?
9. Explain how a source program is related to an object program.

CHAPTER 2

The Programming Process and the Turbo Pascal System

OBJECTIVES

After studying this chapter, you should be able to:

- List the six steps in developing a solution to a programming problem.
- Explain what is meant by understanding a problem.
- Develop algorithms for simple problems.
- Define top-down program design.
- Discuss the characteristics of structured programming.
- Draw flowcharts for simple problem solutions.
- Explain the difference between a single-alternative decision step and a double-alternative decision step.
- Write pseudocode for simple problem solutions.
- Explain what is meant by a loop.
- Access the Turbo Pascal System.
- Type in a simple programming example and execute it.
- Save programs on disk and load them back into the computer's main memory.

OUTLINE

■■■ INTRODUCTION

People who are good programmers are also good problem solvers. Writing a program is a way of solving a problem by using a computer. This chapter will examine problem solving in a systematic way. The steps in reaching a solution to a problem will be explained. Flowcharting and pseudocoding will also be introduced in this chapter as two ways of representing a solution to a programming problem.

■■■ STEPS IN PROBLEM SOLVING

People solve problems every day. Most problems have a number of solutions. There is often more than one way to arrive at the correct answer to a problem. Figure 2–1 shows a maze. There are many ways of getting from the start to the finish in this maze, but one way is considerably shorter than the others. By stopping for a minute and looking ahead, the most direct route can easily be found. Programming problems generally are not this easy to solve, but a little time spent thinking about the problem and possible solutions can save considerable time and trouble later. Here are some basic steps that can help the programmer to develop a solution to a programming problem efficiently:

1. Understand the problem.
2. Develop a solution to the problem.

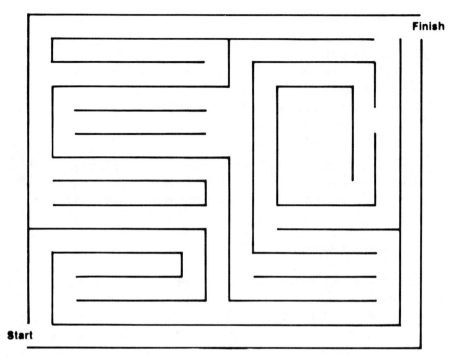

FIGURE 2-1 A MAZE

3. Write the program.
4. Type the program into a computer and run it.
5. Correct any errors in the program.
6. Test the program.

In this chapter, the first two steps will be discussed in detail. Steps 3 through 6 will be covered in the remainder of this text.

Understanding the Problem

It is impossible to get somewhere if it is not clear where you are going. To write a program, it is necessary to know what results are needed. This means the programmer must have a clear idea of what the program's output should be. Once this has been decided, the programmer can determine what input is needed to obtain the output.

Let's practice defining and documenting a simple problem. Suppose you need a program to convert a given number of feet to miles. The output is the number of miles in the specified number of feet. The input is the number of feet to be converted. You will also need to know the conversion formula (that is, how many feet there are in one mile). You now have all of the information needed to solve the problem. This information could be stated as follows:

Problem Definition:
Write a program to convert a given number of feet to miles.
Needed Output:
The number of miles in a given number of feet. This output will be stated as follows:
There are xxx.xx miles in xxxxx.xx feet.
Needed Input:
The number of feet to be converted.

The programmer must not only understand the problem thoroughly, but must also be able to write the statement of the problem in a clear, concise style. This is referred to as documenting the problem.

Developing a Solution

Once the necessary input and output are determined, it is time to write down the steps needed to obtain the correct results from the input. A sequence of steps that can be used to solve a problem is called an **algorithm**. The algorithm must list every step necessary to obtain the correct results from the input. Remember that the computer cannot tell if a step is left out or placed in the wrong order. It depends on the programmer to tell it everything.

Sample Problem

Solving programming problems is like many jobs people do every day. Making a pizza is a good example. The desired output is a pizza that tastes good. First, the exact type of pizza must be determined. In this example, the desired output will be a pepperoni pizza. Once the type of pizza has been decided, it will be apparent what ingredients are needed. For a pepperoni pizza the input might look something like this:

Dough	Toppings
flour	sauce
water	cheese
yeast	pepperoni
salt	

The needed input and output are shown in Figure 2–2.

Next, the steps in making the pizza must be listed. The major steps could look like this:

1. Preheat oven.
2. Prepare dough.
3. Put sauce and toppings on pizza.
4. Bake the pizza.

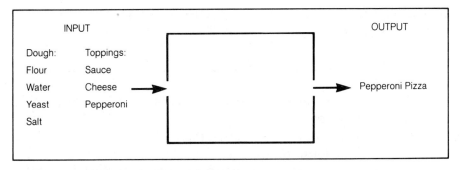

FIGURE 2–2 INPUT AND OUTPUT FOR MAKING A PIZZA

These steps are a basic algorithm for solving the problem of making a pizza. This algorithm can be further refined by breaking each of these steps down into many smaller steps. For example, step 2 could be broken down this way:

1. Read the dough recipe.
2. Get the ingredients ready.
3. Measure each ingredient.
4. Mix the ingredients.
5. Let the dough rise.
6. Grease the pan.
7. Spread the dough in the pan.

Even some of these steps could be broken down further. Step 3 could contain many substeps. Figure 2–3 shows how making a pizza could be broken into many smaller jobs. In Figure 2–3, only step 2, preparing the

FIGURE 2–3 STRUCTURE CHART FOR MAKING A PIZZA

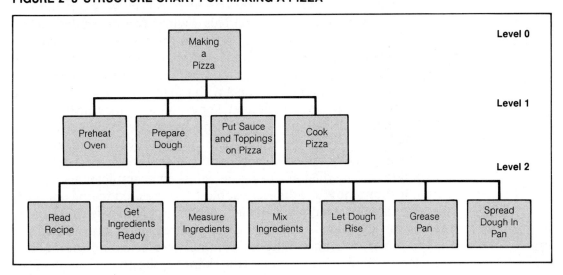

dough, has been broken down further. Of course, this could be done for each of the steps.

**LEARNING
CHECK
2-1**

1. What are the six steps necessary in developing the solution to a programming problem?
2. What is meant by understanding the problem?
3. What is an algorithm?
4. Write an algorithm for a task you have performed, such as making a bed, building a shop project, or cleaning your room.

TOP-DOWN DESIGN

In many ways, writing a program is similar to making a pizza. A small program can probably be written all at once. A large program is much easier to write if it has been divided into **subprograms** or **modules**. Each of these subprograms performs a specific task. Pascal is a **structured programming language**. Structured programming languages have two basic characteristics:

1. They allow a program to be easily divided into subprograms.
2. They allow the programmer to control the order in which statements will be executed in a clear, efficient way.

The first characteristic of structured programming will be discussed here.

Developing a solution to a large problem can be very difficult because of the large amount of detail. This is where **top-down design** becomes helpful. Top-down design refers to the process of breaking a large problem into smaller and smaller subparts. Another way of putting it is that the programmer is going from the general to the specific. This allows the programmer to deal with the major problems first and worry about the specific details later. For example, in making the pizza, the first item dealt with was not how much flour needed to be used in the dough. This would not be dealt with until the subtask of making the dough was actually undertaken. Structure charts are often used in top-down design. The diagram in Figure 2–3 is an example of a structure chart. It shows how the different subtasks are related to one another. Level 0 contains a simple statement of the problem. The subtasks in each subsequent level contain a greater and greater amount of detail.

Top-down design helps the programmer keep an overall view of the problem in mind. It also increases the chance of the programmer realizing early in the programming process whether a particular solution will work. This approach can save time. This style of program development also helps the programmer to write a program that is efficient and logical.

▬▬▬ FLOWCHARTING

One of the ways of visually representing the steps in a program is to use a **flowchart**. Flowcharts contain symbols that have specific meanings. Figure 2–4 shows some of the symbols used in a flowchart. The flowchart for a program adding three numbers together is illustrated in Figure 2–5. Arrows are drawn between the symbols to show the direction of flow. The first symbol represents the beginning of the program. The second symbol is an input step: the three numbers are read into the program. Next is the processing step. Processing steps are where the work of the program is actually done. In this case, the three numbers are added together. The last symbol is a stop step, showing where the program ends. In a flowchart, a **decision step** is represented by a diamond-shaped symbol. A decision step is used when the computer is making a comparison. What would happen if a program was to read a letter and only print the letter if it was a consonant? The steps in solving this problem would look like this:

1. Read letter.
2. Compare letter to list of consonants.
3. If letter is a consonant, print it.

FIGURE 2–4 FLOWCHARTING SYMBOLS

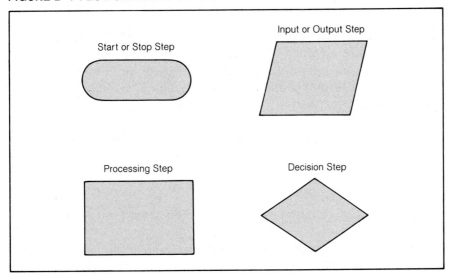

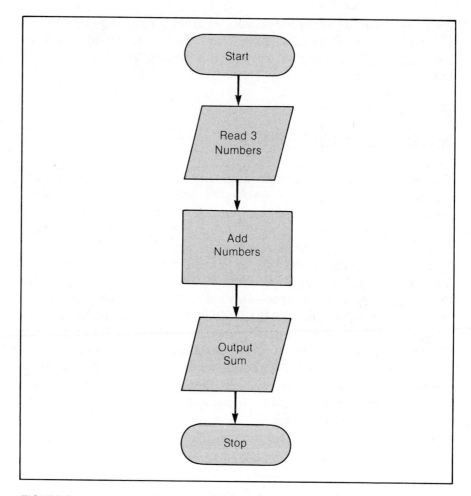

FIGURE 2–5 FLOWCHART FOR FINDING SUM

The flowchart for this program is shown in Figure 2–6. The comparison here is a **single-alternative decision step**. Something is done only if the letter is a consonant. If the letter is a vowel, nothing is done.

A **double-alternative decision step** is one in which one action is taken if the comparison is true and another if the comparison is false. An example would be a program that reads two letters and then prints the one that comes last alphabetically. The algorithm would look like this:

1. Read two letters.
2. Compare the two letters.
3. If the first letter comes alphabetically after the second, then print the first.
4. If the first letter does not come alphabetically after the second, then print the second.

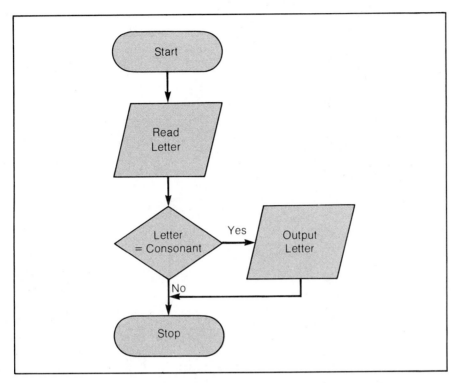

FIGURE 2–6 FLOWCHART SHOWING SINGLE-ALTERNATIVE DECISION STEP

The flowchart for this program is shown in Figure 2–7. In this flowchart, the "Yes" route is taken if the first letter is larger than the second. Otherwise the "No" route is taken.

Loops can also be represented by using flowcharts. A loop allows a particular part of a program to be repeated as many times as needed. Suppose a program needs to be written that will

1. Read 20 numbers.
2. Add the numbers together.
3. Print the total.

This could be written easily with a loop. The flowchart for this program is shown in Figure 2–8. The name "Count" is used to keep track of the number of times the loop has been executed. When the loop has been executed 20 times, (that is, when Count is greater than 20), "Total" will be printed. Notice that before the loop is entered, "Total" is set to zero. This is done so that the first number read can be added to "Total."

Flowcharting makes the logic of a program easier to follow. It helps the programmer visualize how a program should be written.

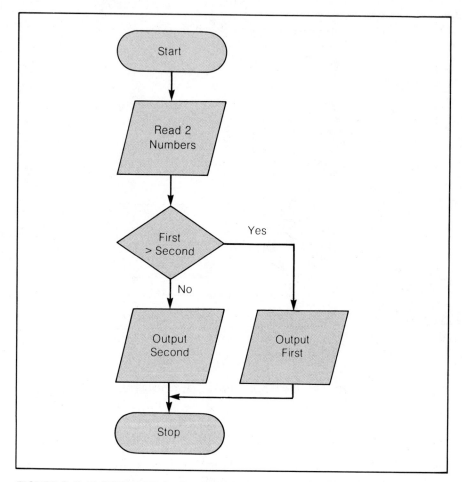

FIGURE 2–7 FLOWCHART SHOWING DOUBLE-ALTERNATIVE DECISION STEP

PSEUDOCODING

Pseudocode is a narrative description of a program's logic. While a flowchart presents the logic of a program graphically, pseudocode often resembles an actual program. Pseudocode uses short English statements to express a program's actions. Pseudocoding is often more useful than flowcharting in developing a program because it is more similar to an actual computer program than a flowchart is.

Pseudocode can be used to represent both simple and complex programming problem solutions. Remember how a flowchart was used to represent a program that read three numbers, added them together, and printed the sum? The following pseudocode represents the same program.

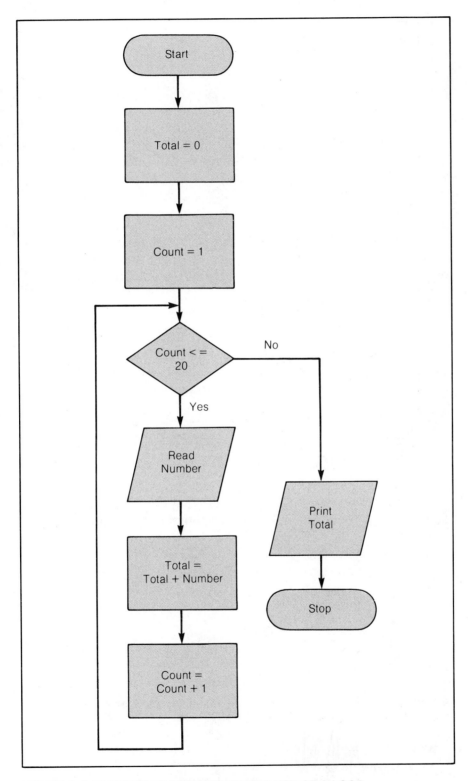

FIGURE 2-8 FLOWCHART DEMONSTRATING USE OF A LOOP

```
Begin
  Read X, Y, Z
  Sum = X + Y + Z
  Print Sum
End
```

The single-alternative decision step requires the program to ask one question. In pseudocode, the question looks like this:

```
If (an expression is true)
  Then statement(s)
```

The action or actions under the "If" are only executed if the expression is true. People often use this type of logic to make decisions. For example, if you like pizza and go to a restaurant, you might decide:

```
If (this restaurant has pizza)
  Then order pizza
```

The double-alternative decision step considers the actions to be executed whether an expression is true or false. The pseudocode of a double-alternative decision step is illustrated below:

```
If (an expression is true)
  Then statement(s)
  Else statement(s)
```

The action or actions following the "Then" are executed if the expression is true; otherwise the actions following the "Else" are executed. The following pseudocode describes a program that reads two numbers and prints the larger of the two. Compare this program to the flowchart in Figure 2–7.

```
Begin
  Read X and Y
  If X > Y
    Then print X
    Else print Y
End
```

Loops also can be represented using pseudocode. Look at the general form of this loop in pseudocode:

```
While (an expression is true) do
  statement(s)
End loop
```

**LEARNING
CHECK
2-2**

1. Give two characteristics of structured programming languages.
2. How is a flowchart different from pseudocode?
3. Create a flowchart from the following pseudocode:

   Begin
       Read the length of a rectangle
       Read the width of a rectangle
       If the rectangle is a square
           Then
               Calculate area
               Print area
           Else
               Calculate perimeter
               Print perimeter
   End

4. Explain how you might write a term paper for a class using top-down design. Create a structure chart that illustrates the solution.
5. Sally has $20.00. She goes to a movie that costs $3.50 and buys popcorn for $1.10. She then buys two books for $4.50 each plus 6 percent sales tax. Write an algorithm that will determine how much money Sally has left.

▬▬▬ USING THE TURBO SYSTEM

This section discusses using Turbo Pascal, Version 4. Version 3 is covered in Appendix H and Version 5 in Appendix I. If you are using Turbo Pascal for the Macintosh (Version 1), refer to Appendix J. Although the editors for each version differ, the Pascal statements are basically the same. Differences are noted in boxes throughout the text.

Version 4 has two compilers. The first one is referred to as a command line compiler. It does not contain an editor for entering programs. If you want to run your programs using this compiler, you will have to use a separate editor to type in your programs and save them on disk. Refer to your system documentation for instructions on using this compiler.

The second compiler includes many more features and is actually a whole programming "system" or "environment." It allows you to type in programs, save them on disk, and run them. Because this second compiler is much more useful, it will be the one explained here and will be referred to as the Turbo Pascal System. To access the Turbo Pascal System, the disk containing the Turbo Pascal compiler must be placed in the drive currently being accessed. If you are using a computer with one hard drive and one floppy drive, check with your instructor about how to access the Turbo Pascal System. If you are using a system with two floppy disk drives, place the Turbo Pascal disk in drive A. To enter the system, type

TURBO <Enter>

The main screen will appear:

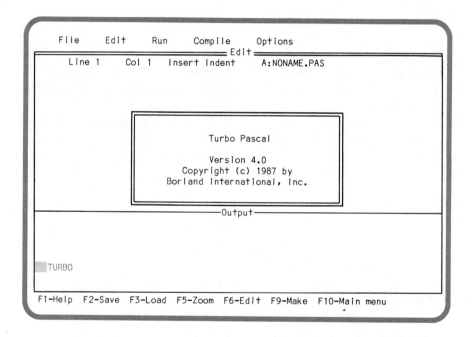

This screen has four parts: the main menu (the top line), the Edit window (the upper empty portion), the output window (the lower empty portion), and the bottom line (the text across the bottom of the screen).

The Main Menu

The main menu lists the following selections:

File   Provides different file-handling options. For example, a file in main memory can be saved on a disk, or a file on a disk can be loaded into main memory.

Edit	Allows a program to be edited.
Run	Executes a program.
Compile	Lists various options available when compiling a program.
Options	This menu allows you to determine how various features in the Turbo Pascal System work. Generally, it is not necessary to change any of these options. If you want to know more about these options, refer to your system documentation.

In order to select an item in the main menu, that item must be highlighted. Use the directional arrow keys to move around and highlight the desired choice. Then press <Enter>.

To leave the main menu and return to the window you were previously working in, press <Esc>. Highlighting Edit and pressing <Enter> will place the cursor (the square of light) in the Edit window so that a program can be edited. Holding down the Alternate key and the E key (<Alt><E>) at the same time will also perform this function. This is one of the nice features of Turbo Pascal; there are often many ways of performing a particular function.

The screen is divided into two windows: the Edit window and the Output window. The name of the window that is currently being used is highlighted and has a double bar at the top. The Edit window is the area in which your program will appear as you type it. You can use the arrow keys to move the cursor around in this window. Any output generated by your program will appear in the Output window.

The Status Line

The line that appears at the top of the Edit window is referred to as the status line:

```
Line 1     Col 1    Insert Indent     A:NONAME.PAS
```

It provides the following information:

Line n	Indicates the vertical line number containing the cursor.
Col n	Indicates the column containing the cursor.

Insert

Indicates whether Insert is on or off. If it is on, any characters typed in will be inserted into existing text. Existing letters will be "pushed over" to make room for the new characters. If Insert is turned off, any new characters typed in will "overwrite" existing characters. The previous text will be lost. You can "toggle" between Insert and Overwrite by pressing the <Ins> key. Press it once and you are in Overwrite; press it again, and you are in Insert.

Indent

Indicates whether the auto-indent feature is on or off. It can be toggled on and off by pressing the <Ctrl><O><I> keys simultaneously. If auto-indent is on, the current line will be indented to the same position as the line immediately above it.

Tab

Indicates whether tabs can be inserted. It is toggled on and off by pressing <Ctrl><O><T>.

A:NONAME.PAS

Indicates the drive and the name of the program currently being edited.

Entering a Program

Let's practice entering a short program. Start the Turbo Pascal System by accessing the disk drive that contains the Turbo Pascal compiler. For example, if you have inserted a disk into drive A, the screen will look like this:

```
A>
```

This indicates that the A drive is being accessed. If the screen appears as follows:

```
B>
```

simply change the accessed drive by entering

```
B>A: <Enter>
```

Now enter the following command (it can be entered using either uppercase or lowercase letters):

```
A>TURBO <Enter>
```

You have now entered the Turbo Pascal System. The main menu will be displayed. To highlight the different menu choices across the top, use the left (←) and right (→) directional arrow keys. Practice high-lighting the different menu choices. Alternately, a menu can be se-lected by entering the first letter of that menu. Now highlight the Edit menu and press <Enter>. Notice that the cursor has moved to the Edit window. This is the window in which you will enter your program. Let's practice typing in a short program. It isn't necessary to understand the program, only to be a careful typist. Enter the program exactly as shown below, pressing <Enter> at the end of each line:

```
PROGRAM GREETING;
BEGIN
    WRITELN ('HI THERE!');
END.
```

If you make any typing mistakes, use the directional arrow keys to move the cursor to the location to be corrected. The backspace key <←> removes the character to the left of the cursor whereas the de-lete key <Del> removes the character at the cursor. After the program is entered, the screen should look like this:

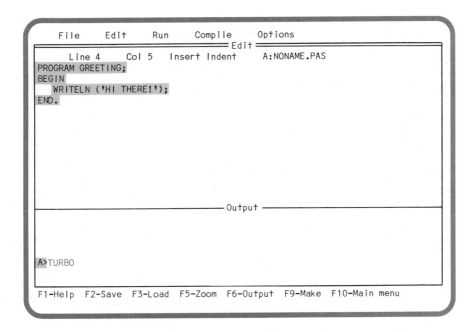

Running a Program

After your program is typed in, press <F10> to return to the main menu from the Edit window. There are two ways to run the program. The first way is to highlight Run and press <Enter>. The second is simply to press R. When the program is executed, some compilation information will appear briefly on the screen, and if there are no errors in the program, the output will be displayed:

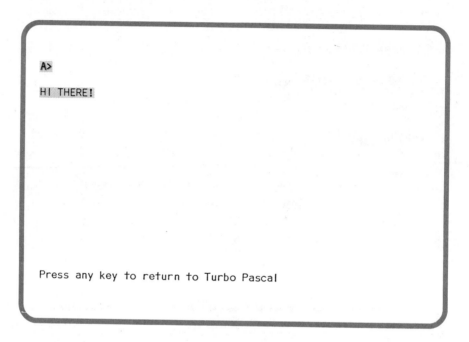

Notice that in addition to the output of the program:

HI THERE!

any other commands that we have entered previously are displayed. In this example, the previous command that we used to access the Turbo System is also displayed:

A>TURBO

If you follow the instruction at the bottom of the screen and press any key, you will be back at the main menu. The program's output will appear in the output window:

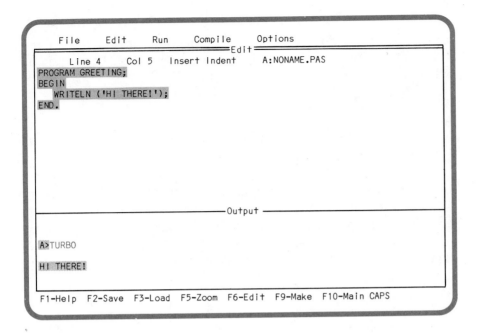

If your program has one or more errors, it cannot be executed until they are corrected. An appropriate error message will be displayed, and the cursor will be placed in the Edit window so that you can correct the error.

Saving a Program

After you have executed the program, save it on a disk by pressing the function key <F2>. Because no name has been specified for this program, it is currently being called NONAME.PAS. The following box will appear on the screen:

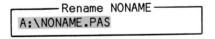

Enter the name you want the program to be saved under. For example:

```
FIRST.PAS <Enter>
```

The program is now saved on disk as FIRST.PAS. This file name has an *extension*, which is that portion of the name following the period. Using an extension is not required. The file could have been named FIRST. However, the extension identifies the file as containing a Pascal program.

There is a second method of saving a file. Go to the main menu by pressing <F10>. Then highlight File. Highlight Save (by using the downward arrow or typing an S) and press <Enter>. The same box will appear asking that the name be entered.

Loading a Program

Let's practice loading a program that has been previously saved. Since FIRST.PAS is the only program we have, we will practice with it. When you have many programs on disk, you will probably want to have the names of them displayed so that you can pick the one you wish to load. If you choose Directory under the File menu, the following will appear:

```
┌─────── Enter Mask ───────┐
│ A:                       │
│                          │
└──────────────────────────┘
```

This indicates that if you press <Enter>, all the files on the disk in drive A will be listed. If you wish, you can change the drive being accessed before pressing <Enter>. After determining the file you wish to load, press <F3>. A box will appear asking for the file name:

```
┌─────── Load File Name ───────┐
│ *.PAS                        │
│                              │
└──────────────────────────────┘
```

Type in FIRST.PAS and press <Enter>. The program we previously created will now appear in the Edit window. Let's modify it as shown below:

```
PROGRAM GREETING;
BEGIN
   WRITELN ('WHAT IS YOUR NAME?');
END.
```

Use the cursor arrows to move to the line to be changed and retype the line. Make certain you are in Overwrite so that you erase the old line. Now run the program in the same way as before. The new message will now be displayed:

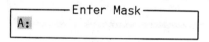

WHAT IS YOUR NAME?

If you want to save this new version of the program, use the same method of saving as previously. The old version of FIRST.PAS will be overwritten by this new version. If you choose not to save the new version, the old version will remain on disk.

Quitting the System

Once you are ready to leave the Turbo Pascal System, go to the main menu and highlight File. Then highlight Quit and press <Enter>. An alternate way of quitting the system is to press the Alternate (<Alt>) and the X keys at the same time. The system prompt will appear, displaying the name of the drive currently being accessed; for example:

 A>

The Function Keys

Below is a list of function keys and the task each performs. Note that some of these functions involve holding down both the Alternate (<Alt>) key and a function key at the same time. Some of these functions may not be clear to you right now. Do not be afraid to try each one. You cannot do any damage to the computer or to the Turbo System.

Key	Purpose
<F1>	Displays a Help screen with information about your position in the system.
<F2>	Saves the file currently in main memory.
<F3>	Allows a program previously saved on disk to be loaded into main memory.
<F5>	Zooms and unzooms the active window. "Zooming" refers to expanding the current active window so that it takes up the entire screen.
<F6>	Switches the cursor to the active window.
<F10>	Causes the main menu to be displayed. If you are currently in the Edit or Output windows, control will be returned to the menu.
<Alt><F1>	Brings up the Help screen that was last referenced.
<Alt><F3>	Allows the user to specify the name of a file to be loaded into main memory.
<Alt><F9>	Compiles a program.
<Alt><C>	Displays the Compile menu.
<Alt><E>	Places you in the Edit window.

<Alt> <F> Displays the File menu.

<Alt> <O> Displays the Options menu.

<Alt> <R> Executes a program.

<Alt> <X> Quits Turbo Pascal and places you back at the system prompt (for example, A>).

LEARNING CHECK 2-3

1. What is the purpose of the File menu?
2. How is a program saved on disk?
3. Alter the program created in this section by changing the statement:

```
WRITELN ('HI THERE!');
```

so that it contains your name between the single quotation marks. For example:

```
WRITELN ('MARVIN K. MOONEY.');
```

Then execute the program.

SUMMARY POINTS

- There are six steps that can be used to develop a solution to a programming problem efficiently: (1) understand the problem, (2) develop a solution to the problem, (3) write the program, (4) type the program into a computer and run it, (5) correct any errors in the program, and (6) test the program.
- Before a problem can be solved, it must be thoroughly understood.
- An algorithm should be developed by listing all steps necessary to solve the problem.
- Top-down design is an efficient way of developing a solution to a problem. This method proceeds from the general to the specific, allowing the programmer to concentrate on major problems first and deal with details later.
- Structure charts graphically represent how a solution to a problem has been broken down into subparts.
- A single-alternative decision step allows for a comparison to be made. If the comparison is true, an action is taken, otherwise nothing

happens. In a double-alternative decision step, one action is taken if the comparison is true and another if it is false.

- Loops allow a specified action to be repeated any number of times.
- Flowcharts are graphic representations of solutions to problems.
- Pseudocode is an English-like description of program logic.
- The Turbo Pascal System allows programs to be entered, edited, executed, and saved on disk.

■ VOCABULARY LIST

Algorithm   Pseudocode
Decision step   Single-alternative decision step
Double-alternative decision step   Structured programming
Flowchart   language
Loop   Subprogram
Module   Top-down design

■ CHAPTER TEST

Vocabulary

Match a term from the numbered column with the description from the lettered column that best fits the term.

1. Pseudocode

    a. A decision step in which an action is taken only if the comparison made in the decision step is true. A different action is taken if the comparison is false.

2. Loop

    b. A narrative description of a program's logic.

3. Flowchart

    c. A programming language that allows a large problem to be methodically divided into smaller subparts. It also allows the programmer to control the order in which program statements will be executed.

4. Top-down design

    d. A sequence of steps that can be used to solve a problem.

5. Subprogram

    e. A decision step in which an action is taken only if the stated comparison is true; otherwise nothing is done.

6. Algorithm

   f. A structure that allows a section of a program to be repeated as many times as needed.

7. Double-alternative decision step

   g. A part of a larger program that performs a specific task.

8. Single-alternative decision step

   h. A method of program design in which a large problem is divided into smaller and smaller subparts.

9. Structured programming language

   i. A method of visually representing the steps in solving a problem.

Questions

1. Why is it necessary to determine what the output of a program should be before determining the input?
2. Think of a task you have performed. What input was needed to complete this task? What was the output? Develop an algorithm for the task.
3. Complete the structure chart in Figure 2–3 by breaking down the three remaining modules in Level 1 (Preheat Oven, Put Sauce and Toppings on Pizza, and Bake Pizza). Follow the pattern that was used to refine the module titled Prepare Dough.
4. Write an algorithm to evaluate the following expression:

$$\frac{14 + 8}{2} \times \frac{3}{16}$$

5. List and explain the purpose of each of the four flowcharting symbols discussed in this chapter.
6. What is the difference between a single-alternative decision step and a double-alternative decision step?
7. Write the pseudocode for the program that will read the scores on 10 tests. Use a loop to do this. The grades will be assigned by the following scale:

   a. A = 90 points or better
   b. B = 82 points to 89 points
   c. C = 74 points to 81 points
   d. D = 60 points to 73 points
   e. F = less than 60 points

Print the correct grade for each score.
8. List the steps for accessing your Turbo Pascal System.
9. Explain how to execute a program that is in the Edit window.
10. What are the different items listed in the Status Line? What is the purpose of each?

CHAPTER 3

The Parts of a Program

OBJECTIVES

After studying this chapter, you should be able to:

- Create valid identifiers to name parts of a program.
- Describe the difference between a program variable and a program constant.
- Identify the six data types discussed in this chapter and describe the characteristics of each type.
- Write constant definition statements.
- Write variable declaration statements.
- Identify the basic parts of a program.
- Explain the purpose of comments in a program.

OUTLINE

■■■ INTRODUCTION

In this chapter, you will begin to learn how programs are written. The basic components of a program will be explained. You will also learn how to name these components. This information will provide a framework when you start to write programs.

■■■ VARIABLES

When the computer stores programs, data, and output, it does not do so randomly. It uses a systematic method to assign a location to each data item and instruction. To visualize the computer's primary storage unit, imagine a block of post office boxes. Each box has an assigned number that acts as an address for the location of that box (see Figure 3–1). Similarly, the primary storage unit in a computer is divided into many separate storage locations. Each location has a specific address, but, unlike a post office box, it can only contain one value at a time. While the contents of the storage location can change, the address stays the same. A storage location whose value can change during program execution is referred to as a **variable**. The programmer may assign

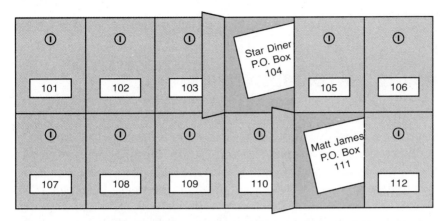

FIGURE 3–1 VARIABLES ARE SIMILAR TO POST OFFICE BOXES

names to these variables. Then it is not necessary to know the exact location where the computer is storing these values. These names are referred to as identifiers. It is a good idea to choose an identifier that describes what is stored in a particular variable.

Let's assume that we wish to write a program to convert a specified number of feet to miles. The pseudocode could be written as follows:

```
Begin
    Read FEET
    MILES = FEET / FEET_IN_A_MILE
    Print MILES
End
```

In this problem, two variables would be needed. FEET would be a good choice to stand for the number of feet to be changed to miles. This is an example of an **input variable**. This value will be put into the computer to get the needed results. The result could be given the name MILES. This is called an **output variable**. It is the result the computer gives after executing the program. The value of the result MILES will change depending on the value of the input variable FEET.

CONSTANTS

We need one more data value in our program that converts feet to miles. We need to know the number of feet in one mile. This value is called a **constant**; it is a value that cannot change during program execution. The number of feet in a mile is always 5,280. We will call this value FEET_IN_A_MILE. Figure 3–2 illustrates the data values that are needed by this program.

CREATING IDENTIFIERS

As we already mentioned, **identifiers** are used to name variables and constants. In addition, they are used to name other parts of programs and objects within programs. There are some rules that need to be followed when creating identifiers. A valid identifier is any string of characters that begins with a lowercase (a–z) or uppercase (A–Z) letter. It may contain any combination of letters, digits (0–9), or the underscore character (_). Here are some examples of valid identifiers:

```
GRADE_POINT
NUM1346
MONTH10
```

One way of making easy-to-read identifiers is to use the underscore character to divide the words:

```
NUM_ITEMS      INCHES_LONG      SALES_TAX
```

Another way is to use a combination of uppercase and lowercase letters:

```
NumItems       InchesLong       SalesTax
```

The Turbo Pascal Compiler treats uppercase and lowercase letters as if they were the same. Because of this, the compiler would see the four identifiers below as being exactly alike:

```
YEARSOLD       yearsold         YearsOld
```

FIGURE 3–2 DATA NEEDED TO CONVERT FEET TO MILES

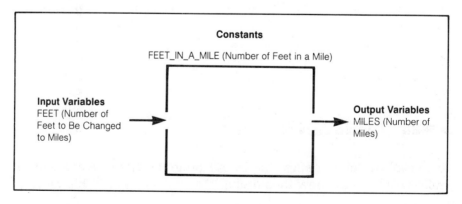

Which of these do you think is easiest to read? The easier the identifiers are to understand, the easier it will be for other people to follow your program. Why are the identifiers listed below invalid?

```
1_MILE
YEARS OLD
Sales#
```

Identifiers may contain any number of characters. However, only the first 63 characters are significant. This means that if two identifiers have the same first 63 characters, the compiler will see them as being identical even if the 64th characters (or any of the remaining characters) are different.

---

1. How is a variable similar to a post office box? How is it not similar to a post office box?
2. Which of the following are valid identifiers?

   LEARNING CHECK 3–1

    a. TOP20   f. 1st
    b. AMOUNT$ g. Look Out
    c. GameScore   h. SALES%
    d. DYLAN_THOMAS   i. outer
    e. N   j. CHEVY1957

3. How many different ways can the identifier "top_10" be written? Name five. The compiler must see all of these variations as being the same.
4. The value of a _____ may change during program execution whereas the value of a _____ may not.

DATA TYPES

All variables in a program must be assigned a data type. The data type assigned to a particular variable depends on what kind of values that variable will contain. We will discuss the five most commonly used data types here.

INTEGER

An **integer** is a positive or negative whole number. It never has a decimal point. If there is no sign in front of the number, it is assumed that the number is positive. Here are some examples:

$$-2532 \quad +48 \quad 7 \quad -10 \quad 0$$

Why is each of the following not a valid integer?

25.48	(decimal point)
+4,687	(comma)
387*	(character other than a digit)

Notice that a comma cannot be used to separate long numbers. The data type INTEGER is used to store integers. In Turbo Pascal, this can be any integer value from -32768 through 32767.

LONGINT

If a variable may need to contain a value outside the ranges of type INTEGER, the variable must be of data type LONGINT, which can store an integer up to 2,147,483,647. However, the data type LONGINT is not available in Turbo Pascal Version 3. If a variable is needed to store a number greater than 32767 when using Version 3, a REAL variable can be used. The data type REAL is discussed next.

REAL

The data type REAL is used to store a **real number**, that is, any number with a decimal point. Variables of this data type can store any number from 10^{-38} through 10^{38}.

There are two possible representations for real numbers. The first, **decimal notation**, is the form in which we most commonly see real numbers. The following are examples of numbers in decimal notation:

$$2567.0 \quad 0.6 \quad -385.0 \quad +467.1121$$

The second method is **exponential notation**. The number is written as a value (the mantissa), which is multiplied by 10 (represented by E) to the stated power (the characteristic). The mantissa always has one nonzero digit before the decimal point. Figure 3–3 illustrates the parts of a number represented in exponential notation. The number in Figure 3–3 would be 4630.0 in decimal notation. Below are some numbers in exponential notation along with their equivalents in decimal notation:

Exponential notation	Decimal notation
4.6300000000E+03	4630.0
−5.2780000000E+04	−52780.0
2.1000000000E−06	0.0000021
−3.1900000000E−02	−0.0319

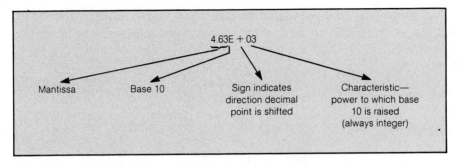

FIGURE 3–3 EXPLANATION OF EXPONENTIAL NOTATION

CHAR

Variables of data type CHAR can contain any single character that the computer can represent. The character is placed in single quotation marks. Some examples are as follows:

'*'   'B'   '2'   '%'   'Y'

What is wrong with these examples?

'0   (missing right quotation mark)
'22'   (more than one character inside quotation marks)
%   (quotation marks missing)

Notice that it is possible for the computer to store a number as a character value. However, because the computer stores character values differently than numeric values, the computer can no longer perform arithmetic operations on these numbers.

STRING

STRING is the data type used to store **character strings** consisting of any characters the computer system is able to represent. The entire string is enclosed in single quotation marks:

'12448 Cloverdale Rd.'
'What are you doing today?'
'578-42-8856'

Below are two incorrect examples:

'Uriah Heep   (missing right quotation mark)
"Double Cheese"   (must use single quotation marks)

What if a string looked like this?

'Don't sit under the apple tree.'

The compiler would see the single quotation mark in Don't as the end of the string. This can be fixed by using two single quotation marks together:

'Don''t sit under the apple tree.'

When this line is printed, only a single quotation mark will appear in Don't. In Turbo Pascal the maximum length of a string is 255 characters.

BOOLEAN

The data type BOOLEAN is probably the most difficult for the beginner to understand. A BOOLEAN variable can be true or false. These are the only two choices. For example, if the variable CORRECT were a BOOLEAN variable, it must be equal to either true or false. It may help to think of a BOOLEAN variable as a switch. The switch is either turned on or off. When we begin writing programs that use BOOLEAN variables, you will realize how useful they are.

RESERVED WORDS

In Turbo Pascal there are certain **reserved words**. These reserved words have specific meanings to the compiler. They cannot be used to name variables or constants. Table 3–1 lists these reserved words. You

TABLE 3–1 RESERVED WORDS

ABSOLUTE	GOTO	RECORD
AND	IF	REPEAT
ARRAY	IMPLEMENTATION	SET
BEGIN	IN	SHL
CASE	INLINE	SHR
CONST	INTERFACE	STRING
DIV	INTERRUPT	THEN
DO	LABEL	TO
DOWNTO	MOD	TYPE
ELSE	NIL	UNIT
END	NOT	UNTIL
EXTERNAL	OF	USES
FILE	OR	VAR
FOR	PACKED	WHILE
FORWARD	PROCEDURE	WITH
FUNCTION	PROGRAM	XOR

can write reserved words in either uppercase or lowercase letters, or in a combination of both. The compiler will see all three of the following as identical:

BEGIN   Begin   begin

---

1. Which data type is each of the following?

   a. FALSE
   b. −1.28
   c. 4678
   d. '$'
   e. 'STOP THAT CAR'
   f. 0.689
   g. '379-50-5288'
   h. 'Marvin K. Mooney'
   i. TRUE
   j. '4'
   k. 9

2. Are these integers valid or invalid?

   a. 785
   b. 678*
   c. 000
   d. −4378
   e. 12.486
   f. 23,100

3. How is the data type STRING different from the data type CHAR?

▬▬▬ PARTS OF A PROGRAM

Just like any other language, Pascal has rules that must be followed. **Syntax rules** are rules that explain how the parts of a language should be put together. Syntax also involves spelling and punctuation. When we write in English, we use the syntax rules of English whether we are aware of them or not. Sentences are capitalized and end with a punctuation mark. Complete sentences need a subject and a verb, and words must be correctly spelled. To most students, these rules are automatic because they have been speaking and writing the English language for years. The syntax rules in Pascal may seem complex and awkward in the beginning, but with practice, the rules will become second nature.

The general structure of a program is shown in Figure 3–4. We will cover some of the parts of Pascal programs here. Other parts will be added as you write more complex programs.

Program Heading

The first line of a program is the program heading. The program heading is not required in Turbo Pascal. However, it is good programming

```
PROGRAM program_name;

CONST
    constant_name = value;

VAR
    variable_name : data_type;

BEGIN

    statement1;
    statement2;
        .
        .
        .
    last_statement;

end.

(The semicolon before the END is optional.)
```

FIGURE 3-4 BASIC STRUCTURE OF A PROGRAM

practice to use one. The program heading starts with the reserved word PROGRAM and contains the program's name. The name may be any valid identifier but should describe the purpose of the program. The heading concludes with a semicolon. The following are examples of valid program headings:

```
PROGRAM AREA;
PROGRAM FindNum;
program Starter1;
```

Format For **Program Heading**
PROGRAM program_name;

In the sample program that converts feet to miles, an appropriate program heading might be:

```
PROGRAM FIND_MILES;
```

Constant Definitions

The constant definition section starts with the reserved word CONST. This section goes after the program heading. If there are no constants, it is omitted. A constant can be of any data type. In the sample program FIND_MILES, the constant definition would be

```
CONST
    FEET_IN_A_MILE = 5280;
```

Now, the identifier FEET_IN_A_MILE can be used anytime you want to refer to the value 5280. The value of this constant cannot be changed during the running of the program. Other examples of constant definitions are listed below (notice that the type of each constant appears after its definition):

```
CONST
    PI = 3.14;            {REAL}
    SPEED = 55;           {INTEGER}
    FLAG = FALSE;         {BOOLEAN}
    NAME = 'GEORGE';      {STRING}
    PERCENT = '%';        {CHAR}
```

Although the reserved word CONST appears only once, any number of constants can be defined. Each constant definition concludes with a semicolon.

Format For **Constant Definition**

```
CONST
    constant_name = value;
    constant_name = value;
```

Variable Declarations

All variables must be declared before they can be used in a program. This is done in the variable declaration section. It starts with the reserved word VAR. This is followed by each variable name and its data type. Each declaration concludes with a semicolon. The following declares four variables (two of type REAL and two of type INTEGER):

```
VAR
    FEET    : REAL;
    MILES   : REAL;
    COUNT   : INTEGER;
    ID_NUM : INTEGER;
```

These declarations could also have been written as

```
VAR
    MILES, FEET    : REAL;
    COUNT, ID_NUM : INTEGER;
```

In the second example, all variables of the same type are placed together, separated by commas. This method saves space and makes it easier to tell which variables are of the same data type. The spaces around the colons and commas are not necessary, but they make the program easier to read. The whole VAR declaration section could have been written on one line without spaces:

```
VAR FEET,MILES:REAL;COUNT,ID_NUM:INTEGER;
```

Putting different parts of the declaration on separate lines and adding blank spaces makes it easier to read.

Format For Variable Declaration

```
VAR
    variable_name : data_type;
    variable_name : data_type;
```

As previously mentioned, type INTEGER can be used to store numbers from −32768 through 32767. If a variable is needed to store values outside this range, it should be declared to be of type LONGINT. For example:

```
VAR
    BIG_NUM : LONGINT;
```

Variable BIG_NUM can store integers from −2,147,483,648 through 2,147,483,647.

DIFFERENCES FOR VERSION 3 USERS

Version 3 does not contain the data type **LONGINT**. If you think a variable may need to contain a value larger than that allowed in **INTEGER** variables, you can declare the variable to be of type **REAL**. The compiler will convert the integer to a real number by adding a decimal point and a zero.

Variables of type CHAR can be declared as follows:

```
VAR
    SYMBOL  : CHAR;
    GRADE   : CHAR;
```

The variables SYMBOL and GRADE may only contain a single character at a time. If you want a variable to contain a character string, such as a person's name or address, you must declare a STRING variable:

```
VAR
    NAME    : STRING[25];
    ADDRESS : STRING[40];
```

The number in brackets after the word STRING is used to indicate the maximum number of characters that are allowed in that string. NAME can have from 0 to 25 characters whereas ADDRESS can have from 0 to 40 characters. The maximum allowable size of a STRING variable is 255. If a variable is declared as data type STRING with no length specified:

```
VAR
    NAME : STRING;
```

the string can have up to 255 characters.

DIFFERENCES FOR VERSION 3 USERS

When using Version 3, a **STRING** variable must always be assigned a length. Therefore, this declaration is valid:

```
VAR
    ADDRESS : STRING[40];
```

but this one is not:

```
VAR
    ADDRESS : STRING;
```

Body of the Program

After the declaration statements comes the reserved word BEGIN. This is the part of the program where the work is done. Statements are placed here to perform the needed tasks. Data can be read and results output. Mathematical operations can be performed and the data can be processed as needed.

▬▬▬ PROGRAM FIND_MILES

Figure 3–5 contains the program that converts feet into miles. One constant and two variables are declared. The statements between the BEGIN and the END perform the processing of the program. It is not

```
PROGRAM FIND_MILES;

{ FIND THE NUMBER OF MILES IN A GIVEN NUMBER OF FEET. }

CONST
    FEET_IN_A_MILE = 5280;

VAR
    FEET, MILES : REAL;

BEGIN { FIND_MILES }

    WRITE ('HOW MANY FEET ARE TO BE CHANGED INTO MILES? ');
    READLN (FEET);
    MILES := FEET / FEET_IN_A_MILE;
    WRITELN ('THERE ARE ', MILES, ' MILES IN ', FEET, ' FEET.');

END.    { FIND_MILES }
```

```
HOW MANY FEET ARE TO BE CHANGED INTO MILES? 52800
THERE ARE   1.0000000000E+01 MILES IN   5.2800000000E+04 FEET.
```

FIGURE 3-5 PROGRAM TO CONVERT FEET TO MILES

important that you understand them completely. They will be discussed briefly here. The first statement asks the user to enter the number of feet to be converted. The user then enters a number and presses the Enter key. The second statement reads the number of feet. The feet are converted to miles by the statement:

```
MILES := FEET / FEET_IN_A_MILE;
```

The last statement displays the results on the monitor screen. All of these statements will be explained in depth later in this book. Examine the output of the program:

```
HOW MANY FEET ARE TO BE CHANGED INTO MILES? 52800
THERE ARE   1.0000000000E+01 MILES IN  5.2800000000E+04 FEET.
```

The values of the real variables are displayed in exponential notation. In Chapter 4, you will learn how to display them in decimal notation.

LEARNING CHECK 3-3

1. Which of the following program headings are valid?

   a. program Search;
   b. PROGRAM TELL ME;
   c. PROGRAM PhoneBill
   d. AVERAGE;
   e. PORGRAM FIND_SQUARE;
   f. program 70Percent;

2. Rewrite the following variable declaration statement so it is more readable.

   VAR GALLON,DISTANCE,TIME:REAL; COUNT:INTEGER;

3. Which of these constant definition statements are correct? What data type is each of the correct ones?

   a. X = 4.35
   b. SCORE : 4;
   c. RESULT = 'THE CORRECT ANSWER IS:';
   d. FLAG = TRUE;

PUNCTUATION

One of the most confusing aspects of Pascal for the beginner is the question of where to put a semicolon. A semicolon is used to separate statements. Because BEGIN is not a statement, there should not be a semicolon after a BEGIN. END is not a statement either. Technically, there should be no semicolon following any statement preceding an END. However, the Turbo Pascal Compiler will allow you to put a semicolon there. Notice the last statement in the program in Figure 3–5:

```
WRITELN ('THERE ARE ', MILES, ' MILES IN ', FEET, ' FEET.');
```

This statement has a semicolon after it even though one is not required. Although technically a semicolon should not be placed before an END, many programmers place one there. The main advantage, as you shall see later, is that it makes it easier to add new statements at a later time. Therefore, in this text we will use a semicolon before an END.

COMMENTS

Comments are used to explain what is going on in a program. Comments have no meaning to the compiler; it simply skips over them. In Pascal, all comments must be enclosed in both parentheses and asterisks:

```
(* This is a comment. *)
```

or in braces:

```
{ Here is another one. }
```

The two types of symbols cannot be mixed. If a comment starts with a brace, it must end with a brace. In this book we will use braces.

Comments may be used anywhere in a program. It is a good idea to include a description of what the entire program does after the program heading. Figure 3–5 contains the following comment that briefly explains the purpose of the program:

```
{ FIND THE NUMBER OF MILES IN A GIVEN NUMBER OF FEET. }
```

There are also comments after the BEGIN and the END in the program:

```
BEGIN     { FIND_MILES}

END.      { FIND_MILES }
```

These comments identify the BEGIN and the END. They are not necessary in this program. However, later you will be writing programs containing many BEGINs and ENDs, and using comments will make the programs easier to understand.

The comments in a program are called the **program documentation**. Well-documented programs make it easier not only for the programmer but also for anyone else trying to understand a program. Comments are particularly useful if a program needs to be changed in the future. It is important to develop the habit of documenting programs as they are written.

LEARNING CHECK 3–4

1. What is the purpose of comments?
2. What are the two ways in which comments can be indicated?
3. Why is there no semicolon after the word BEGIN in the program in Figure 3–5?

▰▰▰ SUMMARY POINTS

- Variables represent values that change during program execution. Constants represent values that do not change during execution.
- Identifiers are used to name parts of a program including variables and constants. An identifier must start with a letter and may contain any letter or digit or the underscore character.
- The data types covered in this chapter are INTEGER, LONGINT, REAL, CHAR, STRING, and BOOLEAN.
- Data type INTEGER can be any positive or negative whole number from −32768 through 32767. The type LONGINT can be used to represent any number up to 2,147,483,647.
- The data type REAL includes any number with a decimal portion. Real numbers can be represented in decimal form or in exponential notation.
- Variables of type CHAR can contain any single character that the computer system can represent. The value must be enclosed in single quotation marks. If more than one character needs to be stored in a variable, the data type STRING must be used. It can store strings up to 255 characters long.
- BOOLEAN variables can be either true or false. They behave like a switch that is on or off.
- Reserved words such as BEGIN or PROGRAM have a specific meaning to the compiler and cannot be used as identifiers.
- The syntax rules of a language are the grammatical rules that determine how parts of the language are put together. Some of the syntax rules of Pascal are covered in this chapter. A program should start with a heading containing the reserved word PROGRAM and the name of the program followed by a semicolon.
- Any constants that the program uses are defined under the constant definitions. This section starts with CONST. The variables are defined under the variable declaration section, which starts with VAR. Each variable must be assigned a data type that indicates the type of values that will be stored in that variable.
- The body of the program contains statements that perform processing. Semicolons are used to separate statements.
- Comments are enclosed { like this } (* like this *) and are used to explain the program to humans. The compiler skips over comments.

▰▰▰ VOCABULARY LIST

Character string	Decimal notation
Comment	Exponential notation
Constant	Identifier

Input variable   Reserved word
Integer   Syntax rules
Output variable   Variable
Program documentation

■■■■ CHAPTER TEST

Vocabulary

Match a term from the numbered column with the description from
the lettered column that best fits the term.

1. Variable

   a. A method of representing a real number in which the whole part of the number is placed before the decimal point and the fractional part after the decimal point.

2. Output variable

   b. Statements in a program that explain to humans what is being done.

3. Reserved word

   c. A value that does not change during program execution.

4. Integer

   d. A group of characters placed within single quotation marks.

5. Identifier

   e. A method of representing a real number by using powers of 10.

6. Comment

   f. A word that has a specific meaning to the compiler and cannot be used as an identifier.

7. Character string

   g. A name chosen by the programmer to name an object in the program.

8. Syntax rules

   h. A variable that contains the results of processing.

9. Program documentation

   i. A variable whose value is entered into the computer and used to obtain the needed results.

10. Decimal notation

   j. A positive or negative whole number.

11. Constant

   k. A storage location the value of which may change during program execution.

12. Input variable

   l. Comments placed in a program that explain it to humans.

13. Exponential notation

   m. Rules that explain how the parts of a language should be put together.

Questions

1. Explain how variables are stored in the computer.
2. State the rules for creating identifiers.
3. Coach Kramer wants to find out the batting average for each member of the girls' softball team. Coach Kramer figures batting averages this way:

$$\frac{\text{number of hits}}{\text{number of times at bat} - \text{number of walks}}$$

    a. Write the pseudocode for a program to find a batting average.
    b. Make a flowchart for this problem.
    c. Write a program heading and variable declaration statements that would be appropriate for this problem.

4. What are the six data types discussed in this chapter? Give an example of each.
5. Are these valid real numbers? If not, change them so they will be valid.

    a. +367.0
    b. −0.7895
    c. $485.21
    d. 8,291.25

6. Write the following declaration statements a different way. Try to make them as easy to read as possible.

```
a. VAR PERCENT : REAL;   SALE_PRICE : REAL;
      NUM : INTEGER;   YEAR : INTEGER;
b. CONST LENGTH=25.00;
```

7. Write variable and constant declaration statements for a program that finds the average of three real numbers, X, Y, and Z. Write a program heading for the program.
8. Identify the mantissa and the characteristic in the following number written in exponential notation. How would this number look if it were written in decimal notation?

```
8.0200000000E−06
```

9. Which of the following are invalid examples of a variable declared as STRING[10]?

    a. koala bear   d. "1234-678"
    b. 'elephant'   e. 'duck-billed platypus'
    c. 'rhinoceros'

10. Insert the necessary punctuation marks in this program.

```
PROGRAM MILEAGE

VAR
     MILES  GALLONS  MPG  REAL
```

```
BEGIN    { MILEAGE }

   WRITE ('HOW MANY MILES DID YOU DRIVE? ')
   READLN (MILES)
   WRITE ('HOW MANY GALLONS OF GAS DID YOU USE? ')
   READLN (GALLONS)
   MPG := MILES / GALLONS
   WRITELN ('YOU GOT ', MPG, ' MILES PER GALLON OF GAS.')

END    { MILEAGE }
```

CHAPTER 4

Reading and Writing Data

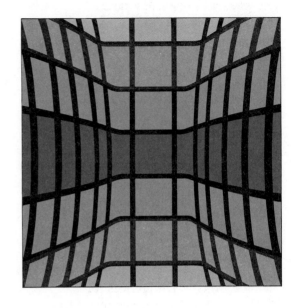

OBJECTIVES

After studying this chapter, you should be able to:

- Use WRITE and WRITELN statements appropriately.
- Explain the difference between the WRITE and WRITELN statements.
- Explain the purpose of prompts and use them appropriately.
- Use READ and READLN statements appropriately.
- Explain the difference between the READ and READLN statements.
- Format real numbers, integers, and character strings.

OUTLINE

■■■■ INTRODUCTION

In Chapter 3, a simple program to convert feet to miles was presented. In order for the program to work, you needed a way to let the computer know the number of feet to be changed to miles. The number of feet was the input data. There had to be a way to enter this data into the computer. Also, you needed a way of finding out what answer the program had obtained. In other words, how could the computer output the answer in a readable form?

In this chapter various ways of entering data into the computer will be presented. In addition, ways of commanding the computer to display results on the monitor screen will be explained.

■■■■ THE WRITE AND WRITELN STATEMENTS

When writing programs, the programmer often wants something displayed on the monitor screen. The WRITE and WRITELN (pronounced "write line") statements can accomplish this action, which is sometimes called writing to the monitor. In most programs the WRITE and WRITELN statements have two basic purposes. The first is to display

prompts for the user. The second is to display results that the program has obtained.

Displaying Prompts

When a program reaches a place where the user is supposed to enter some data, a prompt should be displayed on the monitor. A prompt is a sentence or phrase telling the user that the computer is waiting for the user to enter data. It "prompts" the user to respond. It should also tell the user what type of data is expected. In the FIND_MILES program, the prompt looks like this:

```
WRITE ('HOW MANY FEET ARE TO BE CHANGED INTO MILES? ');
```

This instruction tells the user to type in the number of feet to be changed to miles. Notice that a blank space has been left between the question mark and the ending quotation mark. This space is left so that when the program is run, there will be a space between the prompt and the cursor:

```
HOW MANY FEET ARE TO BE CHANGED INTO MILES?
```

The cursor (represented by the colored rectangle) appears one space after the end of the prompt. The user should now enter the number of feet to be converted and press the Return (or Enter) key.

Displaying Program Results

The WRITE and WRITELN statements are also used to output the results obtained by a program. In program FIND_MILES the following statement displayed the results:

```
WRITELN ('THERE ARE ', MILES, ' MILES IN ', FEET, ' FEET.');
```

When the program was executed, this statement resulted in the following (assuming that the user entered 52800 for the number of feet):

```
THERE ARE  1.0000000000E+01 MILES IN  5.2800000000E+04 FEET.
```

The general format of the WRITE statement is

WRITE (output);

Whatever is to be displayed on the monitor must be in parentheses. If it is a character string, it must also be enclosed in single quotation marks.

The format for the WRITELN statement is

WRITELN (output);

As with the WRITE statement, each value being output must be separated by a comma, and any character strings must be in single quotation marks.

The difference between the WRITE and the WRITELN statements is that after the computer executes a WRITE statement, the cursor remains at the spot where the printing stopped.

Format For WRITE Statement

WRITE (output);

Note: If more than one item is being output, they must be separated by commas.

Format For WRITELN Statement

WRITELN (output);

Note: If more than one item is being output, they must be separated by commas.

However, in the WRITELN statement, after the output is displayed, the cursor returns to the beginning of the next line. The WRITELN statement includes a carriage return, similar to the carriage return on a typewriter. Figure 4–1 contains two short programs that show the difference between the WRITE and WRITELN statements. Notice that the output for the two programs is different. In the first program, several WRITE statements are used. The output is all printed on the same line. Look at the first statement in PROGRAM HELLO1:

```
WRITE ('HI ');
```

There is a space between HI and the quotation mark. If a space had not been left at the end of each string, the output would have looked like this:

```
HITHEREHOW AREYOU DOING?
```

The computer only leaves spaces where the programmer tells it to. There would still be space between HOW and ARE and YOU and DOING because these strings were typed in with spaces between the words. Program HELLO2 outputs each character string on a separate line.

```
PROGRAM HELLO1;

{ DISPLAYS A MESSAGE ON THE MONITOR USING WRITE STATEMENTS. }

BEGIN    { HELLO1 }

    WRITE ('HI ');
    WRITE ('THERE ');
    WRITE ('HOW ARE ');
    WRITE ('YOU DOING?');

END.    { HELLO1 }
```

```
HI THERE HOW ARE YOU DOING?
```

```
PROGRAM HELLO2;

{ DISPLAYS A MESSAGE ON THE MONITOR USING WRITELN STATEMENTS. }

BEGIN    { HELLO2 }

    WRITELN ('HI ');
    WRITELN ('THERE ');
    WRITELN ('HOW ARE ');
    WRITELN ('YOU DOING?');

END.    { HELLO2 }
```

```
HI
THERE
HOW ARE
YOU DOING?
```

FIGURE 4–1 PROGRAMS COMPARING WRITE AND WRITELN STATEMENTS

The WRITELN statement can be used alone to leave blank lines. If the body of HELLO2 were changed like this:

```
WRITELN ('HI');
WRITELN;
WRITELN ('THERE');
WRITELN;
WRITELN ('HOW ARE');
WRITELN;
WRITELN ('YOU DOING?');
```

A blank line would be placed between each line of output:

```
HI

THERE

HOW ARE

YOU DOING?
```

Displaying Literals

WRITE and WRITELN statements can be used to output any type of **literal**. A literal is a value that represents only itself. Prompts are character string literals. Below are some examples of WRITELN statements that output different types of literals:

```
WRITELN (45);              { integer literal }
WRITELN (-0.67);           { real literal }
WRITELN ('#$%SAMPLE');     { character string literal }
```

When these statements are executed, the output will be

```
45
-6.7000000000E-01          (this number is converted
#$%SAMPLE                   to exponential notation)
```

**LEARNING
CHECK
4-1**

1. What two common uses of the WRITE and WRITELN statements are discussed here?
2. What is the purpose of using prompts?
3. What is a literal? Give examples of an integer literal, a real number literal, and a character string literal.
4. What will be output by the following statements? Be careful to get the spacing exactly right.

```
WRITELN ('JON BAUMANN');
WRITELN;
WRITE ('AGE : 15');
WRITE ('GRADE : 9');
WRITELN ('SCHOOL : CITY HIGH');
```

READING INPUT

After the user enters data, the computer needs a way of reading the data and assigning it to variables. The computer uses the READ and READLN statements to do this. The formats for these two statements are

READ (variable[s]);
READLN (variable[s]);

The READ or READLN statement tells the computer to wait until the user enters the needed data. The computer takes the value entered and assigns it to the variable in parentheses. If there is more than one variable, they must be separated by commas. In the FIND_MILES program, the READLN statement is

```
READLN (FEET);
```

As soon as the user types in an integer and presses the Enter key, this value is assigned to the variable FEET.

Format For **READ Statement**
READ (variables[s]); Note: If more than one variable is being read, they must be separated by commas.

Format For **READLN Statement**
READLN (variables[s]); Note: If more than one variable is being read, they must be separated by commas.

In a READ or READLN statement, the value and the variable must be of the same data type. Assume that you run the following short program:

```
PROGRAM CHECK;

VAR
    AGE : INTEGER;

BEGIN    { CHECK }

    WRITE ('ENTER YOUR AGE: ');
    READLN (AGE);

END.    { CHECK }
```

When the program is run, this prompt will appear:

`ENTER YOUR AGE:`

Suppose you type in the letter 'B' in response to the prompt. An error will occur. The compiler cannot assign a letter to a variable of type IN-TEGER. The program will stop executing and an error message will appear.

However, if the variable is of type CHAR or STRING and a number is entered, the compiler will save the number as a character or group of characters. It will convert the number to its character equivalent. Unfortunately, this means that no arithmetic can be performed on it. We will learn more about how numbers can be stored as characters later.

The Difference between READ and READLN

Like the WRITELN statement, the READLN statement includes a carriage return. In Figure 4–2, four integers are added together. The first time the program is run, all four integers are placed on one line. The compiler reads them and adds them together. The numbers are separated by spaces. The number of spaces does not matter.

The second time the program is run, three numbers are typed on one line and the fourth is on the next line. The compiler will keep reading until it finds four numbers, even if it has to go to the next line. The third time the program is run, every number is on a separate line, and the numbers do not necessarily start at the left margin. Again the compiler simply keeps looking until it finds the numbers.

A READ statement could have been used in program ADD1. It would have worked the same way except that a carriage return would not be executed after the data was read. The cursor would remain at the end of the input.

In Figure 4–3, four integers are again added together. In this program, four READ statements are used, one for each integer. When the program is run, all four values are typed on one line. Many values can be read on one line by using a separate READ statement for each value. In a READ statement, the cursor remains on the same line after the data values are read. If there are no more values on the line, the compiler will look for values on the following line. In program ADD2, the four READ statements could have been replaced with a single one:

`READ (NUM1, NUM2, NUM3, NUM4);`

Figure 4–4 illustrates an important difference between the READ and the READLN statements. This program has four separate READLN statements. The first time the program is run, each integer is typed on a separate line. The program works as expected. The second

```
PROGRAM ADD1;

{ THIS PROGRAM READS FOUR INTEGERS AND ADDS THEM TOGETHER. }

VAR
    NUM1, NUM2, NUM3, NUM4, SUM : INTEGER;

BEGIN    { ADD1 }

    WRITE ('TYPE IN THE FOUR NUMBERS TO BE ADDED TOGETHER: ');
    READLN (NUM1, NUM2, NUM3, NUM4);
    SUM := NUM1 + NUM2 + NUM3 + NUM4;
    WRITELN ('THE SUM OF ', NUM1, ', ', NUM2, ', ', NUM3, ' AND ',
             NUM4, ' IS ', SUM);

END.    { ADD1 }
```

```
TYPE IN THE FOUR NUMBERS TO BE ADDED TOGETHER: 4   8   103   15
THE SUM OF 4, 8, 103 AND 15 IS 130

TYPE IN THE FOUR NUMBERS TO BE ADDED TOGETHER: 4   8   103
15
THE SUM OF 4, 8, 103 AND 15 IS 130

TYPE IN THE FOUR NUMBERS TO BE ADDED TOGETHER:       4
8
    103
15
THE SUM OF 4, 8, 103 AND 15 IS 130
```

FIGURE 4-2 PROGRAM ADD1

time the program is run, some of the integers are typed on the same line. Note the output of this program. The compiler has added together the first number on each line. Any other number on the same line is skipped. Because there is only one variable in each READLN statement, the compiler assigns the first value to that variable, and then the

```
PROGRAM ADD2;

{ THIS PROGRAM READS FOUR INTEGERS AND ADDS THEM TOGETHER. }

VAR
    NUM1, NUM2, NUM3, NUM4, SUM : INTEGER;

BEGIN    { ADD2 }

    WRITE ('TYPE IN THE FOUR NUMBERS TO BE ADDED TOGETHER: ');
    READ (NUM1);
    READ (NUM2);
    READ (NUM3);
    READ (NUM4);
    SUM := NUM1 + NUM2 + NUM3 + NUM4;
    WRITELN ('THE SUM OF ', NUM1, ', ', NUM2, ', ', NUM3, ' AND ',
             NUM4, ' IS ', SUM);

END.    { ADD2 }
```

```
TYPE IN THE FOUR NUMBERS TO BE ADDED TOGETHER: 4  8   103   15
THE SUM OF 4, 8, 103 AND 15 IS 130

TYPE IN THE FOUR NUMBERS TO BE ADDED TOGETHER:    4
8
103
15
THE SUM OF 4, 8, 103 AND 15 IS 130
```

FIGURE 4-3 PROGRAM ADD2

cursor advances to the next line. This happens because a READLN statement is being used. This difference is important to remember when using READ and READLN statements. It is important that no data is skipped when it should have been read.

```
PROGRAM ADD3;

{ THIS PROGRAM READS FOUR INTEGERS AND ADDS THEM TOGETHER. }

VAR
    NUM1, NUM2, NUM3, NUM4, SUM : INTEGER;

BEGIN    { ADD3 }

   WRITE ('TYPE IN THE FOUR NUMBERS TO BE ADDED TOGETHER: ');
   READLN (NUM1);
   READLN (NUM2);
   READLN (NUM3);
   READLN (NUM4);
   SUM := NUM1 + NUM2 + NUM3 + NUM4;
   WRITELN ('THE SUM OF ', NUM1, ', ', NUM2, ', ', NUM3, ' AND ',
            NUM4, ' IS ', SUM);

END.    { ADD3 }
```

```
TYPE IN THE FOUR NUMBERS TO BE ADDED TOGETHER: 19
146
2
12
THE SUM OF 19, 146, 2 AND 12 IS 179

TYPE IN THE FOUR NUMBERS TO BE ADDED TOGETHER: 19   208
9
102   12
44
THE SUM OF 19, 9, 102 AND 44 IS 174
```

FIGURE 4–4 PROGRAM ADD3

Reading Character Data

When data of type CHAR is read and more than one character is entered, only the first one will be read. This is different from type STRING, where the entire character string will be read. This is illustrated in Figure 4–5. The first READLN statement assigns 'S' to the CHAR variable INITIAL whereas the second READLN statement assigns the entire name 'Sarah' to the STRING variable NAME.

```
PROGRAM GREETING;

{ THIS PROGRAM DEMONSTRATES THE DIFFERENCE BETWEEN CHAR AND
  STRING VARIABLES. }

VAR
    INITIAL : CHAR;
    NAME    : STRING;

BEGIN    { GREETING }

    WRITE ('PLEASE ENTER YOUR FIRST NAME: ');
    READLN (INITIAL);
    WRITELN ('HI ', INITIAL, '!');
    WRITELN;
    WRITE ('PLEASE ENTER YOUR FIRST NAME AGAIN: ');
    READLN (NAME);
    WRITELN ('HI ', NAME, '!');

END.    { GREETING }
```

```
PLEASE ENTER YOUR FIRST NAME: Sarah
HI S!

PLEASE ENTER YOUR FIRST NAME AGAIN: Sarah
HI Sarah!
```

FIGURE 4–5 PROGRAM GREETING

It is possible to enter more than one STRING variable on a single line. Here is an example:

```
PROGRAM READ_STRING;

VAR
    STR1, STR2 : STRING[4];
```

```
BEGIN    { READ_STRING}

   WRITE ('ENTER TWO STRINGS, EACH FOUR CHARACTERS LONG: ');
   READLN (STR1, STR2);
   WRITELN (STR1);
   WRITELN (STR2);

END.     { READ_STRING }
```

```
ENTER TWO STRINGS, EACH FOUR CHARACTERS LONG: MATT SUE
MATT
 SUE
```

The READLN statement will cause the first four characters to be assigned to STR1 and the next four characters to STR2. Notice that the second string starts with a blank: " SUE." Each blank is treated as a character, just like any other symbol.

DIFFERENCES FOR VERSION 3 USERS

When using READ and READLN statements with Version 3, the following statement should be placed immediately before the program:

```
{$B-}
```

This will cause the READ and READLN statements to function in the same manner as they do in Version 4. Therefore, in order to work properly, the program in Figure 4–2 should be altered as follows:

```
{$B-}
PROGRAM ADD1;

{ THIS PROGRAM READS FOUR INTEGERS AND ADDS THEM TOGETHER. }

VAR
   NUM1, NUM2, NUM3, NUM4, SUM : INTEGER;

BEGIN    { ADD1 }

   WRITE ('TYPE IN THE FOUR NUMBERS TO BE ADDED TOGETHER: ');
   READLN (NUM1, NUM2, NUM3, NUM4);
   SUM := NUM1 + NUM2 + NUM3 + NUM4;
   WRITE ('THE SUM OF ', NUM1, ', ', NUM2, ', ', NUM3, ' AND ',
           NUM4, ' IS ', SUM);

END.     { ADD1 }
```

DIFFERENCES FOR MACINTOSH USERS

When displaying program output, a READLN statement must be placed after a WRITE or WRITELN statement. This READLN statement causes program execution to stop so that the user can examine the program output. The user presses the <Return> key to continue program execution. Therefore, the program in Figure 4–2 should be modified as shown below when using Turbo Pascal for the Macintosh:

```
PROGRAM ADD1;

{ THIS PROGRAM READS FOUR INTEGERS AND ADDS THEM TOGETHER. }

VAR
    NUM1, NUM2, NUM3, NUM4, SUM : INTEGER;

BEGIN    { ADD1 }

    WRITE ('TYPE IN THE FOUR NUMBERS TO BE ADDED TOGETHER: ');
    READLN (NUM1, NUM2, NUM3, NUM4);
    SUM := NUM1 + NUM2 + NUM3 + NUM4;
    WRITE ('THE SUM OF ', NUM1, ', ', NUM2, ', ', NUM3, ' AND ',
           NUM4, ' IS ', SUM);
    READLN;

END.    { ADD1 }
```

▬▬▬▬ FORMATTING OUTPUT

Output is formatted to make it more readable. Formatting means controlling the way the output is displayed.

Let's assume you have a program that reads six integers and prints them in columns. The integers will be called A, B, C, D, E, and F. Each column is to be 10 spaces wide. The following WRITELN statement could be used:

```
WRITELN (A:10, B:10, C:10, D:10, E:10, F:10);
```

Each variable name is followed by a colon and the number of spaces to be allowed for that variable. A WRITELN statement could also be used to set up a heading for these columns. It might look like this:

```
WRITELN ('A':10, 'B':10, 'C':10, 'D':10, 'E':10, 'F':10);
```

This program is given in Figure 4–6. Formatting can be helpful when results are to be printed in columns or in a table.

FIGURE 4–6 PROGRAM COLUMNS

```
PROGRAM COLUMNS;

{ DISPLAYS SIX INTEGERS IN COLUMNS EACH TEN SPACES WIDE. }

VAR
   A, B, C, D, E, F : INTEGER;

BEGIN    { COLUMNS }

   WRITE ('TYPE IN THE 6 INTEGERS: ');
   READLN (A, B, C, D, E, F);
   WRITELN ('A':10, 'B':10, 'C':10, 'D':10, 'E':10, 'F':10);
   WRITELN (A:10, B:10, C:10, D:10, E:10, F:10);

END.    { COLUMNS }
```

```
TYPE IN THE 6 INTEGERS: 11  689  4  121  8  1093
         A         B         C         D         E         F
        11       689         4       121         8      1093
```

LEARNING CHECK 4-2

1. What task do READ and READLN perform? Explain the difference between the READ and READLN statements.

2. Why must a prompt always be followed by a READ or READLN statement?

3. Look at the following input values and then tell what the values of X, Y, and Z will be after each program segment in parts a–d is executed.

```
44   60   99
13   87   12
94
```

```
a. READ (X);          c. READLN (X);
   READ (Y);             READ (Y);
   READ (Z);             READLN (Z);
b. READLN (X, Y);     d. READLN (X);
   READ (Z);             READLN (Y);
                         READLN (Z);
```

Formatting Integers

Formatting integers is quite simple as Figure 4–6 shows. The variable name is followed by a colon and a **field width parameter**. A field width parameter is a value that determines the size of the field in which the output will be displayed. In the program in Figure 4–6 each field is 10 characters long. The output is **right justified** in the field. This means that the last character in the output is placed in the last position in the field. If the number has fewer digits than the length of the field, blank spaces are inserted on the left side of the field. Here's a simple WRITELN statement that displays three integer literals:

```
WRITELN (1:4, 30:4, 469:4);
```

Each literal is placed in a field 4 spaces wide. If the integers are smaller than the field, blanks are placed in front of the integer to "fill out" the field. These blanks will be highlighted in examples by using the letter "b" with a slash (b̸) to represent a blank space. When the preceding statement is executed, the output will be

```
b̸b̸b̸1b̸b̸30b̸469
```

or without the space indicators

```
1   30 469
```

What do you think will happen if the field width parameter is smaller than the number of digits in the integer? For example,

```
WRITELN (1749:3);
```

The compiler will not allow the number to be accidentally "cut off." The entire integer will still be displayed:

```
1749
```

Formatting Real Numbers

In Chapter 3 the results of the FIND_MILES program were displayed in exponential notation. The WRITELN statement looked like this:

```
WRITELN ('THERE ARE ', MILES, ' MILES IN ', FEET, ' FEET.');
```

When 52800 was entered as the number of feet to be changed to miles, the result looked like this:

```
THERE ARE  1.0000000000E+01 MILES IN  5.2800000000E+04 FEET.
```

Usually, you will want results to be output in regular decimal notation. To do this, the real numbers need to be formatted. This WRITELN statement could be rewritten as shown below:

```
WRITELN ('THERE ARE ', MILES:8:2, ' MILES IN ', FEET:8:2, ' FEET.');
```

To format a real number, the variable name is written first, followed by a colon and a field width parameter. Then there is a second colon and another integer. This second integer indicates the number of decimal positions to be displayed. If the number has more than two decimal places, it will be rounded to two decimal places.

Suppose the result of a program is 3748.69812. If a WRITELN statement were written like this:

```
WRITELN (NUM:8:2);
```

the computer would round off the result to two decimal places:

```
3748.70
```

The following table has more examples.

Unformatted Result	WRITE Statement	Result Printed as
1.4895800000E+02	WRITE (NUM:7:2);	148.96
1.7742400000E+01	WRITE (NUM:8:4);	17.7424
2.6839400000E+01	WRITE (NUM:6:2);	26.84
−3.1836700000E−01	WRITE (NUM:7:3);	−0.318

Figure 4–7 shows a program that prints the real number 68.2165 five different ways. We will discuss the output of each of these statements.

```
PROGRAM PRINTNUM;

{ DISPLAYS A REAL NUMBER IN DIFFERENT FORMATS. }

VAR
    REALNUM : REAL;

BEGIN    { PRINTNUM }

    WRITE ('TYPE IN A REAL NUMBER THAT HAS FOUR DECIMAL PLACES: ');
    READLN (REALNUM);
    WRITELN (REALNUM);
    WRITELN (REALNUM:7:4);
    WRITELN (REALNUM:5:2);
    WRITELN (REALNUM:3:2);
    WRITELN (REALNUM:12:2);

END.     { PRINTNUM }
```

```
TYPE IN A REAL NUMBER THAT HAS FOUR DECIMAL PLACES: 68.2165
  6.8216500000E+01
68.2165
68.22
68.22
        68.22
```

FIGURE 4–7 PROGRAM PRINTNUM

1. The first WRITELN statement is

   `WRITELN (REALNUM);`

   This results in the number being printed in exponential notation:

   `6.8216500000E+01`

   Any real number that is not formatted is displayed this way.

2. The second statement displays the number in decimal notation with four decimal places:

   `WRITELN (REALNUM:7:4);`

   The result looks like this:

   `68.2165`

3. The third statement displays the number in decimal notation with two decimal places:

   `WRITELN (REALNUM:5:2);`

   Note that the number has been *rounded* to two decimal places:

   `68.22`

4. In this statement the field width parameter is too small for the number:

   `WRITELN (REALNUM:3:2);`

   Even though the compiler will allow the number of decimal places to be rounded, it will not allow any of the integer portion of the number to be lost:

   `68.22`

   Regardless of how small the field width parameter is, all digits to the left of the decimal point will always be displayed.

5. In this statement, the field width parameter is larger than the number:

   `WRITELN (REALNUM:12:2);`

   The number is right justified in the field:

   `68.22`

   The field is padded with blanks on the left side.

Formatting Character Strings

Character strings are formatted in the same way as integers. When the following statement is executed:

`WRITELN ('TODAY IS THE FIRST DAY OF SPRING!':40);`

the output will be

```
TODAY IS THE FIRST DAY OF SPRING!
```

The string has 33 characters. Therefore, it will be right justified in a field of 40 characters. There will be seven blank spaces on the left side of the field. If the field width parameter is too small:

```
WRITELN ('TODAY IS THE FIRST DAY OF SPRING!':30);
```

the entire string will still be displayed:

```
TODAY IS THE FIRST DAY OF SPRING!
```

The compiler will not allow the programmer to cut off part of the string.

▬▬▬ PROGRAM CIRCLE

We will now write a program that combines a number of things learned in this chapter. In this program, the user will be prompted to enter the diameter of a circle. From this information, the program will calculate the following:

1. The radius of the circle (diameter/2)
2. The circumference of the circle ($\pi \times$ diameter)
3. The area of the circle ($\pi \times$ radius^2)

This information will be displayed in columns that are 15 spaces wide.

Figure 4–8 shows this program. First the diameter is entered and assigned to the variable DIAMETER. From this information, the radius, circumference, and area are calculated. Look at the statement that calculates the circumference:

```
CIRCUMFERENCE := DIAMETER * PI;
```

The identifier PI has not been assigned a value anywhere in this program. This is because the Turbo Pascal compiler automatically assigns the value of pi (approximately 3.14159) to this identifier. Therefore, we can use PI whenever we want without assigning it a value.

The results of this program are printed by using a single WRITELN statement. Each value is rounded off to two decimal places. Each real number is right justified in a field of 15 spaces. Notice that a heading containing labels is placed above the output. The statement generating the heading looks like this:

```
WRITELN ('DIAMETER':15, 'RADIUS':15, 'CIRCUMFERENCE':15, 'AREA':15);
```

Each of these labels is right justified in a field 15 spaces wide so that the label will print above the corresponding number. It is important to label results so that the user can easily understand them.

```
PROGRAM CIRCLE;

{ THIS PROGRAM READS THE DIAMETER OF A CIRCLE IN INCHES.  FROM THIS
  DATA THE RADIUS, CIRCUMFERENCE, AND AREA OF THE CIRCLE ARE THEN
  COMPUTED. }

VAR
    DIAMETER, RADIUS, CIRCUMFERENCE, AREA : REAL;

BEGIN

    WRITE ('WHAT IS THE DIAMETER OF THE CIRCLE IN INCHES: ');
    READLN (DIAMETER);
    RADIUS := DIAMETER / 2;
    CIRCUMFERENCE := DIAMETER * PI;
    AREA := PI * RADIUS * RADIUS;
    WRITELN ('DIAMETER':15, 'RADIUS':15, 'CIRCUMFERENCE':15, 'AREA':15);
    WRITELN (DIAMETER:15:2, RADIUS:15:2, CIRCUMFERENCE:15:2, AREA:15:2);

END.   { CIRCLE }
```

```
WHAT IS THE DIAMETER OF THE CIRCLE IN INCHES: 6
       DIAMETER         RADIUS  CIRCUMFERENCE           AREA
          12.00           6.00          37.70         113.10
```

FIGURE 4–8 PROGRAM CIRCLE

LEARNING CHECK 4-3

1. How will the number −28.3765 be displayed given the following formats? Be sure to indicate any blank spaces by using a "ø."

   a. NUMBER:5:1
   b. NUMBER:6:2
   c. NUMBER:9:2
   d. NUMBER:8:4

2. Write a WRITELN statement that will print eight INTEGER variables in columns six spaces wide. Make up your own variable names.

3. Explain what right justified means.

SUMMARY POINTS

- WRITE and WRITELN statements are used to display prompts and the results of programs. Prompts are used to inform the user that data needs to be entered into the program.
- The WRITELN statement includes a carriage return that causes the cursor to advance to the beginning of the next line whereas when a WRITE statement is used, the cursor remains at the end of the output.
- READ and READLN statements are used to input data to variables. The READLN statement includes a carriage return whereas the READ statement does not.
- Formatting is the process of controlling the physical arrangement of output. When formatting integers or character strings, a single field width parameter is used to determine the size of the field in which the output will be displayed. Output is right justified, which means that if the output is smaller than the field, it is "padded" with blanks on the left side to fill out the field.
- Real numbers can be formatted by using two parameters: the first determines the size of the entire field, and the second determines the number of decimal places that will be displayed.

VOCABULARY LIST

Field width parameter   Prompt
Literal   Right justified

▓▓▓ CHAPTER TEST

Vocabulary

Match a term from the numbered column with the description from the lettered column that best fits the term.

1. Literal

2. Right justified

3. Prompt

4. Field width parameter

a. A message telling the user that data needs to be entered.

b. An integer value that determines the size of an output field.

c. Output displayed so that the last character is in the last position of the output field.

d. An expression containing any combination of numbers, letters, and so forth and representing only itself.

Questions

1. The following numbers are in exponential notation. How would they be displayed if they were formatted like this: NUMBER:7:2?

   a. 2.5783400000E+02
   b. −3.1628910000E+01

   c. 9.7320000000E−03
   d. 4.0000000000E+08

2. Tell where the cursor will be located after each of these statements is executed. What will be output by each statement?

   ```
   a. WRITELN ('TYPE IN A LETTER:');
   b. WRITE ('WHAT IS THE SECOND NUMBER?':30);
   c. WRITE ('WHAT IS YOUR AGE? ');
   d. WRITELN ('THE ANSWER IS 10.':14);
   ```

3. Look at this program segment.

   ```
   READ (X);
   READ (Y);
   READ (Z);
   ```

   Tell what the values of X, Y, and Z will be for each part below if the data is entered as shown:

   a. 4   16   10
      108   7
      32

   b. 16
      81
      1182

   c. 109
      63   70
      2871   532

4. Look at this program segment.

```
READLN (A);
READLN (B);
READLN (C);
```

Tell what the values of A, B, and C will be for each part below if the data is entered as shown.

a. 77   32   0
   188
   16   2871

b. 44
  18   97
  100 82

5. Here's another program segment:

```
READLN (L, M, N);
```

What will the values of L, M, and N be, given the data below?

a. 4   15   82
  91   0
  12

b. 66
  17   18

6. What is formatting? Why do programmers format output?
7. How are real numbers formatted? How is this different from the way in which integers are formatted?
8. What will these statements output to the monitor? (Be sure to indicate blanks.)

```
WRITE ('THAT''S');
WRITE (' ALL');
WRITELN;
WRITELN;
WRITELN ('FOLKS!')
```

■■■ PROGRAMMING PROBLEMS

Level 1

1. Look at the two programs in Figure 4–1. Write a program that places each of the words "HI THERE HOW ARE YOU DOING?" on a separate line.
2. Read four integers. Print them so that they are in columns each 10 spaces wide. Make a heading for each column. Here is a sample of how the output might look:

```
FIRST     SECOND     THIRD    FOURTH
    5         16        101        10
```

Level 2

3. Write a program to display the following:
    First line: your name.
    Second line: your age.
    Third line: blank.
    Fourth line: your address.
4. Write a program that will display your initials in large block letters.
    Use X's or any other appropriate symbols to create the blocks.

CHAPTER 5

Simple Pascal Statements

OBJECTIVES

After studying this chapter, you should be able to:

- Define and explain the purpose of an assignment statement.
- Write valid Pascal assignment statements.
- Name the six arithmetic operators discussed in this chapter and explain what function each performs.
- Write assignment statements using the six arithmetic operators.
- List the order of operations.
- Correctly evaluate expressions containing multiple operators.
- Write statements using parentheses to control the order in which arithmetic operations are performed.
- Explain the purpose of control statements.
- Explain the difference between single- and double-alternative IF statements.
- Write single- and double-alternative IF statements.
- Define and correctly use relational operators.

OUTLINE

▬▬ INTRODUCTION

In Chapter 4, you learned how to read data to variables. This data was entered at the keyboard. In this chapter, you will learn how to assign values directly to variables. You will also learn how to write statements that perform arithmetic. At the conclusion of the chapter, you will learn about a statement that will be very helpful in writing programs. This statement allows the programmer to determine whether a certain part of a program will be executed.

▬▬ ASSIGNMENT STATEMENTS

Computer programs are used to solve problems. In the program converting feet to miles, we needed a way to create a new variable called MILES to hold the result of the computation FEET /

FEET_IN_A_MILE. The number of feet was divided by the number of feet in one mile. An **assignment statement** was used to assign the result of the computation to the variable MILES:

```
MILES := FEET / FEET_IN_A_MILE;
```

This statement should be read "MILES is assigned the value of FEET divided by FEET_IN_A_MILE." The symbol ":=" should not be thought of as an equals sign. The general syntax of the assignment statement is

variable := expression;

An **expression** can be a variable, constant, or any valid combination of variables, constants, or operators. An **operator** is a symbol that stands for a process. The assignment operator is ":=" and stands for the process of placing the result of the expression on the right side of the statement into the variable on the left side of the statement.

Format For **Assignment Statement**
variable := expression;

Finding the average of three whole numbers is a calculation that can be performed in two steps. First, the sum of the three numbers must be found. Then the sum must be divided by three (the number of items being averaged). The first assignment statement could be written as follows (assume SUM, A, B, and C have been declared as type INTEGER):

```
SUM := A + B + C;
```

The sum of A + B + C is now stored in the variable SUM. The second assignment statement could look like this:

```
AVERAGE := SUM / 3;
```

Figure 5–1 shows the data needed by this program. What type of number will AVERAGE be? It could be a whole number, but more than likely it will be a real number. Therefore, AVERAGE must be declared to be of data type REAL. Figure 5–2 contains the computer program that solves this problem.

An assignment statement does not always include an arithmetic operation. It can be used to copy a value from one variable to another:

```
TEMP := SUM;
```

After this statement is executed, the value of TEMP is the same as the value of SUM. The value of SUM remains the same. Later you will see that this type of statement can often be useful.

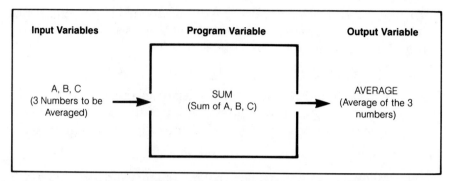

FIGURE 5-1 DATA FOR PROGRAM TO FIND AVERAGE OF THREE NUMBERS

FIGURE 5-2 PROGRAM FIND_AVERAGE

```
PROGRAM FIND_AVERAGE;

{ FINDS THE AVERAGE OF 3 NUMBERS. }

VAR
    SUM, A, B, C : INTEGER;
    AVERAGE      : REAL;

BEGIN    { FIND_AVERAGE }

    WRITE ('WHAT ARE THE 3 NUMBERS? ');
    READLN (A, B, C);
    SUM := A + B + C;
    AVERAGE := SUM / 3;
    WRITELN ('THE AVERAGE IS ', AVERAGE:7:2);

END.    { FIND_AVERAGE }
```

```
WHAT ARE THE 3 NUMBERS? 4   12   26
THE AVERAGE IS   14.00
```

An assignment statement can be used to find the opposite of a number:

```
A := -105;
A := -A;
```

The first statement assigns the value −105 to A. The value of −A is 105. This value, 105, is then stored in A. The original value of A (−105) is lost; it has been replaced by the new value. This statement is the same as multiplying A by −1. Here's another program segment:

```
SUM := 10;
SUM := SUM + 1;
```

The second statement increases the current value of SUM by 1. SUM is now equal to 11.

It is not necessary to have a variable name on the right side of an assignment statement. If COUNT is declared to be of data type INTEGER, this statement would be valid:

```
COUNT := 10;
```

Would the statement below be a valid assignment statement?

```
COUNT := 1.5;
```

No, because 1.5 is a real number and COUNT has been declared to be of data type INTEGER. If you attempted to compile this statement, you would get a "TYPE MISMATCH" error. For the same reason this statement is invalid:

```
COUNT := COUNT + 2.75;
```

What if COUNT had been declared to be of data type REAL? Could there be an assignment statement like the one below?

```
COUNT := 14;
```

Yes, because the compiler can convert a whole number into a real number.

Assignment statements can also be used with STRING and CHAR data types. Here's a program segment:

```
PROGRAM ASSIGN;

VAR
    STAR : CHAR;
    NAME, NEWNAME : STRING;

BEGIN

    STAR := '*';
    NAME := 'MICHAEL DWIGHT';
```

The value of STAR is now *. The variable NAME now contains the value MICHAEL DWIGHT. Remember that in CHAR and STRING data types the value assigned to the variable must be in single quotation marks. Because the variables NAME and NEWNAME are both of the same type (STRING), the value of NAME could be copied to NEWNAME like this:

```
NEWNAME := NAME;
```

NAME is not enclosed in quotation marks because it is a variable name, not a character string. Now both NAME and NEWNAME contain the character string MICHAEL DWIGHT. The following statement is invalid:

```
STAR := NEWNAME;
```

The data type CHAR can contain only one character.

The data type BOOLEAN can be assigned only one of two values: true or false. If ANSWER is declared to be of type BOOLEAN, the assignment statement could look like this:

```
ANSWER := TRUE;
```

or like this:

```
ANSWER := FALSE;
```

In all these examples of assignment statements, the compiler determines the value of the expression to the right of the assignment operator. This result is then assigned to the variable to the left of the assignment operator.

LEARNING CHECK 5-1

1. Given the following declaration statements, which of the assignment statements in parts a–d are valid?

```
VAR
    PERCENT, COST : REAL;
    NUMBER_ITEMS  : INTEGER;
    ITEM_NAME     : STRING;
```

   a. PERCENT := 17.5%;
   b. COST := 156;
   c. NUMBER_ITEMS := 15 + 2;
   d ITEM_NAME := PROTRACTOR;

2. Given the following program segment:

```
VAR
    TREE, PLANT : STRING;

BEGIN

    TREE := 'MAPLE';
```

explain the difference between the following statements:

```
PLANT := 'TREE';
PLANT := TREE;
```

What value will be stored in PLANT after each of these statements is executed?

3. What will be the values of SCORE, NUM, TOTAL, and GRADE after this program is executed?

```
PROGRAM FIND_GRADE;

VAR
    SCORE, NUM, TOTAL : INTEGER;
    GRADE : CHAR;

BEGIN    { FIND_GRADE }

    SCORE := 4 + 2;
    NUM := 12;
    NUM := NUM + 10;
    GRADE := 'A';
    TOTAL := NUM + SCORE;

END.     { FIND_GRADE }
```

ARITHMETIC OPERATORS

Six different **arithmetic operators** will be discussed here. An arithmetic operator is a symbol that stands for a particular arithmetic process, such as addition or subtraction. The first four arithmetic operators are familiar to us:

+ add
− subtract
* multiply
/ divide

The symbols and their meanings are shown in Figure 5–3.

Addition

In the process of addition, the values of the **operands** are added together. This sum is assigned to the variable on the left side of the

Arithmetic Operator	Meaning	Example
+	addition	A + B
−	subtraction	A − B
⋆	multiplication	A ⋆ B
/	division	A / B

FIGURE 5-3 ARITHMETIC OPERATORS

assignment operator. An operand is a value upon which an operation is performed. In this example

15 + 12

the operands are 15 and 12. The arithmetic operator is the plus sign (+). When whole numbers are added together, the result is a whole number. For example, the statement

```
A := 1 + 4 + 5;
```

will result in the value 10 being assigned to A. Although this answer is a whole number, variable A may be declared to be of data type INTE-GER or REAL. As previously mentioned, the compiler can convert a whole number to a real number.

When real numbers are added together, the result must always be of data type REAL. If the result of adding two real numbers together were assigned to an INTEGER variable, it would result in an error when the program was run. Here are some examples of addition with variables of type REAL:

Statement	Value of Variable
TEST1 := 14.5;	TEST1 = 14.5
POINT := 10.00 + TEST1;	POINT = 24.5
SPEED := 35.5 + 0.68 + 1.0;	SPEED = 37.18
DISTANCE1 := 10.25;	DISTANCE1 = 10.25
DISTANCE1 := DISTANCE1 + 5;	DISTANCE1 = 15.25

A whole number and a real number may be added together. The result must be assigned to a variable of type REAL.

Subtraction

In subtraction, the value of the second operand is subtracted from the value of the first. The rules concerning the use of INTEGER and REAL data types are the same as for addition. Given the following declarations, the statements below will evaluate as shown:

```
VAR
    COUNT, YARDS : INTEGER;
    COST, PRICE  : REAL;
```

Statement	Value of Variable
COUNT := 10 - 2;	COUNT = 8
COUNT := COUNT - 6;	COUNT = 2
YARDS := 12 - COUNT;	YARDS = 10
PRICE := 102.50 - 20.00;	PRICE = 82.50
COST := 100 - PRICE;	COST = 17.50

Multiplication

The arithmetic operator for multiplication is the asterisk (*). It is the only sign that may be used for multiplication. In multiplication, the values of the operands are multiplied together, and the result is assigned to the variable on the left side of the assignment operator. If two whole numbers are multiplied together, the result will always be a whole number. As in subtraction and addition, this result may be placed in a variable of either data type INTEGER or REAL. If two real numbers or a whole number and a real number are multiplied together, the result must be assigned to a variable of type REAL.

Division

In Pascal, the arithmetic operator for division is the slash sign (/). The first operand is divided by the second operand.

If one integer is divided by another, the result must always be assigned to a REAL variable. This is because the result will usually be a real number. Two real numbers may be divided by each other. Again, the result must be assigned to a REAL variable. Given the following declarations, the statements below will evaluate as shown:

```
VAR
    COST, PRICE : REAL;
    SUM         : INTEGER;
```

Statement	Value of Variable
PRICE := 10 / 3;	PRICE = 3.33
COST := 12.5 / 2;	COST = 6.25
SUM := 6;	SUM = 6
PRICE := SUM / 0.5	PRICE = 12

As in arithmetic, division by zero is not allowed. Thus the following statement will result in an error:

```
NUM := SCORE / 0;
```

DIV and MOD

The two arithmetic operators DIV and MOD can be used with integers only. The result will always be an integer. The DIV operation truncates, or cuts off, the result of the division process (the quotient) to an integer value. In the following problem the remainder will be cut off.

```
     4   quotient
6 ) 27
    24
     3   remainder
```

In the statement below, A is of data type INTEGER:

```
A := 27 DIV 6;
```

The value of A will be 4. There is never a decimal point in the result of a DIV operation. Here's another example:

```
X := 105 DIV 12;
```

The division problem looks like this:

```
      8   quotient
12 ) 105
     96
      9   remainder
```

The value of X will be 8.

Here's the same problem using the MOD operator:

```
REM := 105 MOD 12;
```

The result of the MOD operation is the remainder of the DIV operation. The value of REM is 9. REM is assigned the value of the remainder. REM must also be declared to be data type INTEGER. Look at the following problems and see if you agree with the answers given.

Problem	Answer
8 DIV 3	2
8 MOD 3	2
140 DIV 12	11
140 MOD 12	8
160 DIV 8	20
160 MOD 8	0

As in regular division, the divisor in a DIV or MOD operation may not be equal to zero. Both of these statements are invalid:

```
A DIV 0
A MOD 0
```

ORDER OF OPERATIONS

In Pascal, arithmetic expressions containing many operations can be written. Here is an example:

4 * 18 + 20 / 5 − 3

In this expression, several steps need to be performed to find the answer. To determine how to solve this problem, it is necessary to have an **order of operations** stating the order in which the arithmetic will be done. The order of operations, shown in Figure 5–4, specified that multiplication and division are performed before addition and subtraction. Any operations on the same level are done from left to right. In the expression above, 4 * 18 and 20 / 5 are both at the same level. First, 4 is multiplied by 18, because we are moving from left to right. Then 20 will be divided by 5. After all of the multiplication and division are done, the addition and subtraction are performed. They will be done from left to right because addition and subtraction are both on the same level. The steps in evaluating the expression will be

1. 4 * 18 = 72
2. 20 / 5 = 4
3. 72 + 4 = 76
4. 76 − 3 = 73

The value of the expression is 73.

In the example above, what if it were necessary to subtract 3 from 5 before doing the rest of the problem? The order in which arithmetic operations are performed can be controlled by using parentheses. The above expression could be written

4 * 18 + 20 / (5 − 3)

In this case the steps would be

1. 5 − 3 = 2
2. 4 * 18 = 72
3. 20 / 2 = 10
4. 72 + 10 = 82

FIGURE 5–4 ORDER OF OPERATIONS

1. Evaluate anything in parentheses.
2. *, /, DIV, and MOD are evaluated before + and − .
3. Arithmetic operators at the same level (such as * and DIV) are evaluated left to right.

The value of the expression would be 82. Expressions in parentheses are always evaluated first. If two sets of parentheses are nested (one inside the other), the innermost one is evaluated first:

$$1500 / (10 * (14 - 4))$$

The steps in evaluating this expression are

1. $14 - 4 = 10$
2. $10 * 10 = 100$
3. $1500 / 100 = 15$

The result is 15. Below is the same problem with no parentheses:

$$1500 / 10 * 14 - 4$$

Now the steps would be

1. $1500 / 10 = 150$
2. $150 * 14 = 2100$
3. $2100 - 4 = 2096$

Obviously, a very different answer is obtained. If you have any doubts about how an expression will be evaluated, always use parentheses. This way you will know exactly how the arithmetic will be done. Adding parentheses when they are not necessary will not hurt anything. It also can make a program easier to understand.

ALGEBRAIC EQUATIONS

Algebraic equations often look like this:

$$\frac{A \times B}{N - 1} \times \frac{X + Y^2}{N + 1}$$

How would this be written in Pascal? Again, parentheses would be needed to control the order in which the arithmetic is performed. The left side would be written

$$A * B / (N - 1)$$

It is not necessary to put A * B in parentheses, but it might help keep things clear. The right side would look like this:

$$(X + Y * Y) / (N + 1)$$

Notice that Y is multiplied by itself to square it. Next the two sides are multiplied together:

$$(A * B / (N - 1)) * ((X + Y * Y) / (N + 1))$$

There are parentheses around each entire term. All of the operations in each term must be performed before the two sides are multiplied together. Be careful when you are using parentheses inside other sets of parentheses. It is very easy to leave one off or put it in the wrong place, resulting in an error when the program is run.

1. Use this program segment to write statements for the problems in parts a–d. Then answer the questions.

```
PROGRAM COMPUTE;

VAR
    NUM1, NUM2, A, B, C : REAL;

BEGIN

    A := 15.0;
    B := 3.0;
    C := 27.0;
```

   a. Subtract A from B. Then multiply the result by two. Assign this value to the variable NUM1. What will the value of NUM1 be?
   b. Divide C by B. Then divide the result by two. Assign the result to NUM2. What will the value of NUM2 be?
   c. Add A and C together. Divide this result by B. Assign the result to A. What will the value of A be?
   d. Subtract B from C. Square the result. Then assign the result to NUM1. Figure out what the value of NUM1 will be.

2. Evaluate the following expressions.

   a. $4 - 6 / 2$
   b. $6.5 + 8.5 - 4.3$
   c. $18 + 16 / 4$
   d. $280 / 7 * 6$
   e. $73.5 / 2.5 * 16.75$
   f. $73.5 / (2.5 * 16.75)$

THE IF STATEMENT

In all the programs written so far, the statements have been executed sequentially. This means the computer has executed statements in the order they occurred in the program. In many programming problems, however, the order in which the statements are executed needs to be controlled.

Control statements allow the programmer to alter the order in which the computer executes the statements in a program. Control statements test a condition; what happens next depends on the outcome of the test. There are two types of control statements: **decision statements** and **loops**. Decision statements allow certain steps in a program to be executed or skipped, depending on the results of the condition. Loops allow a section of a program to be repeated as many times as required. In this section, one type of decision statement will be discussed: the IF statement.

The Single-Alternative IF Statement

In real life, people are constantly making decisions. Most decisions are based on a particular situation. You start making decisions when you awaken in the morning. Some of these decisions might be: is there time for a shower and breakfast? Should you wear a raincoat or a regular coat? If you do not feel well, should you stay in bed?

In order to be useful, computer programs also need to allow for decisions. Computer programs do this by evaluating conditions. These conditions always evaluate as either true or false. For example, is variable A larger than zero? If so, something may be done to A that will not occur if A is less than or equal to zero. Decisions can be written by using an IF statement. Let's say that if a number is less than zero, we want it to be displayed, otherwise we want nothing done. The following statement could be used:

```
IF NUMBER < 0
    THEN WRITELN (NUMBER:7);
```

If the value of NUMBER were -5, the following would be output when this statement was executed:

If the value of NUMBER were 23, nothing would happen. Program execution would simply continue with the next statement.

Format For **Single-Alternative IF Statement**
IF condition   THEN statement;

This is referred to as a single-alternative IF (or IF/THEN) statement. If the tested condition is true, the statement after the THEN is executed. Otherwise, nothing happens. Its general format is

```
IF condition
    THEN statement;
```

The IF/THEN statement is a single Pascal statement. It has a semicolon only at the end of the statement, so there is no semicolon after the THEN. We could write the statement all on one line:

```
IF NUMBER < 0 THEN WRITELN (NUMBER:7);
```

Putting it on two lines and indenting the second one makes the program logic easier to follow.

Comparisons are frequently made in IF statements by using **relational operators**. Relational operators compare one operand with another. The relational operators in Pascal are listed in Figure 5–5. The same operators are used in mathematics, although some of the symbols are slightly different.

Here is an example of an IF/THEN statement:

```
IF Z = Y
    THEN Z := Z + 10;
```

This is read "IF Z is equal to Y, then assign the value of Z plus 10 to Z." In this example, Z will be increased by 10 only if Z is equal to Y. This statement could be changed to the opposite:

```
IF Z <> Y
    THEN Z := Z + 10;
```

In this case, the value of Z will be increased by 10 only if it is *not* equal to Y. If Z is equal to Y, the compiler will simply skip to the next statement.

Relational operators may also be used with character data. Look at how the following expressions are evaluated.

Expression	Evaluates as
'A' < 'D'	true
'JIMINY' < 'JIM'	false
'PARTRIDGE' = 'PARTRIDGE'	true
'P' = 'p'	false
'P' <> 'Q'	true

FIGURE 5–5 RELATIONAL OPERATORS

Operator	Meaning	Example
=	equals	X = Y
<>	does not equal	X <> Y
>	greater than	X > Y
>=	greater than or equal to	X >= Y
<	less than	X < Y
<=	less than or equal to	X <= Y

Notice that for the compiler to see two characters as being equal, they must both be uppercase or lowercase. This is also true of character strings. The compiler will not see 'Yesterday' and 'yesterday' as being the same.

You may wonder how the computer is able to determine that a given character string is less than, equal to, or greater than another character string. We know that A comes before C, but how does the computer know this? It can make this comparison because the computer assigns characters an internal ordering it is able to recognize. This ordering is referred to as the computer's **collating sequence**. In other words, the computer sees characters as a sequence of values, just the same as integers. There are many different collating sequences. The one used by Turbo Pascal is called the ASCII code; it is shown in Appendix E. Turn to Appendix E and locate the ASCII code for 'J'. It is 74. Now find 'C', which is 67. To evaluate the expression 'C' < 'J', the computer would compare these two values, 67 and 74. Because 67 is less than 74, this expression evaluates as true. Conversely, the expression '#' > '{' would be false because 35 is not greater than 123.

Let's write a simple program using the IF/THEN statement. The local record store is having a sale. All of the albums are marked down to $5. If you buy six or more albums, you get 10 percent off the total price. The flowchart for this problem is shown in Figure 5–6. First, the number of albums to be bought needs to be read. This number will be multiplied by the price per album, $5. Now we will need to determine whether the number of albums being bought is greater than or equal to six. If it is, the price charged will be only 90 percent of the total (100% − 10% = 90%). For this problem, the IF/THEN statement could be

```
IF ALBUMS >= 6
   THEN COST := COST * 0.90;
```

It also could be written as

```
IF ALBUMS > 5
   THEN COST := COST * 0.90;
```

Either way, 10 percent is taken from the total price if six or more albums are being purchased. Figure 5–7 contains the complete program.

The Double-Alternative IF Statement

The IF/THEN statement is called a single-alternative IF statement because there is only one choice. If the condition is false, nothing is done. Suppose the discount on the records is a little different. Consider this pricing arrangement:

one to five albums: $5.00 each
six or more albums: $4.85 each

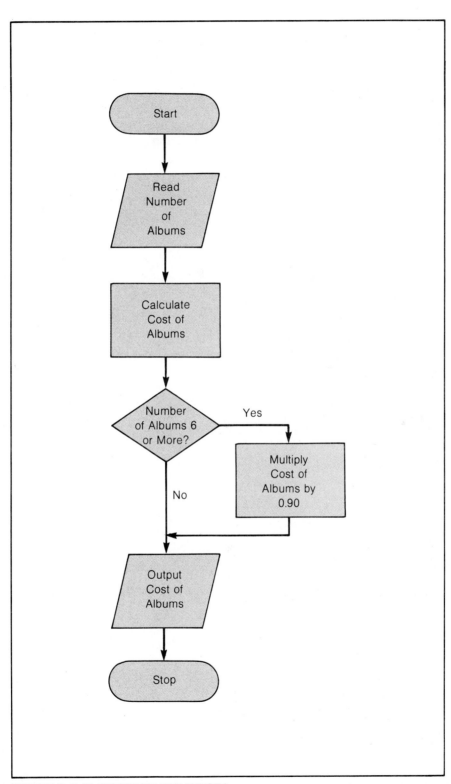

FIGURE 5-6 FLOWCHART FOR PRICE1

```
PROGRAM PRICE1;

{ FIND THE TOTAL COST OF THE RECORD ALBUMS.  THE ALBUMS ARE $5.00
EACH.  IF 6 OR MORE ARE BOUGHT, THERE IS A 10% DISCOUNT. }

VAR
   ALBUMS : INTEGER;
   COST   : REAL;

BEGIN   { PRICE1 }

   {   DETERMINE THE NUMBER OF ALBUMS. }
   WRITE ('HOW MANY ALBUMS ARE BEING BOUGHT? ');
   READLN (ALBUMS);

   { DETERMINE THE TOTAL COST. }
   COST := ALBUMS * 5.00;

   { IF THERE ARE 6 OR MORE ALBUMS, SUBTRACT 10%. }
   IF ALBUMS >= 6
      THEN COST := COST * 0.90;

   { OUTPUT THE FINAL COST. }
   WRITELN ('THE COST OF THE ALBUMS IS $', COST:6:2);

END.    { PRICE1 }
```

```
HOW MANY ALBUMS ARE BEING BOUGHT? 7
THE COST OF THE ALBUMS IS $ 31.50

HOW MANY ALBUMS ARE BEING BOUGHT? 4
THE COST OF THE ALBUMS IS $ 20.00
```

FIGURE 5-7 PROGRAM PRICE1

Look at the flowchart for this problem in Figure 5–8. The easiest way to write this program would be to use a double-alternative IF (IF/THEN/ELSE) statement. It has the following format:

   IF condition
     THEN statement1
     ELSE statement2;

FIGURE 5–8 FLOWCHART FOR PRICE2

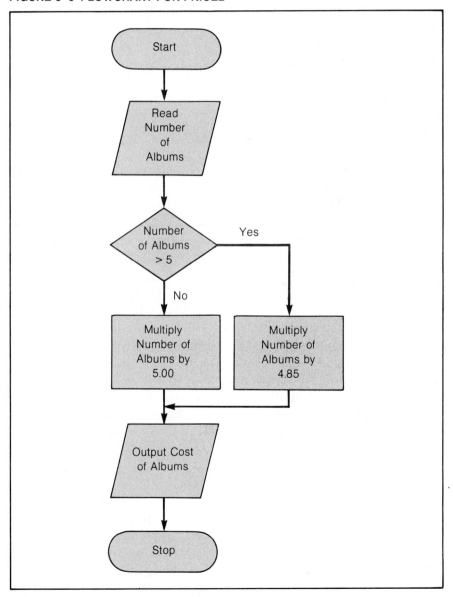

In this case, if the stated condition is true, the statement following the THEN is executed. If it is false, the statement following the ELSE is executed. One or the other of the statements will always be executed. Notice that there is a semicolon only at the very end of the statement. The IF/THEN/ELSE statement is a single Pascal statement. For the problem computing the cost of the albums, the IF/THEN/ELSE statement could look like this:

```
IF ALBUMS <= 5
    THEN COST := ALBUMS * 5.00
    ELSE COST := ALBUMS * 4.85;
```

This statement could be rearranged and still produce the same results:

```
IF ALBUMS > 5
    THEN COST := ALBUMS * 4.85
    ELSE COST := ALBUMS * 5.00;
```

Figure 5–9 shows the complete program for this problem.

Format For **Double-Alternative IF Statement**

IF condition
  THEN statement1
  ELSE statement2;

■■■■ USING UNITS

The Turbo Pascal system contains a number of predefined *units* that allow the programmer to perform tasks such as controlling output going to the printer or to the display screen. These units consist of collections of constants, variables, and program statements. They allow the user to perform commands that are related to the IBM PC. We will discuss how you can use two of these units here. For more information on using units, refer to your Turbo Pascal documentation.

Sending Output to the Printer

So far, all the output from programs has been displayed on the monitor screen. Suppose you want the output printed on paper? This is important if you need to turn in an assignment showing your teacher that your program works properly. One way of doing this (if you are using an IBM PC or a PC-compatible) is simply to display the output on the screen and then hold down the Shift and the Print Screen (PrtScr) keys at the same time. Everything on the screen will be sent to the printer. But, what if your program's output takes up more than a single screen? Output can be transferred to the printer by using the unit named PRINTER. In order to inform the compiler that a particular program is

FIGURE 5-9 PROGRAM PRICE2

```
PROGRAM PRICE2;

{ FIND THE TOTAL COST OF THE RECORD ALBUMS.  THE ALBUMS ARE $5.00
  EACH IF 5 OR FEWER ARE BOUGHT.  IF 6 OR MORE ARE BOUGHT, THEY ARE
  $4.85 EACH. }

VAR
   ALBUMS : INTEGER;
   COST   : REAL;

BEGIN   { PRICE2 }

   { DETERMINE THE NUMBER OF ALBUMS. }
   WRITE ('HOW MANY ALBUMS ARE BEING BOUGHT? ');
   READLN (ALBUMS);

   { COST IS $5.00 PER ALBUM FOR UP TO FIVE ALBUMS, $4.85 EACH
     IF MORE THAN 5 ALBUMS ARE BOUGHT. }
   IF ALBUMS <= 5
      THEN COST := ALBUMS * 5.00
      ELSE COST := ALBUMS * 4.85;

   { OUTPUT THE FINAL COST. }
   WRITELN ('THE COST OF THE ALBUMS IS $', COST:6:2);

END.   { PRICE2 }
```

```
HOW MANY ALBUMS ARE BEING BOUGHT? 5
THE COST OF THE ALBUMS IS $ 25.00

HOW MANY ALBUMS ARE BEING BOUGHT? 6
THE COST OF THE ALBUMS IS $ 29.10
```

going to use PRINTER, it must be declared in a USES statement. Then, any output sent to the printer must be preceded by the word LST (which stands for "list"). When the following program is executed:

```
PROGRAM PAPER;

USES
    PRINTER;

BEGIN    { PAPER }

    WRITELN ('THIS STATEMENT WAS DISPLAYED ON THE SCREEN.');
    WRITELN (LST, 'BUT, THIS WAS SENT RIGHT TO THE PRINTER.');

END.     { PAPER }
```

the output of the first WRITELN appears on the screen:

```
THIS STATEMENT WAS DISPLAYED ON THE SCREEN.
```

However, the second statement is transferred to the printer:

```
BUT, THIS WAS SENT RIGHT TO THE PRINTER.
```

DIFFERENCES FOR VERSION 3 USERS

When sending output to the printer using Version 3, simply place the word LST in front of the output:

```
WRITELN (LST, 'THIS OUTPUT WILL BE PRINTED.');
```

No USES statement is required.

DIFFERENCES FOR MACINTOSH USERS

When sending output directly to the printer, place the word PRINTER (rather than LST as on the IBM) in front of output to be transferred to the printer. The following program segment demonstrates how the output of a WRITELN statement can be sent to the printer:

```
PROGRAM PAPER;
```

(Box continued on next page)

```
USES
    PASPRINTER;

BEGIN
    WRITELN (PRINTER, 'THIS OUTPUT WILL BE PRINTED
    ON PAPER.');
```

Note that PRINTER uses the PASPRINTER unit.

The CLRSCR and GOTOXY Statements

The CLRSCR and GOTOXY statements both use the CRT unit. This unit allows the user to perform tasks that involve using the display screen. Therefore, the following USES statement must be placed in any programs using the CLRSCR and GOTOXY statements:

```
USES
    CRT;
```

When the following statement is executed, the screen goes blank, and the cursor is placed in the upper left corner of the screen.

```
CLRSCR;
```

This is useful when you wish to clear the screen before program output is displayed.

The GOTOXY statement allows the cursor to be moved to a specified position (or coordinate) on the screen. For example,

```
GOTOXY (10, 20);
WRITELN ('This message starts at column 10, row 20.');
```

will move the cursor to column 10, row 20, and the output will begin at that point. The column number is always given first and the row number second. The position at the upper left corner of the screen is (1, 1). This statement allows output to be attractively positioned on the screen.

DIFFERENCES FOR VERSION 3 USERS

When CLRSCR and GOTOXY are used, no USES statement is required.

DIFFERENCES FOR MACINTOSH USERS

The following program segment will clear the screen and position the cursor at column 10, row 20 on the screen:

```
PROGRAM DEMONSTRATE;

BEGIN   { DEMONSTRATE }

    CLEARSCREEN;
    GOTOXY (10, 20);
    WRITELN ('The cursor has been moved to column 10, row 20.');

END.    { DEMONSTRATE }
```

LEARNING CHECK 5-3

1. Given the following program segment, tell whether the expressions in parts a–g will evaluate as true or false.

```
PROGRAM ONE;

VAR
    I, J, K       : INTEGER;
    ANSWER, MORE : BOOLEAN;
    ADDRESS      : STRING;

BEGIN   { ONE }

    I := 10;
    J := 12;
    K := 0;
    ANSWER := TRUE;
    MORE := FALSE;
    ADDRESS := '101 S. Main';
```

a. I >= J
b. ANSWER <> MORE
c. K < I
d. ADDRESS = '101 S. Main'
e. J = 12
f. MORE = TRUE
g. J = K + 1

2. What is the difference between an IF/THEN statement and an IF/THEN/ELSE statement? Give appropriate examples of each.

3. Given the program segment below, determine what output will
   be generated by the control statements that follow.

```
PROGRAM EXAMPLE;

VAR
    FLOWER          : STRING;
    QUANTITY, MANY : INTEGER;

BEGIN    { EXAMPLE }

    QUANTITY := 2 * 8;
    FLOWER := 'ZINNIA';
    MANY := QUANTITY - 3;
a. IF FLOWER > 'ZINNIA'
      THEN WRITELN ('THIS IS THE RIGHT FLOWER.')
      ELSE WRITELN ('KEEP LOOKING.');
b. IF MANY = 12
      THEN WRITELN ('MANY IS A DOZEN.');
c. IF QUANTITY >= 16
      THEN WRITELN ('THERE ARE ENOUGH.')
      ELSE WRITELN (FLOWER);
```

■■■■ SUMMARY POINTS

- Assignment statements are used to assign values to variables. The assignment operator ":=" is used. The value of the expression to the right of the operator is assigned to the variable to the left.
- The arithmetic operators for addition (+), subtraction (−), multiplication (*), and division (/) can be used with integers or real numbers. In the case of division, the result will always be a real number. The DIV and MOD operators are used with integers. DIV results in the quotient value of integer division whereas MOD produces the remainder of integer division.
- The value of an arithmetic expression is found by following the order of operations, which determines the order in which arithmetic operations are performed. This order can be changed by using parentheses.
- The IF statement is used to test a condition. The action taken next depends on the result of the test. In a single-alternative IF (an IF/THEN) statement, an action is taken only if the condition is true. In a double-alternative IF (an IF/THEN/ELSE) statement, one action is taken if the condition is true, and another if it is false.

■ The relational operators are $<$, $<=$, $>$, $>=$, $=$, and $<>$; they are used to compare two operands.

■■■■ VOCABULARY LIST

Arithmetic operator	Loop
Assignment statement	Operand
Collating sequence	Operator
Control statement	Order of operations
Decision statement	Relational operator
Expression	

■■■■ CHAPTER TEST

Vocabulary

Match a term from the numbered column with the description from the lettered column that best fits the term.

1. Loop

    a. The internal ordering that the computer assigns to the characters it is able to recognize.

2. Assignment statement

    b. Any valid combination of variables, constants, operators, and parentheses.

3. Operand

    c. A symbol that stands for an arithmetic process, such as addition or subtraction.

4. Control statement

    d. A value on which an operation is being performed.

5. Relational operator

    e. The rules that determine the order in which arithmetic operations will be performed.

6. Collating sequence

    f. A statement that allows the programmer to determine whether a statement (or a group of statements) will be executed and how many times.

7. Arithmetic operator

    g. An operator that compares one operand with another.

8. Order of operations

    h. A statement that allows a value to be stored in a variable.

9. Expression

    i. A symbol that stands for a process.

10. Decision statement

   j. A structure that allows a given section of a program to be executed as many times as necessary.

11. Operator

   k. A statement that determines whether a specified portion of a program will be executed.

Questions

1. Explain in your own words what an assignment statement does.
2. Why can an integer value be assigned to a variable of type REAL whereas a real value cannot be assigned to a variable of type INTEGER?
3. The program shown in Figure 5–2 has two assignment statements:

```
SUM := A + B + C;
AVERAGE := SUM / 3;
```

Using parentheses, write these two statements as one statement.
4. List each of the relational operators and tell what each does.
5. Write an assignment statement to represent each of the following equations.

  a. $X = \dfrac{Y^2}{2}$

  b. $A = Y + Z \times 3$

  c. $B = \dfrac{X + 10}{4 \times 8} + 2$

  d. $Z = 12 + (-A) - \dfrac{A + B}{X}$

6. Evaluate the following expressions containing DIV and MOD.

  a. 18 DIV 2 − 1

  b. 16 * 2 + 27 MOD 3

  c. 6 + 14 MOD 5 − 2

  d. (8 + 10) DIV 4

7. What is a control statement?
8. What are the two types of control statements? What is the purpose of each?
9. Evaluate the following expressions as true or false.

  a. 6 * 3 <> 16

  b. 'b' < 'd'

  c. 102 − 77 = 77

  d. 476.32 <= 476.0

▬▬▬ PROGRAMMING PROBLEMS

Level 1

1. Write a program to determine the cost of a movie ticket. The customer's age is entered at the keyboard. If the age is 12 or less, the cost

of the ticket is $2.00. If the customer's age is 13 or more, the cost is $3.50. Display the cost of the ticket on the monitor screen with an appropriate label.

2. Write a program to print an integer only if it is even. (Hint: think about how the MOD operator could be used to do this.)

Level 2

3. Patricia McGill's band charges its clients $78.00 an hour for every hour up to midnight and time-and-a-half for every hour after midnight. Write a program to allow Patricia to enter the client's name and the number of hours worked before and after midnight. The program should display the client's name and the amount owed.

4. Sally wants to buy the following items:

sweater:	$35.00
skirt:	$28.50
blouse:	$22.95
bracelet:	$12.25

   The clothing store is having a sale next Tuesday. Everything except jewelry will be 15 percent off. Write a program to tell Sally how much the items she wants would cost now. Also figure out how much the items would cost if Sally waited until they were on sale. Both amounts should be printed at the end of the program.

5. WJCR 1414 Radio is giving $140 to the fourteenth person to call in. Billie needs the money for her new 10-speed bike. She has figured that each call takes 6.4 seconds to be answered after it begins ringing at the radio station. It then takes 12.8 seconds for the radio station to answer the phone and tally the call. It will take her 5.8 seconds to dial the call. Write a program that Billie can use to determine how many seconds she should wait before calling the radio station.

Level 3

6. Write a program to convert a given number of minutes and seconds to the correct fraction of an hour. For example, if 25 minutes, 30 seconds is entered, the program should determine that this is 0.425 of an hour.

7. Steve Hoffman works weekends at a carpet-cleaning business. Write a program that he can use to determine how much to bill a customer. The charges are as follows:

   a. $1.00 per square yard for normal carpets.
   b. $1.20 per square yard for extra dirty carpets.

    c. $0.05 extra per square yard if the carpet is to be deodorized.

    d. $0.25 extra per square yard if the carpet is to be treated with
       soil protector.

Allow Steve to enter the length and width of a room in feet and have the program compute the number of square yards. Assume that the rooms are rectangular. Use prompts to find out if the carpet is extra dirty or if it needs to be deodorized or treated with soil protector. Display the amount of the bill on the monitor screen.

CHAPTER 6

Control Statements

OBJECTIVES

After studying this chapter, you should be able to:

- Use compound statements appropriately.
- Write programs that use nested IF/THEN/ELSE statements.
- Explain how nested IF/THEN/ELSE statements work.
- Write statements containing BOOLEAN operators.
- Evaluate expressions containing BOOLEAN operators.
- Write programs that use WHILE/DO loops.
- Explain how the execution of a WHILE/DO loop is controlled by a BOOLEAN expression.

OUTLINE

▆▆▆ INTRODUCTION

As discussed in the last chapter, control statements can be divided into two groups: decision statements and loops. The IF statement is a type of decision statement. In this chapter you will learn how IF statements can be placed inside one another. You will also learn how to use one type of loop: the WHILE/DO loop.

▆▆▆ COMPOUND STATEMENTS

So far the programs you have written have contained simple Pascal statements. But what if it were necessary to write an IF/THEN statement to do more than one thing? The following IF/THEN statement checks to see if a whole number is positive. If the number is positive, it will be squared.

```
IF X >= 0
   THEN X := X * X;
```

How could the computer be instructed to print this result only if X were a positive number? This result could be achieved by using two separate IF/THEN statements:

```
IF X >= 0
   THEN X := X * X;
IF X >= 0
   THEN WRITELN (X);
```

116

But a simpler way would be to use a **compound statement**. In this case, the compound statement could be written like this:

```
IF X >= 0
    THEN
    BEGIN
        X := X * X;
        WRITELN (X)
    END;    { THEN }
```

A compound statement is a group of statements bracketed by the words BEGIN and END. It can contain any number of individual statements. The compiler treats this group of statements as if it were a single statement. If the IF statement in the above example is true, all of the statements between the BEGIN and the END will be executed.

```
Format For Compound IF Statement

    IF condition
        THEN
        BEGIN
            statement1;
            statement2;
                •
                •
                •
            last_statement;
        END;
```

The body of a Pascal program starts with a BEGIN and concludes with an END. Therefore, the body of a program is one compound statement. It is possible to have many compound statements within a program. Some compound statements may be inside others. It is important to have a BEGIN and an END for each one. Otherwise the compiler will not know where each compound statement starts and finishes.

A program is needed that will determine the amount of fabric required to complete a home economics project. Each student has a choice of making an apron or a vest. Aprons take 2.0 yards of fabric and vests take 3.25 yards. A flowchart for this program is shown in Figure 6-1. First, the student is asked to enter the name of the item being made. An IF/THEN/ELSE statement is used to determine which item has been chosen. Then the amount of fabric needed is assigned to the

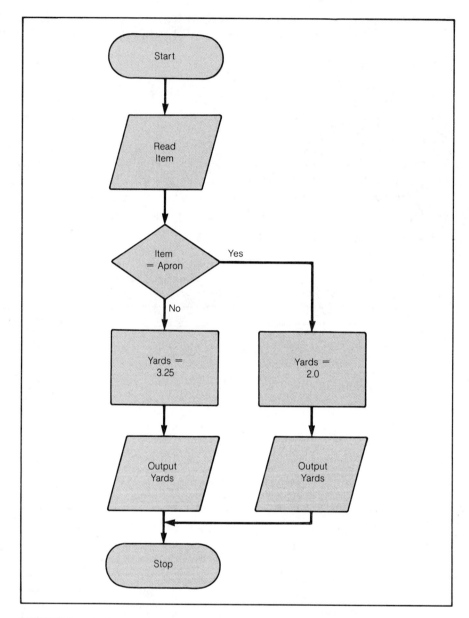

FIGURE 6-1 FLOWCHART FOR HOME ECONOMICS PROJECT PROBLEM

variable YARDS, and this value is displayed. Figure 6–2 shows the complete program. There are two compound statements in this program. The first compound statement starts with the expression IF ITEM = 'APRON' and contains two single statements:

```
YARDS := 2.0;
WRITELN ('YOU WILL NEED ', YARDS:7:2,
    ' YARDS OF FABRIC FOR YOUR APRON.');
```

```
PROGRAM SEWING;

{ THIS PROGRAM TELLS HOME ECONOMICS STUDENTS HOW MUCH FABRIC THEY
   WILL NEED FOR THEIR SEWING PROJECT.   THE PROJECTS TAKE:
        1.   APRON - 2.0 YARDS
        2.   VEST  - 3.25 YARDS   }

VAR
    ITEM  : STRING;
    YARDS : REAL;

BEGIN    { SEWING }

    WRITE ('WHICH PROJECT ARE YOU MAKING, AN APRON OR A VEST? ');
    READLN (ITEM);

    { CALCULATE AMOUNT OF FABRIC NEEDED FOR THE ITEM. }
    IF ITEM = 'APRON'
       THEN
       BEGIN
          YARDS := 2.0;
          WRITELN ('YOU WILL NEED ', YARDS:7:2,
             ' YARDS OF FABRIC FOR YOUR APRON.');
       END    { THEN }
       ELSE
       BEGIN
          YARDS := 3.25;
          WRITELN ('YOU WILL NEED ', YARDS:7:2,
             ' YARDS OF FABRIC FOR YOUR VEST.');
       END;    { ELSE }

END.   { SEWING }
```

```
WHICH PROJECT ARE YOU MAKING, AN APRON OR A VEST? APRON
YOU WILL NEED    2.00 YARDS OF FABRIC FOR YOUR APRON.
```

FIGURE 6-2 PROGRAM SEWING

The second compound statement is in the ELSE portion of this IF/THEN/ELSE statement. Be careful *not* to put a semicolon after the reserved word END that comes before the ELSE portion of an IF/THEN/ELSE statement. The entire IF/THEN/ELSE statement is a single statement.

When the prompt,

```
WHICH PROJECT ARE YOU MAKING, AN APRON OR A VEST?
```

is displayed on the screen, the user must enter APRON in capital letters in order for the expression IF ITEM = 'APRON' to evaluate as true. Any other response (such as "Apron") will cause the ELSE portion of the statement to be executed.

■■■■ NESTED IF/THEN/ELSE STATEMENTS

It is possible to place one IF/THEN/ELSE statement inside another. Sometimes this is necessary when several conditions must be checked. For example, how would a program be written to find the largest of three numbers? The numbers need to be compared with one another in an orderly way to determine the largest one. One way is to use **nested statements**. A flowchart that solves the problem of finding the largest of three numbers is shown in Figure 6–3. The following program segment reads and determines the largest of three integer values, A, B, and C:

```
READLN (A, B, C);
IF A > B
   THEN IF A > C
           THEN BIGGEST := A
           ELSE BIGGEST := C
   ELSE IF B > C
           THEN BIGGEST := B
           ELSE BIGGEST := C;
```

First, A is compared with B. If A is larger than B, then A is compared to C. If A is larger than C, A must be the largest number of the three, so it is assigned to BIGGEST. Otherwise, C is assigned to BIGGEST because we know that it is bigger than both A and B. The ELSE portion of the outer IF/THEN/ELSE statement is executed only if B is larger than or equal to A. Here B is compared to C, and the larger of the two is assigned to BIGGEST.

Notice that there is an IF/THEN/ELSE statement nested within the THEN portion of the outer statement and another IF/THEN/ELSE statement nested within the ELSE portion of the outer statement. Each inner IF/THEN/ELSE statement must be nested completely within one portion of the outer IF/THEN/ELSE statement.

Format For **Nested IF/THEN/ELSE Statement**

IF condition1
   THEN IF condition2
      THEN IF condition3
         THEN statement1
         ELSE statement2
      ELSE statement3
   ELSE statement4;

FIGURE 6–3 FLOWCHART TO DETERMINE THE LARGEST OF THREE NUMBERS

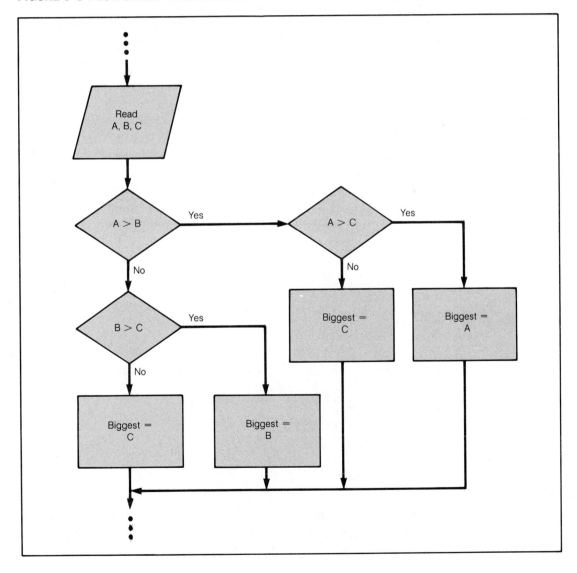

How does the compiler know which ELSE goes with which IF clause? The compiler starts from the innermost THEN and matches it to the IF clause closest to it. It works from the inside out, matching each IF/THEN with the corresponding ELSE. Carefully indenting each statement helps to make the logic of nested statements easier to follow. Each ELSE clause should start in the same column as its corresponding THEN clause. This is not a Pascal rule, but it makes the program easier to read.

Smiley's Pizza Pub needs a program to calculate the cost of pizza for its customers. Pizzas come in three sizes:

    9 inch: $4.50
    12 inch: $5.75
    16 inch: $7.50

A thick-crusted pizza costs 50 cents extra regardless of the size of the pizza. The cost of each extra topping is as follows:

    9 inch: $0.50
    12 inch: $0.65
    16 inch: $0.90

Figure 6–4 shows the flowchart for the pizza cost problem. IF/THEN/ELSE statements must be used to (1) determine the basic cost depending on size, (2) determine if the customer wants a thick crust, and (3) determine the cost of any extra toppings.

First the cost of the basic pizza must be determined. This depends on the size of the pizza. A series of single-alternative IF statements can be used to assign this cost:

```
IF SIZE = 9
   THEN COST := 4.50;
IF SIZE = 12
   THEN COST := 5.75;
IF SIZE = 16
   THEN COST := 7.50;
```

Each pizza will fall into one of these categories since these are the only sizes of pizza available. The same result could be accomplished by using nested IF/THEN/ELSE statements:

```
IF SIZE = 9
   THEN COST := 4.50
   ELSE IF SIZE = 12
           THEN COST := 5.75
           ELSE COST := 7.50;
```

It is important that a semicolon be placed only at the end of this nested statement. One disadvantage of this method is that if an invalid size is entered (such as 14), the cost assigned will be $7.50. In fact, any value entered other than 9 or 12 will result in a value of $7.50 being assigned

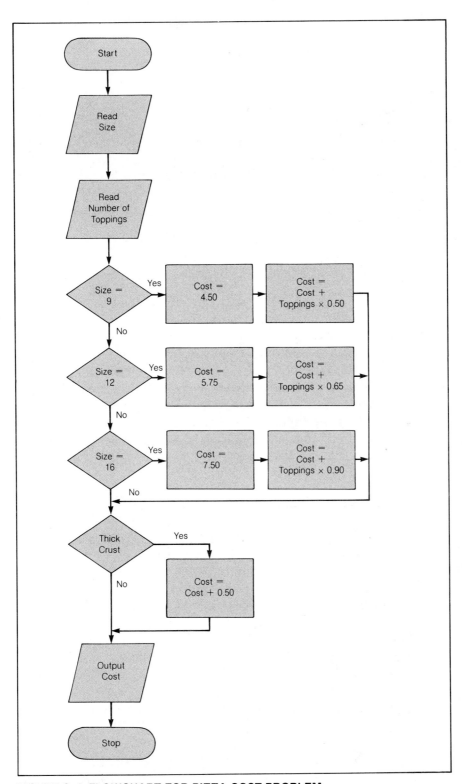

FIGURE 6-4 FLOWCHART FOR PIZZA COST PROBLEM

to COST. This nested IF statement could be altered to handle invalid values as shown below:

```
IF SIZE = 9
   THEN COST := 4.50
   ELSE IF SIZE = 12
           THEN COST := 5.75
           ELSE IF SIZE = 16
                   THEN COST := 7.50
                   ELSE WRITELN ('NO PIZZA AVAILABLE IN THIS SIZE.');
```

Now if the user typed in 14 for the pizza size, the following message would appear:

```
NO PIZZA AVAILABLE IN THIS SIZE.
```

If this happened, the program should go back to the beginning of this section and prompt the user to reenter the size. We will learn how to do this later in this chapter.

Figure 6–5 contains the complete pizza cost program. Notice that the user is prompted to enter the size and then the number of toppings. Because the cost of each topping depends on the size of the pizza, compound statements are used to assign the basic cost and the cost of the toppings at the same time. If the customer wants a thick crust, this charge is added on. Then the total cost of the pizza is displayed.

LEARNING CHECK 6–1

1. Change Figure 6–2 so that fabric for an additional project can be determined. The project added should be pants that take 3.75 yards of fabric. Use compound statements and nested IF/THEN/ELSE statements.
2. How is the compiler able to recognize compound statements?
3. What is the advantage of nesting IF/THEN/ELSE statements?
4. Rewrite the following program segment, using one compound statement instead of three IF/THEN statements:

```
IF LETTER = 'A'
   THEN VOWELS := VOWELS + 1;
IF LETTER = 'A'
   THEN CONT := TRUE;
IF LETTER = 'A'
   THEN WRITELN ('THIS LETTER IS A VOWEL.');
```

```
PROGRAM PIZZA;

{ THIS PROGRAM COMPUTES THE COST OF PIZZAS FOR SMILEY'S PIZZA PARLOR.
  THE COST OF A PIZZA IS:
        9 INCH - $4.50
       12 INCH - $5.75
       16 INCH - $7.50
  EACH EXTRA TOPPING COSTS:
        9 INCH - $0.50
       12 INCH - $0.65
       16 INCH - $0.90
  PIZZAS WITH THICK CRUST ARE $0.50 EXTRA, REGARDLESS OF THE SIZE.

  MAJOR VARIABLES:
     COST     - THE COST OF THE PIZZA
     SIZE     - THE SIZE OF THE PIZZA
     TOPPINGS - THE NUMBER OF DESIRED TOPPINGS
     CRUST - THICK CRUST? }

VAR
   COST : REAL;
   SIZE, TOPPINGS : INTEGER;
   CRUST : STRING;

BEGIN   { PIZZA }

   { DETERMINE THE SIZE OF THE PIZZA. }
   WRITELN ('WHAT SIZE PIZZA DO YOU WANT? ');
   WRITE ('THE CHOICES ARE: 9, 12, OR 16 INCHES: ');
   READLN (SIZE);

   { DETERMINE THE NUMBER OF TOPPINGS. }
   WRITELN ('HOW MANY TOPPINGS WOULD YOU LIKE? ');
   WRITE ('ENTER A WHOLE NUMBER UP TO 6: ');
   READLN (TOPPINGS);

   { DETERMINE COST OF PIZZA BASED ON SIZE AND NUMBER OF TOPPINGS. }
   IF SIZE = 9
      THEN
      BEGIN
         COST := 4.50;
         COST := COST + (TOPPINGS * 0.50);
      END
```

FIGURE 6-5 PROGRAM PIZZA

(Figure continued on next page)

```
        ELSE IF SIZE = 12
                THEN
                BEGIN
                    COST := 5.75;
                    COST := COST + (TOPPINGS * 0.65);
                END
                ELSE
                BEGIN
                    COST := 7.50;
                    COST := COST + (TOPPINGS * 0.90);
                END;    { ELSE }

    { ADD $0.50 IF THICK-CRUST. }
    WRITELN ('DO YOU WANT A THICK CRUST? ');
    WRITE ('ANSWER YES OR NO: ');
    READLN (CRUST);
    IF CRUST = 'YES'
        THEN COST := COST + 0.50;

    { DISPLAY THE TOTAL COST. }
    WRITELN ('THE COST OF YOUR PIZZA IS $', COST:7:2);

END.    { PIZZA }
```

```
WHAT SIZE PIZZA DO YOU WANT?
THE CHOICES ARE: 9, 12, OR 16 INCHES: 9
HOW MANY TOPPINGS WOULD YOU LIKE?
ENTER A WHOLE NUMBER UP TO 6: 3
DO YOU WANT A THICK CRUST?
ANSWER YES OR NO: NO
THE COST OF YOUR PIZZA IS $   6.00
```

FIGURE 6-5 PROGRAM PIZZA (Cont.)

BOOLEAN OPERATORS

So far, the arithmetic operators ($+$, $-$, $*$, $/$, DIV, and MOD) and the relational operators ($=$, $<$, $<=$, $>$, $>=$, and $<>$) have been covered. Now you will learn how to use a third type of operator: the **BOOLEAN**

operator. BOOLEAN operators are used only with BOOLEAN expressions. These are expressions that always evaluate as either true or false. The BOOLEAN operators in Turbo Pascal are NOT, AND, OR, and XOR.

NOT is a unary operator. This means that it is used alone with a BOOLEAN expression. Consider the following statements:

```
X := 2;
IF X > 0
   THEN WRITELN (X:2);
```

The BOOLEAN expression "X > 0" evaluates as true so the WRITELN statement is executed. Now suppose the NOT operator is added:

```
X := 2;
IF NOT (X > 0)
   THEN WRITELN (X:2);
```

NOT has the effect of reversing the expression. It now is false. Therefore, the WRITELN statement is not executed. Suppose the value of X is changed:

```
X := -1
IF NOT (X > 0)
   THEN WRITELN (X:2);
```

This expression now becomes true because X is *not* greater than 0. Therefore, the WRITELN statement is executed.

AND is used to combine two BOOLEAN expressions. For example, the expression

```
IF (HEIGHT > 72) AND (WEIGHT > 150)
```

will evaluate as true only if HEIGHT > 72 and WEIGHT > 150 are both true. Both of these expressions must be true for the entire expression to be true.

OR is also used to combine two BOOLEAN expressions. In this case, only one of the expressions needs to evaluate as true for the entire expression to evaluate as true. In the expression

```
IF (HEIGHT > 72) OR (WEIGHT > 150)
```

if either HEIGHT > 72 *or* WEIGHT > 150 is true, the entire expression will evaluate as true.

An expression containing the XOR or *exclusive or* is true only if one of the expressions within it is true. In the expression

```
IF (HEIGHT > 72) XOR (WEIGHT > 150)
```

if HEIGHT is 80 and WEIGHT is 145, then the expression is true. However, if HEIGHT is 80 and weight is 160, then both expressions are true and the result of the XOR expression is false. Only one of the two expressions can be true.

The BOOLEAN operators are evaluated in this order:

1. NOT
2. AND
3. OR
4. XOR

This means an expression using NOT will be evaluated first, then AND, OR, and lastly XOR. Consider the following expression:

```
NOT (10 < 12) OR (10 * 3 = 30)
```

This expression is evaluated in this order:

1. Expressions in parentheses are evaluated left to right: (10 < 12) evaluates as true; (10 * 3 = 30) evaluates as true.
2. NOT is evaluated before OR; NOT (TRUE) evaluates as false.
3. (FALSE) OR (TRUE) evaluates as true.

Therefore, the entire expression evaluates as true. When you are evaluating a complex BOOLEAN expression, it is important to perform each step in the correct order. Dividing the expression into small parts makes this simpler.

The programmer can use parentheses to change the order in which the expression will be evaluated. This is done in the same way as with arithmetic and relational operators. If the programmer wanted the OR operation to be evaluated before the NOT, the expression could be written

```
NOT ((10 < 12) OR (10 * 3 = 30))
```

The steps to evaluate this expression are

```
1. NOT ((TRUE) OR (TRUE))
2. NOT (TRUE) = FALSE
```

This expression would evaluate as false. The parentheses have changed the meaning of the expression.

Now we will write a program that uses BOOLEAN operators to determine an appropriate activity for a given day. The program should ask the user two questions:

```
IS TODAY A SCHOOLDAY?
```

and

```
IS TODAY SUNNY?
```

There are four different combinations of answers to these two questions. Depending on the combination, an activity should be displayed as shown below:

Combination	Message
SCHOOLDAY AND SUNNY	GO TO SCHOOL TODAY.
SCHOOLDAY AND NOT SUNNY	WEAR RAINCOAT TO SCHOOL TODAY.

```
NOT SCHOOLDAY AND NOT SUNNY    WATCH TV TODAY.
NOT SCHOOLDAY AND SUNNY        PLAY BALL TODAY!
```

Each combination can be checked by using BOOLEAN operators. Then the corresponding message can be displayed. For example in the following expression:

```
IF SCHOOLDAY AND SUNNY
   THEN WRITELN ('GO TO SCHOOL TODAY.');
```

the WRITELN statement will be executed only if it is both a schoolday and sunny. You may wonder why this statement isn't written:

```
IF (SCHOOLDAY = TRUE) AND (SUNNY = TRUE)
   THEN WRITELN ('GO TO SCHOOL TODAY.');
```

This is because SCHOOLDAY itself has the value of true or false. This value has already been assigned to SCHOOLDAY in the expression SCHOOLDAY := TRUE or SCHOOLDAY := FALSE. This complete program is shown in Figure 6–6.

Study the following BOOLEAN expressions and make certain that you understand how each is evaluated.

Expression	Evaluates as
NOT (1 * 4 - 5)	TRUE
(18 < 16) OR (7 + 2 = 9)	TRUE
(18 < 16) XOR (7 + 2 = 9)	TRUE
(18 < 16) AND (7 + 2 = 9)	FALSE
(2 + 8 <= 11) AND (17 * 2 = 34)	TRUE
(2 + 8 <= 11) XOR (17 * 2 = 34)	FALSE
NOT (12 > 8 - 2)	FALSE

WHILE/DO LOOPS

In Chapter 4, a program was written to calculate the radius, circumference, and area of a circle. It probably would have been faster to figure these results by hand than to write this program. But, suppose it were necessary to calculate these values for a thousand circles. This is an example of a situation in which a computer can really save time. The computer can easily do the same job over and over again. In this section we will discuss how to create loops that allow the programmer to execute a particular portion of a program as many times as needed.

There are three loop statements in Pascal: the WHILE/DO, REPEAT/UNTIL, and FOR loops. The WHILE/DO loop is explained here; the REPEAT/UNTIL and FOR loops are discussed in Chapter 8.

```
PROGRAM ACTIVITY;

{ THIS PROGRAM DETERMINES WHAT ACTIVITY WILL BE DONE ON A PARTICULAR
  DAY. }

VAR
   ANSWER1, ANSWER2 : STRING;
   SCHOOLDAY, SUNNY : BOOLEAN;

BEGIN    { ACTIVITY }

   { DETERMINE WHETHER TODAY IS A SCHOOLDAY. }
   WRITELN ('IS TODAY SCHOOLDAY? ');
   WRITE ('ENTER YES OR NO: ');
   READLN (ANSWER1);
   IF ANSWER1 = 'YES'
      THEN SCHOOLDAY := TRUE
      ELSE SCHOOLDAY := FALSE;

   { DETERMINE WHETHER TODAY IS SUNNY. }
   WRITELN ('IS TODAY SUNNY? ');
   WRITE ('ENTER YES OR NO: ');
   READLN (ANSWER2);
   IF ANSWER2 = 'YES'
      THEN SUNNY := TRUE
      ELSE SUNNY := FALSE;

   { DISPLAY APPROPRIATE ACTIVITY. }
   IF SCHOOLDAY AND SUNNY
      THEN WRITELN ('GO TO SCHOOL TODAY.');

   IF SCHOOLDAY AND NOT SUNNY
      THEN WRITELN ('WEAR RAINCOAT TO SCHOOL TODAY.');

   IF NOT SCHOOLDAY AND NOT SUNNY
      THEN WRITELN ('WATCH TV TODAY.');

   IF NOT SCHOOLDAY AND SUNNY
      THEN WRITELN ('PLAY BALL TODAY!');

END.    { ACTIVITY }
```

```
IS TODAY SCHOOLDAY?
ENTER YES OR NO: YES
IS TODAY SUNNY?
ENTER YES OR NO: NO
WEAR RAINCOAT TO SCHOOL TODAY.
```

FIGURE 6-6 PROGRAM ACTIVITY

The following program segment contains a simple WHILE/DO loop (assume all of the variables are of type INTEGER):

```
COUNT := 1;
TOTAL := 0;
WHILE COUNT <= 10 DO
BEGIN
    READLN (NUMBER);
    TOTAL := TOTAL + NUMBER;
    COUNT := COUNT + 1;
END;   { WHILE }

WRITELN ('The total of the 10 numbers is ', TOTAL:8);
```

The BOOLEAN expression COUNT $<=$ 10 controls the execution of this loop. As long as this expression evaluates as true, the body of the loop will be executed. Note that the body of the loop is a compound statement containing three simple statements. Each time through the loop, a value is read to NUMBER and NUMBER is added to TOTAL; then COUNT is incremented by one. As long as COUNT is less than or equal to 10, the loop will execute. Therefore, this loop will execute 10 times. Then control will pass to the first statement after the loop, and the value of TOTAL will be output.

Format For **WHILE/DO Statement**

WHILE BOOLEAN expression DO
   statement;

When using WHILE/DO loops, the BOOLEAN expression controlling loop repetition is evaluated before each repetition. Loops are useful when checking to see if the user has entered valid data. Below is the program segment for determining the size of pizza ordered in the program in Figure 6–5:

```
{ DETERMINE THE SIZE OF THE PIZZA. }
WRITELN ('WHAT SIZE PIZZA DO YOU WANT?');
WRITE ('THE CHOICES ARE: 9, 12, OR 16 INCHES: ');
READLN (SIZE);
```

With slight alteration this segment can check to make certain that the user has entered a valid size (9, 12, or 16):

```
{ DETERMINE THE SIZE OF THE PIZZA. }
WRITELN ('WHAT SIZE PIZZA DO YOU WANT? ');
WRITE ('THE CHOICES ARE:9, 12, OR 16 INCHES: ');
READLN (SIZE);
```

```
WHILE (SIZE <> 9) AND (SIZE <> 12) AND (SIZE <> 16) DO
BEGIN
    WRITELN ('PLEASE REENTER SIZE OF PIZZA.');
    WRITE ('THE CHOICES ARE 9, 12, OR 16 INCHES: ');
    READLN (SIZE);
END;    { WHILE }
```

As long as the user enters an invalid value, the WHILE/DO loop will continue to execute. Otherwise, the program will continue to the next statement.

The following facts are important to remember when using WHILE/DO loops:

1. Any variables used in the BOOLEAN expression that controls loop repetition must be assigned a value before entering the loop. In the example above, SIZE was assigned a value before the loop was first entered.

2. The variables used in the BOOLEAN expression that controls loop repetition must be modified at some point in the loop to avoid a situation where the loop executes indefinitely. For example,

```
NUM := 1;
WHILE NUM <= 10 DO
    SUM := NUM + SUM;
```

This loop will execute indefinitely (that is, until the computer's resources are used up) because the value of NUM will always be less than 10. This is referred to as an **infinite loop**.

3. Watch for errors caused by "off-by-one" loops. Suppose you want to write a program to print the numbers 1 through 5 using a WHILE/DO loop. A beginning programmer might write a program similar to Figure 6–7 and assume that the WHILE/DO loop will terminate as soon as NUMBER is greater than 5. In this case, however, one extra number (the 6) will be printed. This is referred to as an "off-by-one" error. Remember that the WHILE/DO loop executes until the BOOLEAN expression is evaluated and found to be false.

4. After execution of the loop, control returns to the top of the loop where the BOOLEAN expression is evaluated again.

1. What is a BOOLEAN operator? What are the four BOOLEAN operators discussed here?
2. What is an infinite loop?
3. Evaluate each of the following expressions.

    a. NOT (10 <> 0) AND (4 * 7 >= 18)
    b. (6 / 2 = 3) OR (14 > 23)
    c. ((11 - 8) * 2 = 6) AND NOT (14 <> 14)

4. Create a WHILE/DO loop that will count by fives up to 100.

LEARNING CHECK 6-2

FIGURE 6-7 PROGRAM DEMONSTRATING "OFF-BY-ONE" ERROR

```
PROGRAM NUMBERS;

VAR
   NUMBER : INTEGER;

BEGIN    { NUMBERS }

   NUMBER := 0;

   WHILE NUMBER <= 5 DO
   BEGIN
      NUMBER := NUMBER + 1;
      WRITE (NUMBER:5);
   END;    { WHILE }

   WRITELN;

END.    { NUMBERS }
```

Since the condition is "<=5" a 6 will also be printed.

    1   2   3   4   5   6

■■■■■ SUMMARY POINTS

- Compound statements consist of any number of individual statements inside a BEGIN-END pair. The compiler treats the entire compound statement as a single statement.
- Control statements such as the IF/THEN/ELSE statement can be nested, or placed inside one another.
- BOOLEAN expressions always evaluate as either true or false. They are used to control the execution of statements. The BOOLEAN operators are NOT, AND, OR, and XOR.
- Loops allow a specified portion of a program to be executed repeatedly. In the WHILE/DO loop, a BOOLEAN expression is evaluated before the loop is entered. The loop is executed as long as the expression remains true. Once it is false, control passes to the first statement after the loop.

■■■■■ VOCABULARY LIST

BOOLEAN operator
Compound statement
Infinite loop
Nested statement

■■■■■ CHAPTER TEST

Vocabulary

Match a term from the numbered column with the description from the lettered column that best fits the term.

1. Infinite loop

2. BOOLEAN operator

a. An operator that combines two BOOLEAN expressions with the resulting expression evaluating as true or false.

b. A control statement nested within another.

3. Nested statement

    c. A loop that will execute indefinitely.

4. Compound statement

    d. A statement enclosed in a BEGIN-END pair.

Questions

1. Look at the following program segment:

```
IF OUNCES = 40
   THEN SIZE := 'JUMBO'
   ELSE IF OUNCES = 25
           THEN SIZE := 'LARGE'
           ELSE IF OUNCES = 18
                   THEN SIZE := 'REGULAR'
                   ELSE WRITELN ('PRODUCT DOES NOT COME IN THIS SIZE.');
```

What will the value of SIZE be if OUNCES is equal to each of the values below?

a. 18

b. 40

c. 20

d. 50

e. 25

2. Why is the body of a Pascal program a compound statement?
3. How is the BOOLEAN operator XOR different from the OR operator?
4. Using the program segment below, evaluate the BOOLEAN expressions that follow:

```
VAR
    ANSWER  : BOOLEAN;
    X, Y, Z : INTEGER;

BEGIN

    ANSWER := TRUE;
    X := 4;
    Y := 3;
    Z := 12;
```

a. NOT ANSWER
b. (X * Y = Z) AND (X = 4)
c. (X + Z = 10) OR (4 * 4 = 10)
d. ANSWER AND (X + Y * 10 = 14)

5. What types of tasks are well suited for loops?
6. Describe a job you have done that involves repeating a task over and over again until a certain condition is met.
7. Examine the program segment below. How many times will the

WHILE/DO loop be executed? What will the value of Y be at the end of each loop repetition? What will the value of X be?

```
Y := 1;
X := Y;
WHILE Y < 11 DO
BEGIN
    Y := Y + X;
    X := X + 1;
    WRITELN (X, Y);
END;    { WHILE }
```

8. At what point does a WHILE/DO loop stop executing?
9. What is meant by an "off-by-one" loop error?
10. Which of the following program segments contain infinite loops?

```
a. X := 10;
   WHILE X < 10 + X DO
       X := X + 120;
b. X := 10;
   WHILE X < 20 DO
       X := X - 10;
```

▬▬▬ PROGRAMMING PROBLEMS

Level 1

1. Write a program segment that prompts the user to enter an integer that is (1) positive, (2) even, and (3) less than one hundred. If the integer entered is negative, odd, or greater than or equal to one hundred, an appropriate error message should be displayed, and the user should be prompted to enter a different number. Use a WHILE/DO loop to prompt the user until a valid integer has been entered.

2. Write a program to read an outdoor temperature and output the appropriate sport for that temperature using the following guidelines:

Sport	Temperature
Swimming	temp > 85
Tennis	70 < temp ≤ 85
Golf	32 < temp ≤ 70
Skiing	10 < temp ≤ 32
Checkers	temp ≤ 10

Level 2

3. The football coach would like a program to determine if a given student is a likely candidate for the high school football team. The coach feels that students should meet the following criteria to be candidates:

    a. Male
    b. Weight more than 130 pounds
    c. Height taller than 5'8"
    d. Grade point average of at least 2.5

    Write a program to allow the coach to enter the student's name and the above data. A message should then be displayed stating whether the person is a likely candidate. Use nested IF statements.

4. Steve Cavanaugh works for Uptown Lumber Company on weekends and evenings. He receives $3.60 an hour for the first 15 hours and $3.75 for the hours over 15. State income tax is taken out of his weekly check as follows:

    6 percent is taken out if he makes $50.00 or less per week.
    7 percent is taken out if he makes more than $50.00 per week.

    Write a program to calculate Steve's weekly paycheck. Write it so Steve enters the number of hours he works in a given week and the amount of his paycheck will be calculated and displayed on the screen.

Level 3

5. Ms. Hasselschartz, the librarian, would like a program to calculate library fines. Fines are charged on the following basis:

    general books
        paperbacks: 15¢/day
        other general books: 20¢/day
    magazines: 25¢/day
    reference books
        encyclopedias: 50¢/day
        other reference books: 35¢/day

    Write a program using nested IF/THEN/ELSE statements. Use a WHILE/DO loop so that as many fines as needed can be calculated.

6. The coordinate system is divided into four parts called quadrants. They are numbered as shown in the diagram below:

```
              |
      II      |      I
      x−      |      x+
      y+      |      y+
              |
   _____|_____
              |
      III     |      IV
      x−      |      x+
      y−      |      y−
              |
              |
```

In each quadrant the signs of the coordinates x and y are as indicated in the diagram. Write a program to read two values (X and Y) and output the quadrant in which that point will be found. Use a WHILE/DO loop to read the coordinates of five points. The output should be similar to the following: The point 4, −5 is located in quadrant IV.

CHAPTER 7

Procedures

OBJECTIVES

After studying this chapter, you should be able to:

- Define the term standard procedure.
- Define the term user-defined procedure.
- Write user-defined procedures.
- Explain the relationship between actual parameters and formal parameters.
- Explain the difference between a value parameter and a variable parameter.
- Trace through programs using value and variable parameters.
- Use value and variable parameters appropriately.
- Explain the difference between a local and a global variable.
- Identify the scope of the identifiers contained in a program.

OUTLINE

INTRODUCTION

As Chapter 2 explained, structured programming languages offer two features:

1. They allow programs to be easily divided into subprograms.
2. They allow the programmer to control the order in which statements will be executed in a clear, efficient way.

You already have learned how to control the order in which statements are executed by using decision statements (the IF statement) and loops (the WHILE/DO loop). This chapter will discuss dividing a program into subprograms. In Pascal, these subprograms are called **procedures**. Each procedure can be written separately. Then all the procedures can be combined to form a single program. This "divide and conquer" method makes the process of writing a program more manageable. There are two types of procedures: standard and user defined.

STANDARD PROCEDURES

A **standard** (or **built-in**) **procedure** is a part of the Pascal compiler. The programmer can use it to perform certain tasks automatically. Examples of standard procedures are READ, READLN, WRITE, and

WRITELN. Each of these procedures serves a specific purpose. For example, in the following statement:

```
WRITELN ('WHAT IS YOUR NAME?');
```

the WRITELN procedure instructs the compiler to display the message contained in single quotation marks on the monitor screen. In addition, because WRITELN rather than WRITE was used, the cursor will be advanced to the beginning of the next line. The character string WHAT IS YOUR NAME? is referred to as the **actual parameter** (or **argument**). An actual parameter is a value that is manipulated by the procedure. In this example, the procedure causes the character string to be displayed on the screen.

Turbo Pascal also contains several standard procedures for use with the data type STRING. They include STR, VAL, DELETE, and INSERT.

The STR procedure converts an integer or real value into a string of characters. For example:

```
NUMBER := 625;
STR (NUMBER:3, NUMBER_STRING);
```

When these statements are executed, the numeric value 625 contained in the variable NUMBER will be converted to the string '625' and assigned to NUMBER_STRING (which must be of type STRING).

The VAL procedure is the opposite of the STR procedure. It converts a string to an integer or real value. When the following statements are executed:

```
VAR
    STRING1, STRING2 : STRING;
    NUM1, NUM2, ERROR_POS : INTEGER;

BEGIN

    STRING1 := '624';
    VAL (STRING1, NUM1, ERROR_POS);
```

the value 624 will be assigned to NUM1 and the value 0 will be assigned to ERROR_POS. On the other hand, the statements

```
STRING2 := '5*6';
VAL (STRING2, NUM2, ERROR_POS);
```

will result in NUM2 being undefined and ERROR_POS containing a 2, because the second character of STRING2 is not a digit. The purpose of ERROR_POS is to indicate whether the string is a valid number. If it is, ERROR_POS will be assigned a value of 0; if it isn't, ERROR_POS will contain the location of the first nonnumeric character in the string. This makes the VAL procedure very useful when checking for invalid

user input. Below is a program segment in which the user is supposed
to enter his or her height:

```
PROGRAM FIND_HEIGHT;

VAR
    HEIGHT_STRING : STRING;
    HEIGHT        : REAL;
    ERROR         : INTEGER;

BEGIN  { FIND_HEIGHT }

    WRITE ('ENTER YOUR HEIGHT IN INCHES: ');
    READLN (HEIGHT_STRING);
    VAL (HEIGHT_STRING, HEIGHT, ERROR);

    WHILE ERROR <> 0 DO
    BEGIN
        WRITE ('PLEASE REENTER YOUR HEIGHT IN INCHES: ');
        READLN (HEIGHT_STRING);
        VAL (HEIGHT_STRING, HEIGHT, ERROR);
    END;    { WHILE }

END.   { FIND_HEIGHT }
```

The height entered by the user is assigned to HEIGHT_STRING, which
is a string variable. Then the VAL function is used to assign the height
to the real variable HEIGHT. If the value of ERROR is zero, you know
that HEIGHT_STRING is a valid number and that this number has
been assigned to HEIGHT. If ERROR is any value other than zero, the
user has entered an invalid number. The WHILE/DO loop will then
prompt the user to reenter the number until a valid one is entered. This
type of error checking can protect the program from user mistakes.

DIFFERENCES FOR MACINTOSH USERS

On the Macintosh, the STR2NUM function is used in place of the
VAL procedure. (Functions are discussed in Chapter 10. Briefly,
functions return a value, whereas procedures do not.) The following USES statement must be inserted at the beginning of the
program:

```
USES
    SANE;
```

The STR2NUM function can be used as follows:

(Box continued on next page)

```
PROGRAM CONVERTNUM;

USES SANE;

VAR
    NUMBER : EXTENDED;
    NUMSTRG : DECSTR;

BEGIN

    READLN (NUMSTRG);
    NUMBER := STR2NUM (NUMSTRG);
    WRITELN (NUMBER:8:2);
```

Notice that the value entered must be assigned to a variable of type DECSTR (NUMSTRG). After NUMSTRG is converted to a numeric value, it is assigned to NUMBER which must be of type EXTENDED. The data type EXTENDED permits a larger range of real numbers than the data type REAL. If the value of NUMSTRG is an invalid number, STR2NUM returns the value NAN(017).

The DELETE procedure deletes a substring from an already existing string. For example,

```
SAYING := 'TIC TAC TOE';
DELETE (SAYING, 5, 4);
```

deletes a substring four characters long, starting at the fifth position in TIC TAC TOE. The value TIC TOE will be assigned to SAYING.

The INSERT procedure performs the opposite task of DELETE. It inserts a string into an already existing string. For example, these statements

```
SAYING := 'TIC TOE';
INSERT ('TAC ', SAYING, 5);
```

will result in SAYING being changed to TIC TAC TOE. The first two values must be strings, the third is an integer value that indicates the position at which the first substring will be inserted into the second one.

The INC (increment) procedure increments a variable to the next ordinal value. The following WHILE loop uses the INC procedure to output the numbers from 1 through 20:

```
COUNT := 1;
WHILE COUNT <= 20 DO
```

```
BEGIN
   WRITE (COUNT:4);
   INC (COUNT);
END;   { WHILE }
```

in this example, the INC procedure replaces the statement

```
COUNT := COUNT + 1;
```

The DEC (decrement) procedure decrements a variable to the previous ordinal value.

DIFFERENCES FOR VERSION 3 USERS

The INC and DEC procedures are not available in Version 3.

DIFFERENCES FOR MACINTOSH USERS

The INC and DEC procedures are not available on the Macintosh.

USER-DEFINED PROCEDURES

User-defined procedures, unlike standard procedures, are written by the programmer. The syntax for these procedures is similar to that for a complete program. It is helpful to think of a procedure as a program within a program. The following procedure reads 10 test scores and determines the highest score, the lowest score, and the average of all the scores. At the end of the procedure, the three values are output:

```
PROCEDURE TEST_SCORES;

{ READ THE SCORES AND DETERMINE AND DISPLAY HIGH SCORE,
  LOW SCORE, AND AVERAGE. }

CONST
   NUM_TESTS = 10;
```

```
VAR
    SCORE, HIGH, LOW, COUNT, TOTAL : INTEGER;
    AVERAGE : REAL;

BEGIN   { TEST_SCORES }

    TOTAL := 0;
    WRITE ('ENTER FIRST SCORE: ');
    READLN (SCORE);            { READ FIRST SCORE }
    HIGH := SCORE;             { SET HIGH SCORE TO FIRST SCORE }
    LOW :=  SCORE;             { SET LOW SCORE TO FIRST SCORE }
    TOTAL := TOTAL + SCORE; { ADD FIRST SCORE TO TOTAL POINTS }
    COUNT := 1;

    { READ EACH OF THE SCORES. }
    WHILE COUNT < NUM_TESTS DO
    BEGIN
        COUNT := COUNT + 1;
        WRITE ('ENTER NEXT SCORE: ');
        READLN (SCORE);
        IF SCORE > HIGH          { IF NEW SCORE HIGHER THAN CURRENT HIGH }
            THEN HIGH := SCORE; { SET HIGH TO SCORE }
        IF SCORE < LOW           { IF NEW SCORE LOWER THAN CURRENT LOW }
            THEN LOW := SCORE;  {SET LOW TO SCORE }
        TOTAL := TOTAL + SCORE;
    END;   { WHILE }

    { CALCULATE AVERAGE. }
    AVERAGE := TOTAL / COUNT;

    { DISPLAY THE RESULTS. }
    WRITELN;
    WRITELN ('HIGH':10, 'LOW':10, 'AVERAGE':10);
    WRITELN ('SCORE':10, 'SCORE':10, 'SCORE':10);
    WRITELN ('------------------------------------');
    WRITELN (HIGH:10, LOW:10, AVERAGE:10:2);

END;   { TEST_SCORES }
```

The first line of this procedure is the procedure heading. It starts with the reserved word PROCEDURE and contains the procedure's name. The procedure has both a constant definition section and a variable declaration section, just like a main program. The body of the procedure starts with BEGIN and concludes with END. Notice that the END is followed by a semicolon, rather than a period as it is in the main program.

Procedures are placed immediately before the BEGIN of a main program.

Format For **Procedure**
PROCEDURE procedure_name (formal parameter list);
local declaration section;
BEGIN
procedure_body;
END;

Format For **Procedure Call**
procedure_name (actual parameter list);

Calling a Procedure

In order to execute a procedure, you must use a **procedure call.** The procedure call can be placed in the main program at the point at which you want the procedure to be executed. In this example, the call will simply contain the procedure's name:

`TEST_SCORES;`

Examine Figure 7–1 which shows the program containing procedure TEST_SCORES. Procedure TEST_SCORES has been placed after the main program's variable declarations but before the program body. The procedure has been divided from the main program by a row of asterisks. This is not necessary, but makes it easier for readers to identify the boundaries of the procedure. The body of the main program consists of one statement, a call to procedure TEST_SCORES. When this program is executed, the main program body will be executed first. When execution reaches the procedure call, control will transfer to the first line of the procedure. When the procedure has finished executing, control will return to the main program.

Using Parameters

The procedure TEST_SCORES in Figure 7–1 actually contains two tasks:

1. Reading the data and calculating the high, low, and average scores.
2. Displaying the results.

```
PROGRAM ANALYZE_SCORES;

{ THIS PROGRAM READS A GROUP OF TEST SCORES.  THE HIGHEST, LOWEST,
  AND AVERAGE ARE DETERMINED.  THEN THESE RESULTS ARE DISPLAYED. }

{*****************************************************************}

PROCEDURE TEST_SCORES;

{ READ THE SCORES AND DETERMINE AND DISPLAY HIGH SCORE, LOW SCORE,
  AND AVERAGE. }

CONST
    NUM_TESTS = 10;

VAR
    SCORE, HIGH, LOW, COUNT, TOTAL : INTEGER;
    AVERAGE                        : REAL;

BEGIN   { TEST_SCORES }

    TOTAL := 0;
    WRITE ('ENTER FIRST SCORE: ');
    READLN (SCORE);    { READ FIRST SCORE }
    HIGH := SCORE;     { SET HIGH SCORE TO FIRST SCORE }
    LOW := SCORE;      { SET LOW SCORE TO FIRST SCORE }
    TOTAL := TOTAL + SCORE; { ADD FIRST SCORE TO TOTAL POINTS }
    COUNT := 1;

    { READ EACH OF REMAINING SCORES. }
    WHILE COUNT < NUM_TESTS DO
    BEGIN
        COUNT := COUNT + 1;
        WRITE ('ENTER NEXT SCORE: ');
        READLN (SCORE);
        IF SCORE > HIGH           { IF NEW SCORE HIGHER THAN CURRENT HIGH }
            THEN HIGH := SCORE;   { SET HIGH TO SCORE }
        IF SCORE < LOW            { IF NEW SCORE LOWER THAN CURRENT LOW }
            THEN LOW := SCORE;    { SET LOW TO SCORE }
        TOTAL := TOTAL + SCORE;  { KEEP TRACK OF TOTAL POINTS SCORED }
    END;    { WHILE }

    { CALCULATE AVERAGE. }
    AVERAGE := TOTAL / COUNT;

    { DISPLAY RESULTS. }
    WRITELN;
    WRITELN ('HIGH':10, 'LOW':10, 'AVERAGE':10);
    WRITELN ('SCORE':10, 'SCORE':10, 'SCORE':10);
    WRITELN ('----------------------------------');
    WRITELN (HIGH:10, LOW:10, AVERAGE:10:2);

END;    { TEST_SCORES }
```

FIGURE 7–1 PROGRAM ANALYZE_SCORES

(Figure continued on next page)

```
{**************************************************************}

BEGIN   { MAIN }

  TEST_SCORES;

END.    { MAIN }
```

```
ENTER FIRST SCORE: 78
ENTER NEXT  SCORE: 84
ENTER NEXT  SCORE: 81
ENTER NEXT  SCORE: 92
ENTER NEXT  SCORE: 75
ENTER NEXT  SCORE: 95
ENTER NEXT  SCORE: 79
ENTER NEXT  SCORE: 90
ENTER NEXT  SCORE: 84
ENTER NEXT  SCORE: 90

        HIGH      LOW    AVERAGE
       SCORE     SCORE    SCORE
    ------------------------------------
         95        75     84.80
```

FIGURE 7-1   PROGRAM ANALYZE_SCORES (Cont.)

In general, it is good programming practice to write programs so that each procedure performs a single task. This is especially important when you begin to write larger, more complex programs. In this program, it is not all that critical because procedure TEST_SCORES is relatively short and easy to understand. However, the program ANALYZE_SCORES can be rewritten so that it contains two procedures, one to read the scores and determine the results and the second to display them.

Examine Figure 7-1 again. Notice that all of the variables used by procedure TEST_SCORES are declared in the procedure. If this procedure is divided into two procedures, both will have to use the variables HIGH, LOW, and AVERAGE. To allow both procedures to use these variables, they will have to be declared in the main program. The program containing these two procedures is shown in Figure 7-2. Notice the procedure heading for the second procedure, DISPLAY_RESULTS:

```
PROCEDURE DISPLAY_RESULTS (HIGH, LOW : INTEGER; AVERAGE : REAL);
```

```
PROGRAM ANALYZE_SCORES;

{ THIS PROGRAM READS A GROUP OF TEST SCORES.  THE HIGHEST, LOWEST,
  AND AVERAGE ARE DETERMINED.  THEN THESE RESULTS ARE DISPLAYED. }

CONST
   NUM_TESTS = 10;

VAR
   HIGH, LOW : INTEGER;
   AVERAGE   : REAL;

{*******************************************************************}

PROCEDURE READ_AND_CALCULATE (VAR HIGH, LOW : INTEGER;
                              VAR AVERAGE   : REAL);

{ READ THE SCORES AND DETERMINE HIGH SCORE, LOW SCORE, AND AVERAGE.
  THESE VALUES ARE RETURNED TO THE CALLING PROGRAM. }

VAR
   SCORE, COUNT, TOTAL : INTEGER;

BEGIN    { READ_AND_CALCULATE }

   TOTAL := 0;
   WRITE ('ENTER FIRST SCORE: ');
   READLN (SCORE);          { READ FIRST SCORE }
   HIGH := SCORE;           { SET HIGH SCORE TO FIRST SCORE }
   LOW := SCORE;            { SET LOW SCORE TO FIRST SCORE }
   TOTAL := TOTAL + SCORE;  { ADD FIRST SCORE TO TOTAL POINTS }
   COUNT := 1;

   { READ EACH OF REMAINING SCORES. }
   WHILE COUNT < NUM_TESTS DO
   BEGIN
      COUNT := COUNT + 1;
      WRITE ('ENTER NEXT SCORE: ');
      READLN (SCORE);
      IF SCORE > HIGH          { IF NEW SCORE HIGHER THAN CURRENT HIGH }
         THEN HIGH := SCORE;    { SET HIGH TO SCORE }
      IF SCORE < LOW           { IF NEW SCORE LOWER THAN CURRENT LOW }
         THEN LOW := SCORE;     { SET LOW TO SCORE }
      TOTAL := TOTAL + SCORE;  { KEEP TRACK OF TOTAL POINTS SCORED }
   END;    { WHILE }

   { CALCULATE AVERAGE. }
   AVERAGE := TOTAL / COUNT;

END;    { READ_AND_CALCULATE }

{*******************************************************************}
```

FIGURE 7-2 PROGRAM ANALYZE_SCORES WITH PARAMETERS

(Figure continued on next page)

```
PROCEDURE DISPLAY_RESULTS (HIGH, LOW : INTEGER; AVERAGE : REAL);

{ DISPLAYS THE HIGH SCORE, LOW SCORE, AND AVERAGE OF ALL SCORES. }

BEGIN   { DISPLAY_RESULTS }

   WRITELN;
   WRITELN ('HIGH':10, 'LOW':10, 'AVERAGE':10);
   WRITELN ('SCORE':10, 'SCORE':10, 'SCORE':10);
   WRITELN ('------------------------------------');
   WRITELN (HIGH:10, LOW:10, AVERAGE:10:2);

END;   { DISPLAY_RESULTS }

{******************************************************************}

BEGIN   { MAIN }

   READ_AND_CALCULATE (HIGH, LOW, AVERAGE);
   DISPLAY_RESULTS (HIGH,LOW, AVERAGE);

END.   { MAIN }
```

```
ENTER FIRST SCORE: 78
ENTER NEXT SCORE: 84
ENTER NEXT SCORE: 81
ENTER NEXT SCORE: 92
ENTER NEXT SCORE: 75
ENTER NEXT SCORE: 95
ENTER NEXT SCORE: 79
ENTER NEXT SCORE: 90
ENTER NEXT SCORE: 84
ENTER NEXT SCORE: 90

        HIGH      LOW   AVERAGE
       SCORE    SCORE     SCORE
   ------------------------------------
         95       75     84.80
```

FIGURE 7-2   PROGRAM ANALYZE_SCORES WITH PARAMETERS (Cont.)

Each of the variables declared in the main program and used by the procedure is listed in the heading. These are referred to as **parameters**. Parameters are used to pass values between procedures and the calling program. There are two types of parameters: **formal parameters** and actual parameters. The variables listed in the procedure heading are formal parameters. Procedure DISPLAY_RESULTS has three formal parameters, two of type INTEGER and one of type REAL. If there is more than one parameter of the same type, these parameters may be listed together, separated by commas. If there is more than one parameter type, the parameters of different types are separated by semicolons. A formal parameter is a variable name representing a value (the actual parameter) to be passed to the procedure from the calling program. When this procedure is called, the actual parameters must be listed in the procedure call. The following statement could be used to call procedure DISPLAY_RESULTS:

```
DISPLAY_RESULTS (HIGH, LOW, AVERAGE);
```

Notice that the data types of the actual parameters are not listed in the procedure call. When this statement is executed, program control will transfer to DISPLAY_RESULTS, and the current values of HIGH, LOW, and AVERAGE in the main program will be assigned to the corresponding formal parameters in the procedure heading.

Parameters are substituted based on their position in the parameter list. The value of the first actual parameter is assigned to the first formal parameter, the value of the second actual parameter to the second formal parameter, and so forth. Therefore, the name of the actual parameter need not be the same as that of the corresponding formal parameter. All of the following are valid procedure calls for DISPLAY_RESULTS:

```
DISPLAY_RESULTS (HIGHEST, LOWEST, AVE);
DISPLAY_RESULTS (98, 67, 82.5);
DISPLAY_RESULTS (H, L, 45 + 50);
```

The actual parameters can be variables or expressions as long as they evaluate to the data type of the formal parameter. Figure 7–3 demonstrates how actual parameters are substituted for formal parameters.

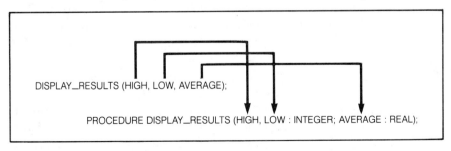

DISPLAY_RESULTS (HIGH, LOW, AVERAGE);

PROCEDURE DISPLAY_RESULTS (HIGH, LOW : INTEGER; AVERAGE : REAL);

FIGURE 7–3 SUBSTITUTING ACTUAL PARAMETERS FOR FORMAL PARAMETERS

1. Give two examples of standard procedures.
2. Write three different valid procedure calls for this procedure heading:

   PROCEDURE PR_TABLE (ITEM : INTEGER; COST, TAX, TOTAL_COST :
                            REAL);

3. Which of the following are valid procedure headings?

   a. PROCEDURE GAME (LIFE : BOOLEAN);
   b. PROCEDURE TOOLS (WRENCH, HAMMER : CHAR; NUM_WRENCH,
                            NUM_HAMMER : INTEGER);
   c. PROCEDURE SET_TABLE (PLACES, GLASSES, KNIVES, FORKS);
   d. VOLUME (HEIGHT, WIDTH, DEPTH);

4. Assume that you have written a program that requires the user to enter a numeric value. How can the VAL procedure be used to allow the user to reenter a value if a character value was accidentally entered?

Value and Variable Parameters

Examine the procedure heading for procedure READ_AND_CALCULATE in Figure 7–2:

```
PROCEDURE READ_AND_CALCULATE (VAR HIGH, LOW  :  INTEGER;
                              VAR AVERAGE    :  REAL);
```

The reserved identifier VAR is placed in front of the formal parameters because these are **variable parameters**. If it is necessary for the values determined in a procedure to be returned to the calling program, a variable parameter must be used. A variable parameter is a two-way parameter. It passes its value to the procedure, and any changes to the parameter are returned to the calling program.

The parameters passed to DISPLAY_RESULTS were **value parameters**. Value parameters work in only one direction. They pass values to procedures but cannot pass a value back to the calling program. This means that if the value of a parameter is changed in a procedure, the value will not be changed in the calling program. None of the values of the parameters should be changed by procedure DISPLAY_RESULTS. Its purpose is merely to display them. Therefore, in this situation, value parameters should be used.

However, procedure READ_AND_CALCULATE must determine the values of HIGH, LOW and AVERAGE. The main program needs to know these new values. Therefore, variable parameters must be used so that the new values will be returned to the calling program.

Using VAR in front of the parameters indicates to the compiler that any changes to these variables should be returned to the calling program.

Figure 7–4 demonstrates the difference between value and variable parameters. Examine the first program, TOTAL1. In procedure SUM1, the total of three numbers is assigned to variable X, which is then displayed. After SUM1 has been executed, the value of variable A (the corresponding parameter) is output. The value of A is the same as it was before SUM1 was called. Although the value of the formal parameter X was changed in procedure SUM1, this new value is not returned to the main program. This is because X is a value parameter.

Value parameters protect variables from being changed accidentally. However, sometimes the new value of a variable should be returned to the calling program. TOTAL2 contains the same program except that X is now a variable parameter. Notice that the new value of X is returned to the calling program. When A is printed in the main program, its value is the same as the value that was assigned to X in SUM2.

When a variable parameter is used, it must be a variable name in the procedure call. It cannot be an expression or a constant. This is because a value will be returned in this parameter. Suppose a procedure call looked like this:

```
CHECK (X / 2);
```

What if the procedure heading looked like this:

```
PROCEDURE CHECK (VAR TOT : REAL);
```

After procedure CHECK is executed, how would the value of TOT be returned in X/2? A value can be assigned to a variable, but not to an expression or a constant. Because of this, only value parameters may be expressions or constants.

Advantages of Using Procedures

Dividing a program into subprograms, each of which performs a specific task, makes writing a program easier. The programmer needs to work on only one small part at a time rather than on a single large program. If you think of tasks you have performed, you can readily see that this is true. For example, cleaning a messy room might seem overwhelming if the job is tackled all at once. But dividing it into subtasks and dealing with these one at a time makes the job seem less formidable. Your energy is focused on each separate part rather than on the whole. This is more efficient than wandering randomly around the room, doing part of one job and then part of another. Also, by performing each subtask from start to finish in turn, the end result is likely to be more thorough.

```
PROGRAM TOTAL1;

{ THIS PROGRAM DEMONSTRATES THAT WHEN A VALUE PARAMETER IS CHANGED IN
  A PROCEDURE, THE NEW VALUE IS NOT RETURNED TO THE CALLING PROGRAM.
  THIS PROGRAM CALLS PROCEDURE SUM1 TO ADD THE THREE NUMBERS TOGETHER
  AND ASSIGN THE TOTAL TO X.  ALTHOUGH THE VALUE OF VARIABLE X IS
  CHANGED IN PROCEDURE SUM1, THIS RESULT IS NOT RETURNED TO THE MAIN
  PROGRAM. }

VAR
   A, B, C : REAL;

{*********************************************************************}

PROCEDURE SUM1 (X, Y, Z : REAL);

{ ADDS X, Y, AND Z TOGETHER AND PLACES THE RESULT IN X. }

BEGIN  { SUM1 }

   X := X + Y + Z;
   WRITELN ('THE VALUE OF X IN PROCEDURE SUM1 IS ', X:6:2);

END;   { SUM1 }

{*********************************************************************}

BEGIN   { MAIN }

   WRITE ('TYPE IN 3 NUMBERS TO BE ADDED TOGETHER: ');
   READLN (A, B, C);
   SUM1 (A, B, C);
   WRITELN ('THE VALUE OF A IN THE MAIN PROGRAM IS ', A:6:2);

END.   { MAIN }
```

```
TYPE IN 3 NUMBERS TO BE ADDED TOGETHER: 5  8  6
THE VALUE OF X IN PROCEDURE SUM1 IS  19.00
THE VALUE OF A IN THE MAIN PROGRAM IS   5.00
```

FIGURE 7–4   COMPARING VALUE AND VARIABLE PARAMETERS   *(Figure continued on next page)*

```
PROGRAM TOTAL2;

{ THIS PROGRAM DEMONSTRATES THAT WHEN A VARIABLE PARAMETER IS CHANGED
  IN A PROCEDURE, THE NEW VALUE IS RETURNED TO THE CALLING PROGRAM.
  THIS PROGRAM CALLS PROCEDURE SUM2 TO ADD THREE NUMBERS TOGETHER AND
  ASSIGN THE SUM TO X.   THIS NEW VALUE OF X IS RETURNED TO THE CALLING
  PROGRAM. }

VAR
    A, B, C : REAL;

{*********************************************************************}

PROCEDURE SUM2 (VAR X : REAL; Y, Z : REAL);

{ ADDS X, Y, AND Z TOGETHER AND PLACES THE RESULT IN X.   THIS NEW VALUE
  OF X IS RETURNED TO THE MAIN PROGRAM. }

BEGIN   { SUM2 }

    X := X + Y + Z;
    WRITELN ('THE VALUE OF X IN PROCEDURE SUM2 IS ', X:6:2);

END;    { SUM2 }

{*********************************************************************}

BEGIN   { MAIN }

    WRITE ('TYPE IN 3 NUMBERS TO BE ADDED TOGETHER: ');
    READLN (A, B, C);
    SUM2 (A, B, C);
    WRITELN ('THE VALUE OF A IN THE MAIN PROGRAM IS ', A:6:2);

END.    { MAIN }
```

```
TYPE IN 3 NUMBERS TO BE ADDED TOGETHER: 5  8  6
THE VALUE OF X IN PROCEDURE SUM2 IS  19.00
THE VALUE OF A IN THE MAIN PROGRAM IS  19.00
```

FIGURE 7–4   COMPARING VALUE AND VARIABLE PARAMETERS (Cont.)

Remember the discussion of how to divide a programming problem into tasks using a structure chart? Structure charts are very helpful when writing programs using procedures. When the program is written, each box in the structure chart can be written as a separate procedure. The structure chart provides a guideline for determining the tasks that each procedure will perform.

In this section, a program will be developed to determine the quantity of art supplies needed for an art class. Each student is required to make one of three projects. The projects and the supplies needed for each are as follows:

Project	Supplies
Ceramic vase	0.5 pounds of clay
	5 ounces of glaze
	1 brush
Water color	1 box water colors
	1 canvas
	1 brush
Charcoal sketches	4 pieces of charcoal
	8 pieces of newsprint

The program should prompt the user to enter the name of the project and the number of students choosing to make that project. The program should then calculate and print the total quantity of supplies needed. This programming problem contains two major tasks:

1. Determine the quantity of supplies needed based on the types of projects.
2. Display the quantity of supplies.

Step 2 is fairly simple. However, step 1 could be divided further:

1a. Determine quantity of supplies needed for vases.
1b. Determine quantity of supplies needed for water colors.
1c. Determine quantity of supplies needed for sketches.

A structure chart showing the substeps needed to solve this problem is shown in Figure 7–5.

When this program is written, the first procedure will be named DETERMINE_PROJECT and the second procedure DISPLAY_SUP-PLIES. Because there are three substeps under DETERMINE_ PROJECT, each will be written as a separate procedure. These three procedures will be nested inside DETERMINE_PROJECT. Procedures can be nested inside other procedures. Each of these procedures will be called by the procedure DETERMINE_PROJECT.

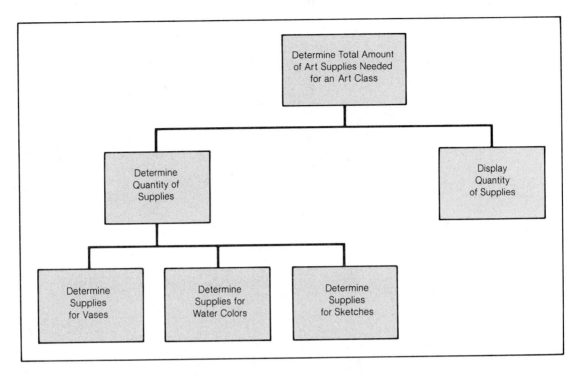

FIGURE 7-5   STRUCTURE CHART FOR ART SUPPLIES PROGRAM

The Scope of Identifiers

The completed art supplies program is shown in Figure 7–6. Notice that the three procedures PROJECT1, PROJECT2, and PROJECT3 are placed immediately after the local declaration section of DETER-MINE_PROJECT. Because these three procedures are nested inside DETERMINE_PROJECT, they can only be called by DETERMINE_PROJECT. Attempting to call them from DISPLAY_SUPPLIES (or the main program) would result in an error. If it were necessary for DISPLAY_SUPPLIES to access one of the procedures, such as PROJECT1, that procedure would have to be moved outside DE-TERMINE_PROJECT. Then it could be called by DISPLAY_SUPPLIES.

Variables declared in a procedure are called **local variables.** This means that they are local to the procedure in which they are declared and can only be used in that procedure (or any procedure nested in it). If an attempt is made to use them elsewhere, an undeclared identifier error will occur. In Figure 7–6, the procedure DETERMINE_PROJECT

```
PROGRAM ART;

{ THIS PROGRAM DETERMINES THE QUANTITY OF SUPPLIES NEEDED FOR AN ART
  CLASS.  EACH STUDENT IS ALLOWED TO MAKE ONE PROJECT.  THE PROJECTS
  AND THE SUPPLIES NEEDED FOR EACH ARE LISTED BELOW:

NAME OF PROJECT          SUPPLIES NEEDED
   1.   VASE              0.5 POUNDS OF CLAY
                          5 OUNCES OF GLAZE
                          1 BRUSH

   2.   WATER COLORS      1 BOX WATER COLORS
                          1 CANVAS
                          1 BRUSH

   3.   SKETCHES          4 PIECES OF CHARCOAL
                          8 PIECES OF NEWSPRINT

THE NAME AND QUANTITY OF EACH PROJECT TO BE MADE ARE ENTERED AT THE
KEYBOARD.  WHEN ALL THE DATA IS ENTERED, THE AMOUNT OF SUPPLIES NEEDED
IS DISPLAYED ON THE MONITOR. }

VAR
    PAINTS, CANVAS, CHARCOAL, PAPER, BRUSH : INTEGER;
    CLAY, GLAZE                            : REAL;

{*********************************************************************}

PROCEDURE DETERMINE_PROJECT (VAR PAINTS, CANVAS, CHARCOAL, PAPER, BRUSH :
                             INTEGER; VAR CLAY, GLAZE : REAL);

{  DETERMINES THE QUANTITY OF SUPPLIES NEEDED TO MAKE THE PROJECTS. }

VAR
    PROJECT : STRING;
    NUM     : INTEGER;
    ANSWER  : CHAR;

{*********************************************************************}

PROCEDURE PROJECT1 (NUM : INTEGER; VAR BRUSH : INTEGER;
                    VAR CLAY, GLAZE : REAL);

{ DETERMINES THE QUANTITY OF SUPPLIES NEEDED TO MAKE CERAMIC VASES. }

BEGIN    { PROJECT1 }

    CLAY  := CLAY + NUM * 0.5;
    GLAZE := GLAZE + NUM * 5.0;
    BRUSH := BRUSH + NUM;

END;    { PROJECT1 }

{*********************************************************************}
```

FIGURE 7–6 PROGRAM ART

(Figure continued on next page)

```
PROCEDURE PROJECT2 (NUM : INTEGER; VAR PAINTS, CANVAS, BRUSH : INTEGER);

{ DETERMINES THE QUANTITY OF SUPPLIES NEEDED TO MAKE WATER COLORS. }

BEGIN   { PROJECT2 }

    PAINTS := PAINTS + NUM;
    CANVAS := CANVAS + NUM;
    BRUSH := BRUSH + NUM;

END;   { PROJECT2 }

{******************************************************************}

PROCEDURE PROJECT3 (NUM : INTEGER; VAR CHARCOAL, PAPER : INTEGER);

{ DETERMINES THE QUANTITY OF SUPPLIES NEEDED TO MAKE CHARCOAL SKETCHES. }

BEGIN   { PROJECT3 }

    CHARCOAL := CHARCOAL + 4 * NUM;
    PAPER := PAPER + 8 * NUM;

END;   { PROJECT3 }

{******************************************************************}

BEGIN   { DETERMINE_PROJECT }

    PAINTS   := 0;
    CANVAS   := 0;
    CHARCOAL := 0;
    PAPER    := 0;
    BRUSH    := 0;
    CLAY     := 0;
    GLAZE    := 0;

    ANSWER := 'Y';
    WHILE ANSWER = 'Y' DO
    BEGIN
        WRITE ('ENTER THE TYPE OF PROJECT (VASE, COLORS, OR SKETCHES): ');
        READLN (PROJECT);
        WRITE ('ENTER THE QUANTITY OF THIS PROJECT TO BE MADE: ');
        READLN (NUM);
        IF PROJECT = 'VASE'
            THEN PROJECT1 (NUM, BRUSH, CLAY, GLAZE)
            ELSE IF PROJECT = 'COLORS'
                    THEN PROJECT2 (NUM, PAINTS, CANVAS, BRUSH)
                    ELSE IF PROJECT = 'SKETCHES'
                            THEN PROJECT3 (NUM, CHARCOAL, PAPER);
```

FIGURE 7–6   PROGRAM ART (Cont.)   *(Figure continued on next page)*

```
            WRITELN;
            WRITE ('ARE THERE MORE PROJECTS (Y/N)? ');
            READLN (ANSWER);
      END;    { WHILE }

END;    { DETERMINE_PROJECT }

{***********************************************************************}

PROCEDURE DISPLAY_SUPPLIES (PAINTS, CANVAS, CHARCOAL, PAPER, BRUSH :
                            INTEGER; CLAY, GLAZE : REAL);

{ DISPLAY THE TOTAL AMOUNT OF ALL SUPPLIES NEEDED. }

BEGIN    { DISPLAY_SUPPLIES }

   WRITELN;
   WRITELN;
   WRITELN ('THE FOLLOWING ART SUPPLIES WILL BE NEEDED:');
   WRITELN ('--------------------------------------------');
   WRITELN;
   WRITELN (CLAY:7:2, ' POUNDS OF CLAY');
   WRITELN (GLAZE:7:2, ' OUNCES OF GLAZE');
   WRITELN (PAINTS:7, ' SETS OF WATER COLORS');
   WRITELN (CANVAS:7, ' CANVASES');
   WRITELN (CHARCOAL:7, ' PIECES OF CHARCOAL');
   WRITELN (PAPER:7, ' SHEETS OF NEWSPRINT');
   WRITELN (BRUSH:7, ' BRUSHES');

END;    { DISPLAY_SUPPLIES }

{***********************************************************************}

BEGIN    { MAIN }

   DETERMINE_PROJECT (PAINTS, CANVAS, CHARCOAL, PAPER, BRUSH, CLAY,
                GLAZE);

   DISPLAY_SUPPLIES (PAINTS, CANVAS, CHARCOAL, PAPER, BRUSH, CLAY,
                GLAZE);

END.    { MAIN }
```

FIGURE 7–6   PROGRAM ART (Cont.)

(Figure continued on next page)

```
ENTER THE TYPE OF PROJECT (VASE, COLORS, OR SKETCHES): VASE
ENTER THE QUANTITY OF THIS PROJECT TO BE MADE: 8

ARE THERE MORE PROJECTS (Y/N)? Y
ENTER THE TYPE OF PROJECT (VASE, COLORS, OR SKETCHES): SKETCHES
ENTER THE QUANTITY OF THIS PROJECT TO BE MADE: 10

ARE THERE MORE PROJECTS (Y/N)? Y
ENTER THE TYPE OF PROJECT (VASE, COLORS, OR SKETCHES): COLORS
ENTER THE QUANTITY OF THIS PROJECT TO BE MADE: 7

ARE THERE MORE PROJECTS (Y/N)? N


THE FOLLOWING ART SUPPLIES WILL BE NEEDED:
------------------------------------------

    4.00 POUNDS OF CLAY
   40.00 OUNCES OF GLAZE
       7 SETS OF WATER COLORS
       7 CANVASES
      40 PIECES OF CHARCOAL
      80 SHEETS OF NEWSPRINT
      15 BRUSHES
```

FIGURE 7-6   PROGRAM ART (Cont.)

has three local variables: PROJECT, NUM, and ANSWER. These variables cannot be used in the main program or in procedure DISPLAY_SUPPLIES. However, they may be used in DETERMINE_PROJECT and those procedures nested inside it: PROJECT1, PROJECT2, and PROJECT3.

Global variables are those variables declared in the main program. In program ART, the global variables are PAINTS, CANVAS, CHARCOAL, PAPER, BRUSH, CLAY, and GLAZE. These variables can be used anywhere in the program. Whenever we have used a global variable in a procedure, we have used a parameter to pass that variable to the procedure. This is not required, however. These variables could be used in a procedure without being passed as parameters. This might seem easier than using parameters. But this approach can lead to many problems. For example, any changes made to the variables in the procedure would be returned to the calling program. It would not be possible to have value parameters. By listing the parameters in the procedure heading, it is easy to see which variables are used in that procedure. Often a number of programmers will work together on a large program. Each may write certain procedures. Using parameters makes such cooperation easier. There is no problem if the variable names in the procedures do not match those in the calling program. All that matters is that all parameters are listed and are in the correct order. This also means that, if necessary, the same procedure can be easily used in any number of different programs.

Each identifier in a program has a **scope block**. A scope block is that portion of the program in which a paticular identifier is defined. For example, the scope block for GLAZE is the entire program whereas the scope block for ANSWER is DETERMINE_PROJECT and those procedures nested inside DETERMINE_PROJECT. The scope block for a global variable is always the entire program, whereas that for a local variable is the procedure in which it is declared and any procedures nested inside it.

Procedures also have scope blocks. The scope block for DETERMINE_PROJECT is the entire program, whereas the scope block for PROJECT1 is DETERMINE_PROJECT. These scope blocks indicate the area in which the procedure can be called.

Figure 7–7 contains program ART with its scope blocks marked. Any variable or procedure declared inside a particular block can be used inside that block and any block nested in that block.

Documenting Procedures

The procedures written in this chapter have been short and easy to understand. In large programs, procedures may become much more complex and numerous. There may be many parameters. Because of this, procedures should be documented in the same way as a main program. There should be a general statement of the purpose of the procedure after the heading. This should include a description of the parameters passed to the subprogram. The documentation should also describe any values returned to the calling program.

1. How does the programmer indicate that a particular parameter is a variable parameter?
2. Refer to the program in Figure 7–2. List the scope of all the variables in this program. What is the scope of procedure READ_AND_CALCULATE?
3. Study the following program. Determine the values of the variables R1, R2, I1, and I2 after this program is executed.

LEARNING CHECK 7-2

```
PROGRAM EXAMPLE;

VAR
    R1, R2 : REAL;
    I1, I2 : INTEGER;
    YES    : BOOLEAN;

{********************************************************************}

PROCEDURE CHANGE (VAR PR1, PR2 : REAL; PI1, PI2 : INTEGER; CONT :
                  BOOLEAN);

BEGIN   { CHANGE }

   PR1 := PI1 + PI2;
   IF CONT
      THEN PI1 := PI2 - 6;

END;   { CHANGE }

{********************************************************************}

BEGIN   { MAIN }

   R1 := 104.55;
   R2 := 86.73;
   YES := TRUE;
   I1 := 66;
   I2 := 0;
   CHANGE (R1, R2, I1, I2, YES);

END.   { MAIN }
```

```
PROGRAM ART;

{ THIS PROGRAM DETERMINES THE QUANTITY OF SUPPLIES NEEDED FOR AN ART
  CLASS.  EACH STUDENT IS ALLOWED TO MAKE ONE PROJECT.  THE PROJECTS
  AND THE SUPPLIES NEEDED FOR EACH ARE LISTED BELOW:

NAME OF PROJECT            SUPPLIES NEEDED
  1.  VASE                 0.5 POUNDS OF CLAY
                           5 OUNCES OF GLAZE
                           1 BRUSH

  2.  WATER COLORS         1 BOX WATER COLORS
                           1 CANVAS
                           1 BRUSH

  3.  SKETCHES             4 PIECES OF CHARCOAL
                           8 PIECES OF NEWSPRINT

THE NAME AND QUANTITY OF EACH PROJECT TO BE MADE ARE ENTERED AT THE
KEYBOARD.  WHEN ALL THE DATA IS ENTERED, THE AMOUNT OF SUPPLIES NEEDED
IS DISPLAYED ON THE MONITOR. }

VAR
    PAINTS, CANVAS, CHARCOAL, PAPER, BRUSH : INTEGER;
    CLAY, GLAZE                            : REAL;

{***********************************************************************}

PROCEDURE DETERMINE_PROJECT (VAR PAINTS, CANVAS, CHARCOAL, PAPER, BRUSH :
                            INTEGER; VAR CLAY, GLAZE : REAL);

{ DETERMINES THE QUANTITY OF SUPPLIES NEEDED TO MAKE THE PROJECTS. }

VAR
    PROJECT : STRING;
    NUM     : INTEGER;
    ANSWER  : CHAR;

{***********************************************************************}

PROCEDURE PROJECT1 (NUM : INTEGER; VAR BRUSH : INTEGER;
                    VAR CLAY, GLAZE : REAL);

{ DETERMINES THE QUANTITY OF SUPPLIES NEEDED TO MAKE CERAMIC VASES. }

BEGIN   { PROJECT1 }

    CLAY := CLAY + NUM * 0.5;
    GLAZE := GLAZE + NUM * 5.0;
    BRUSH := BRUSH + NUM;

END;    { PROJECT1 }

{***********************************************************************}

PROCEDURE PROJECT2 (NUM : INTEGER; VAR PAINTS, CANVAS, BRUSH : INTEGER);

{ DETERMINES THE QUANTITY OF SUPPLIES NEEDED TO MAKE WATER COLORS. }

BEGIN   { PROJECT2 }

    PAINTS := PAINTS + NUM;
    CANVAS := CANVAS + NUM;
    BRUSH := BRUSH + NUM;

END;    { PROJECT2 }

{***********************************************************************}

PROCEDURE PROJECT3 (NUM : INTEGER; VAR CHARCOAL, PAPER : INTEGER);

{ DETERMINES THE QUANTITY OF SUPPLIES
  NEEDED TO MAKE CHARCOAL SKETCHES. }
```

FIGURE 7–7   PROGRAM ART WITH SCOPE BLOCKS INDICATED

```
BEGIN   { PROJECT3 }

   CHARCOAL := CHARCOAL + 4 * NUM;
   PAPER := PAPER + 8 * NUM;

END;   { PROJECT3 }
```

```
{*********************************************************************}

BEGIN   { DETERMINE_PROJECT }

   PAINTS   := 0;
   CANVAS   := 0;
   CHARCOAL := 0;
   PAPER    := 0;
   BRUSH    := 0;
   CLAY     := 0;
   GLAZE    := 0;

   ANSWER := 'Y';
   WHILE ANSWER = 'Y' DO
   BEGIN
      WRITE ('ENTER THE TYPE OF PROJECT (VASE, COLORS, OR SKETCHES): ');
      READLN (PROJECT);
      WRITE ('ENTER THE QUANTITY OF THIS PROJECT TO BE MADE: ');
      READLN (NUM);
      IF PROJECT = 'VASE'
         THEN PROJECT1 (NUM, BRUSH, CLAY, GLAZE)
         ELSE IF PROJECT = 'COLORS'
                 THEN PROJECT2 (NUM, PAINTS, CANVAS, BRUSH)
                 ELSE IF PROJECT = 'SKETCHES'
                         THEN PROJECT3 (NUM, CHARCOAL, PAPER);
      WRITELN;
      WRITE ('ARE THERE MORE PROJECTS (Y/N)? ');
      READLN (ANSWER);
   END;   { WHILE }

END;   { DETERMINE_PROJECT }
```

```
{*********************************************************************}

PROCEDURE DISPLAY_SUPPLIES (PAINTS, CANVAS, CHARCOAL, PAPER, BRUSH :
                           INTEGER; CLAY, GLAZE : REAL);

{ DISPLAY THE TOTAL AMOUNT OF ALL SUPPLIES NEEDED. }

BEGIN   { DISPLAY_SUPPLIES }

   WRITELN;
   WRITELN;
   WRITELN ('THE FOLLOWING ART SUPPLIES WILL BE NEEDED:');
   WRITELN ('-------------------------------------------');
   WRITELN;
   WRITELN (CLAY:7:2, ' POUNDS OF CLAY');
   WRITELN (GLAZE:7:2, ' OUNCES OF GLAZE');
   WRITELN (PAINTS:7, ' SETS OF WATER COLORS');
   WRITELN (CANVAS:7, ' CANVASES');
   WRITELN (CHARCOAL:7, ' PIECES OF CHARCOAL');
   WRITELN (PAPER:7, ' SHEETS OF NEWSPRINT');
   WRITELN (BRUSH:7, ' BRUSHES');

END;   { DISPLAY_SUPPLIES }
```

```
{*********************************************************************}

BEGIN   { MAIN }

   DETERMINE_PROJECT (PAINTS, CANVAS, CHARCOAL, PAPER, BRUSH, CLAY,
                      GLAZE);

   DISPLAY_SUPPLIES (PAINTS, CANVAS, CHARCOAL, PAPER, BRUSH, CLAY,
                     GLAZE);

END.   { MAIN }
```

FIGURE 7-7   PROGRAM ART WITH SCOPE BLOCKS INDICATED (Cont.)

▬▬ SUMMARY POINTS

- Procedures allow programs to be divided into subparts, each of which performs a specific task. This simplifies the process of writing a program.
- There are two types of procedures: standard and user defined.
- Standard procedures, such as READ, are "built into" the compiler.
- User-defined procedures are written by the programmer to perform specific tasks needed by a program. The format of a user-defined procedure is similar to that of an entire program.
- Parameters are used to communicate between a procedure and the calling program. When a procedure is called, the actual parameters listed in the call statement replace the formal parameters listed in the procedure heading.
- Parameters can be placed into two categories: value or variable. Value parameters do not return their values to the calling program, whereas variable parameters do. Variable parameters are preceded by the reserved identifier VAR in the formal parameter list.
- Global variables are declared in the main program and can be used anywhere in that program, whereas local variables are declared in a procedure and can be used only in that procedure.
- The scope of an identifier is that portion of a program in which it is defined.

▬▬ VOCABULARY LIST

Actual parameter   Procedure
Argument   Scope block
Built-in procedure   Standard procedure
Formal parameter   User-defined procedure
Global variable   Value parameter
Local variable   Variable parameter

▬▬ CHAPTER TEST

Vocabulary

Match a term from the numbered column with the description from the lettered column that best fits the term.

1. Scope block

2. Local variable

3. Variable parameter

4. Procedure

5. Global variable

6. Value parameter

7. Actual parameter

8. Standard procedure

9. Formal parameter

10. User-defined procedure

11. Procedure call

a. A statement causing a procedure to be executed.

b. A parameter whose value is passed to a procedure and also passed back to the calling program.

c. That portion of a program in which a specific identifier can be used.

d. An identifier listed in a procedure heading that represents a value to be passed to the procedure by the calling program through an actual parameter.

e. A variable declared in the declaration section of a main program.

f. A value passed to a procedure when it is called and manipulated by that procedure. It is substituted for its corresponding formal parameter.

g. A procedure the programmer writes to perform a specific task.

h. A variable declared in a procedure. It is undefined outside that procedure.

i. A subprogram used to perform a specific task.

j. A procedure "built in" to the Pascal compiler.

k. A parameter whose value is passed to the procedure, but any changes made to the parameter are not passed back to the calling program.

Questions

1. Explain the difference between actual parameters and formal parameters and how each is used in a procedure and its calling program.
2. Given the following program segment, evaluate the expressions in parts a–c.

```
VAR
    STR1, STR2 : STRING;
    NUM        : INTEGER;
    ERROR      : INTEGER;
```

```
BEGIN
    STR1 := 'BEWARE JABBERWOCK';

a. DELETE (STR1, 1, 3);
b. INSERT ('THE', STR1, 8);
c. INSERT (' MY SON', STR1, 18);
```

3. How is a variable parameter different from a value parameter?
4. What is an advantage of using value parameters? What is an advantage of using variable parameters?
5. Write a valid procedure call for each of the following procedure headings:

```
PROCEDURE MONEY (NET, GROSS : REAL; CATEGORY : CHAR);
PROCEDURE SIZE (VAR TALL, SHORT, MEDIUM : INTEGER);
PROCEDURE CLASS (GEOLOGY, ALGEBRA, GYM, ENG_LIT : CHAR);
```

6. Why must the actual parameter for a variable parameter be a variable and not an expression or a constant?
7. After the following program is run, what will be the values of these variables: AGE, GRADE, HEIGHT, WEIGHT, and HONORS?

```
PROGRAM EXAMPLE;

VAR
   AGE, GRADE     : INTEGER;
   HEIGHT, WEIGHT : REAL;
   HONORS         : BOOLEAN;

PROCEDURE CHANGE (VAR NEW_HEIGHT : REAL; NEW_WEIGHT : REAL; VAR
                  NEW_HONORS : BOOLEAN; NEW_AGE, NEW_GRADE : INTEGER);

BEGIN   { CHANGE }

   NEW_HONORS := TRUE;
   NEW_WEIGHT := 108;
   NEW_GRADE := NEW_GRADE + 1;
   NEW_AGE := 18;
   NEW_HEIGHT := NEW_HEIGHT + 0.5;

END;   { CHANGE }

{*********************************************************************}

BEGIN   { MAIN }

   HONORS := FALSE;
   AGE := 17;
   HEIGHT := 62.5;
```

```
    WEIGHT := 110;
    GRADE := 10;
    CHANGE (HEIGHT, WEIGHT, HONORS, AGE, GRADE);

  END.    { MAIN }
```

8. Explain the difference between a global and a local variable.
9. List the local variables and the global variables in program ANALYZE_SCORES in Figure 7–1.

![] **PROGRAMMING PROBLEMS**

Level 1

1. Write a procedure having the following parameters passed to it:

    a. Three integers corresponding to the day, month, and year of a person's birthday.
    b. Three integers corresponding to today's date.

   The procedure should then calculate the person's age in years (disregarding additional months and days). Then the procedure should display the person's birthday and age in years using a format similar to the following:

BIRTHDATE	AGE
8/5/72	16

2. Urbank's Well Drilling Company drills water and oil wells for businesses and individuals. A water well costs $15 per foot to drill. An oil well costs $20 per foot to drill for the first 10,000 feet. Below that, it costs $35 per foot. Write a procedure to determine how much it will cost to drill a given well. The cost should be returned to the calling program.

Level 2

3. Write a program to help an art student determine the cost of framing a piece of artwork. The program should prompt the student for the length and the width of the item. First the amount of glass needed (in square inches) and the cost of the glass should be determined. Assume the glass costs 2 cents per square inch. Next the cost of the framing material should be determined. The wood used for framing costs $1.45 per foot. Use procedures as appropriate.

4. The marketing division of a cookie manufacturer wants a program to report the results of a customer survey of its four kinds of cookies.

Customers gave each kind of cookie a rating of 0 to 10. The program should read the ratings for each of the four kinds of cookies. Write a procedure that can be called four times to read each cookie's rating and then return the average rating to the calling program. When all the data on the cookies is obtained, the program should call a second procedure to display a table containing the results. At the bottom of the table, a message should be displayed stating which cookie had the best overall rating. Use the following data:

Chocolate Chip	Oatmeal	Lemon	Peanut Butter
7	4	3	5
9	6	5	2
5	7	4	6
10	8	7	4
6	8	4	8
9	7	5	3
8	8	6	2
6	7	2	4
9	8	5	8
8	6	6	7

Level 3

5. Write a procedure to determine if a positive integer is prime. An integer is prime if it can only be divided by itself and 1. For example, the numbers 3, 11, and 19 are prime. The integer should be passed to the procedure as a value parameter. A BOOLEAN parameter named PRIME should be passed to the procedure. PRIME should be a variable parameter. If the number is prime, the value of PRIME returned to the calling program should be true, otherwise it should be false.

6. Write a program to determine the greatest common divisor of two positive integers. The greatest common divisor of two numbers is the largest integer that can be divided into both numbers evenly. For example, the greatest common divisor of 15 and 10 is 5. The program should prompt the user to enter two positive integers and then display the greatest common divisor. Use procedures as appropriate.

CHAPTER 8

More Control Statements

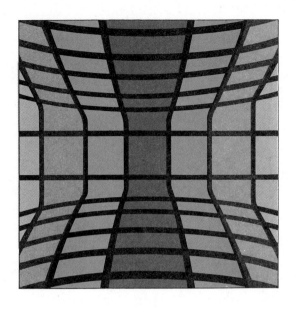

OBJECTIVES

After studying this chapter, you should be able to:

- Explain how sentinel values can be used to control loops.
- Explain how BOOLEAN flags can be used to control loops.
- Use a FOR loop when appropriate.
- Explain how the FOR loop works.
- List the rules for using a FOR loop.
- Explain what is meant by an ordinal data type.
- Use a REPEAT/UNTIL loop when appropriate.
- Explain how the REPEAT/UNTIL loop works.
- Use a CASE statement when appropriate.
- Explain how the CASE statement works.

OUTLINE

▬ INTRODUCTION

Chapter 6 introduced the WHILE/DO loop. In this chapter, you will learn how to use two other types of loops: the FOR and the REPEAT/-UNTIL loops. Each of these loops is well suited to certain situations.

▬ CONTROLLING LOOPS

One of the most difficult aspects of using loops is getting them to stop executing at the proper time. This section discusses three basic methods of controlling loop repetition: (1) counting loops, (2) sentinel values, and (3) BOOLEAN flags.

Counting Loops

A **counting loop** is a loop in which the number of repetitions necessary is determined before loop execution begins. The following program segment contains a counting loop:

```
COUNT := 2;
WHILE COUNT <= 10 DO
BEGIN
    WRITELN (COUNT:3);
    COUNT := COUNT + 2;
END;   { WHILE }
```

This loop will count by two's from 2 through 10. Each time through the loop the value of COUNT is incremented by two. When the value of COUNT exceeds 10, the loop will stop.

Sentinel Values

Another method of controlling repetition of a loop is to use a **sentinel value**. A sentinel value is a special data value that would not occur naturally in the input. It is used specifically to indicate the end of the input data. For example, if all data values for a given program will be nonnegative numbers, the sentinel value could be a negative number such as -1. The following program segment continues to read data until a value of -1 is encountered:

```
TOTAL := 0;
READ (NUMBER);
WHILE NUMBER <> -1 DO
BEGIN
    WRITELN (NUMBER:4);
    TOTAL := TOTAL + NUMBER:
    READ (NUMBER);
END;   { WHILE }
```

The first value must be read to NUMBER before the loop is entered. Subsequent values are read at the end of the loop immediately before the BOOLEAN expression is tested again.

The READ statement immediately before the loop is called a **priming read.** This allows NUMBER to be equal to the first data value before the condition in the WHILE/DO loop is tested. For this reason it is necessary to use two READ statements: one to initialize the variable NUMBER before the loop is entered and one at the bottom of the loop to read the remaining input. The second READ statement should appear as the last statement in the loop, immediately before control is passed back to the top of the loop.

Figure 8–1 contains a loop controlled by a sentinel value. The program reads a list of positive numbers, counts them, and determines the largest and smallest values. The sentinel value is 0. As soon as a 0 is entered, the loop will stop, and the results will be displayed.

BOOLEAN Flags

Often it is desirable to repeat a loop until a certain condition is read. For example, a program might read a series of values until a certain value is found. This can be accomplished by initializing a BOOLEAN variable called a **flag** to either true or false and then resetting the value after

```
PROGRAM READ_NUMBERS;

{ THIS PROGRAM READS A SERIES OF POSITIVE REAL NUMBERS UNTIL A
  SENTINEL VALUE IS ENCOUNTERED.  THE NUMBER OF NUMBERS ENTERED
  IS DETERMINED, ALONG WITH THE LARGEST AND THE SMALLEST. }

VAR
   NUMBER, SMALLEST, LARGEST : REAL;
   COUNTER                   : INTEGER;

BEGIN   { READ_NUMBERS }

   COUNTER := 0;
   WRITE ('ENTER A POSITIVE NUMBER (ENTER 0 TO QUIT): ');
   READLN (NUMBER);
   SMALLEST := NUMBER;  { INITIALIZE SMALLEST TO FIRST NUMBER }
   LARGEST := NUMBER;   { INITIALIZE LARGEST TO FIRST NUMBER }

   { LOOP TO READ NUMBERS, COUNT THEM, AND DETERMINE LARGEST
     AND SMALLEST. }
   WHILE NUMBER <> 0 DO
   BEGIN
      IF NUMBER > LARGEST        { SEE IF NEW NUMBER IS BIGGER }
         THEN LARGEST := NUMBER; { IF IT IS, ASSIGN IT TO LARGEST }
      IF NUMBER < SMALLEST        { SEE IF NEW NUMBER IS SMALLER }
         THEN SMALLEST := NUMBER; { IF IT IS, ASSIGN IT TO SMALLEST }
      COUNTER := COUNTER + 1;
      WRITE ('ENTER NEXT NUMBER (ENTER 0 TO QUIT): ');
      READLN (NUMBER);
   END;    { WHILE }

   { DISPLAY RESULTS.}
   WRITELN;
   WRITELN ('THE NUMBER OF VALUES ENTERED IS ', COUNTER:8);
   WRITELN ('THE LARGEST NUMBER IS ', LARGEST:8:2);
   WRITELN ('THE SMALLEST NUMBER IS ', SMALLEST:8:2);

END.   { READ_NUMBERS }
```

```
ENTER A POSITIVE NUMBER (ENTER 0 TO QUIT): 15.4
ENTER NEXT NUMBER (ENTER 0 TO QUIT): 12
ENTER NEXT NUMBER (ENTER 0 TO QUIT): 8
ENTER NEXT NUMBER (ENTER 0 TO QUIT): 26
ENTER NEXT NUMBER (ENTER 0 TO QUIT): 13
ENTER NEXT NUMBER (ENTER 0 TO QUIT): 0

THE NUMBER OF VALUES ENTERED IS        5
THE LARGEST NUMBER IS    26.00
THE SMALLEST NUMBER IS     8.00
```

FIGURE 8–1   A LOOP CONTROLLED BY A SENTINEL VALUE

a certain condition occurs. Initializing a variable means to set it to a starting value. The loop is then controlled by checking the status of the BOOLEAN variable. Consider again the program in Figure 8–1. This program can be altered so that the loop is controlled by a BOOLEAN flag rather than a sentinel value. Figure 8-2 shows this program. The BOOLEAN variable DONE is set to false before the WHILE/DO loop is first entered. The WHILE/DO loop is controlled by the expression

```
WHILE NOT DONE DO
```

Each time the loop is executed, a value is read to NUMBER. When a value of zero is read to NUMBER, DONE is set to true; therefore, the loop will not be executed again.

1. What are the three basic ways of controlling a loop?
2. What is a sentinel value?
3. What method is used to control the loop in the following program segment?

LEARNING CHECK 8-1

```
VAR
    VALID : BOOLEAN;
    LETTER : CHAR;

BEGIN
    VALID := TRUE;
    WHILE VALID DO
    BEGIN
        READLN (LETTER);
        IF (LETTER >= 'A') AND (LETTER <= 'F')
            THEN WRITELN ('YOUR GRADE IS A ', LETTER)
            ELSE VALID := FALSE;
    END;    { WHILE }
```

THE FOR LOOP

The FOR loop is used when the number of times a group of instructions should be executed can be determined. Therefore, the FOR loop is useful when writing counting loops. Below is an example of a FOR loop:

```
FOR COUNTER := 1 TO 7 DO
    WRITE (COUNTER:3);
WRITELN;
```

```
PROGRAM READ_NUMBERS;

{ THIS PROGRAM READS A SERIES OF POSITIVE REAL NUMBERS, DETERMINES
  THE TOTAL NUMBER OF NUMBERS ENTERED, AND THE LARGEST AND SMALLEST
  NUMBER ENTERED.  A BOOLEAN FLAG NAMED "DONE" IS USED TO CONTROL
  LOOP REPETITION. }

VAR
   NUMBER, SMALLEST, LARGEST : REAL;
   COUNTER                   : INTEGER;
   DONE                      : BOOLEAN;

BEGIN   { READ_NUMBERS }

   COUNTER := 0;
   DONE := FALSE;
   WRITE ('ENTER A POSITIVE NUMBER (ENTER 0 TO QUIT): ');
   READLN (NUMBER);
   SMALLEST := NUMBER;  { INITIALIZE SMALLEST TO FIRST NUMBER }
   LARGEST := NUMBER;   { INITIALIZE LARGEST TO FIRST NUMBER }

   { LOOP TO READ NUMBERS, COUNT THEM, AND DETERMINE LARGEST
     AND SMALLEST. }
   WHILE NOT DONE DO
   BEGIN
      IF NUMBER > LARGEST          { SEE IF NEW NUMBER IS BIGGER }
         THEN LARGEST := NUMBER;   { IF IT IS, ASSIGN IT TO LARGEST }
      IF NUMBER < SMALLEST         { SEE IF NEW NUMBER IS SMALLER }
         THEN SMALLEST := NUMBER;  { IF IT IS, ASSIGN IT TO SMALLEST }
      COUNTER := COUNTER + 1;
      WRITE ('ENTER NEXT NUMBER (ENTER 0 TO QUIT): ');
      READLN (NUMBER);
      { IF NO MORE NUMBERS, SET FLAG TO TRUE. }
      IF NUMBER = 0
         THEN DONE := TRUE;
   END;   { WHILE }

   { DISPLAY RESULTS. }
   WRITELN;
   WRITELN ('THE NUMBER OF VALUES ENTERED IS ', COUNTER:8);
   WRITELN ('THE LARGEST NUMBER IS ', LARGEST:8:2);
   WRITELN ('THE SMALLEST NUMBER IS ', SMALLEST:8:2);

END.   { READ_NUMBERS }
```

```
ENTER A POSITIVE NUMBER (ENTER 0 TO QUIT): 9
ENTER NEXT NUMBER (ENTER 0 TO QUIT): 4.5
ENTER NEXT NUMBER (ENTER 0 TO QUIT): 16
ENTER NEXT NUMBER (ENTER 0 TO QUIT): 2.8
ENTER NEXT NUMBER (ENTER 0 TO QUIT): 0

THE NUMBER OF VALUES ENTERED IS        4
THE LARGEST NUMBER IS     16.00
THE SMALLEST NUMBER IS     2.80
```

FIGURE 8-2   A LOOP CONTROLLED BY A BOOLEAN FLAG

This loop will be repeated seven times. The output will look like this:

```
1   2   3   4   5   6   7
```

Notice that no BEGIN or END is used in this example. The loop body contains only one statement. If it were a compound statement, a BEGIN and an END would be needed. The variable COUNTER is referred to as the **loop control variable** (**lcv** for short). Its value controls whether the loop will be executed.

In this FOR loop, the compiler performs the following steps automatically:

1. COUNTER is initialized to 1 (the starting value).
2. Each time through the loop, the expression COUNTER $<= 7$ is evaluated. If it evaluates as true, the loop is executed. Otherwise, control passes to the first statement after the loop.
3. One is added to the value of COUNTER each time through the loop.

If the starting value is greater than the ending value, a FOR loop will not be executed at all. When the following statement is executed

```
FOR COUNTER := 8 TO 7 DO
    WRITE (COUNTER:3);
WRITELN;
```

no values will be output. Control will simply pass to the next statement. The FOR loop also has a "DOWNTO" format. For example, the following loop

```
FOR COUNTER := 10 DOWNTO 2 DO
    WRITE (COUNTER:3);
WRITELN;
```

will result in COUNTER being decremented by one before each execution:

```
10   9   8   7   6   5   4   3   2
```

Format For **The FOR Loop**
   The "TO" Format

FOR lcv := starting_value TO ending_value DO
    statement;

> ### Format For **The "DOWNTO" Format**
>
> FOR lcv := starting_value DOWNTO ending_value DO
>   statement;

When using a FOR loop, the loop control variable must be an **ordinal data type.** For a data type to be ordinal, each value of that type (except the first) must have a unique predecessor, and each value (except the last) must have a unique successor. Of the data types covered so far, the types INTEGER, LONGINT, CHAR, and BOOLEAN are ordinal data types. The data type REAL is not ordinal. For example, what would the unique successor of 26.55 be? Would it be 26.551 or 26.56, or some other number? Figure 8–3 shows two loops controlled by loop control variables of type CHAR.

The data type BOOLEAN is also an ordinal type. Its values are true and false. But, since it only has two values, it is generally not useful as a loop control variable.

Rules for Using the FOR Loop

Several rules apply to using the FOR loop:

1. As previously stated, the loop control variable must be an ordinal data type. The starting and ending values must belong to the same ordinal type. Given this declaration

   ```
   VAR
        COUNTER : INTEGER;
   ```
   this statement is valid:
   ```
   FOR COUNTER := 1 TO 20 DO
   ```
   but this is not:
   ```
   FOR COUNTER := 'a' TO 'h' DO
   ```

2. The starting and ending values can be constants, variables, or expressions, as long as they are of the same ordinal type:

   ```
   FOR X := (2 * 10) TO (200 - 50) DO
      WRITELN (X);
   ```

3. The loop control variable should be locally declared; that is, it should be declared in the procedure in which it is used. This makes program logic easier to follow.

4. The value of the loop control variable cannot be changed in the loop.

```
PROGRAM EXAMPLE_A;

VAR
   LETTER : CHAR;

BEGIN    { EXAMPLE_A }

   FOR LETTER := 'A' TO 'G' DO
        WRITELN ('WE ARE ON LOOP ', LETTER);

END.    { EXAMPLE_A }
```

```
WE ARE ON LOOP A
WE ARE ON LOOP B
WE ARE ON LOOP C
WE ARE ON LOOP D
WE ARE ON LOOP E
WE ARE ON LOOP F
WE ARE ON LOOP G
```

```
PROGRAM EXAMPLE_B;

VAR
   LETTER : CHAR;

BEGIN    { EXAMPLE_B }

   FOR LETTER := 'G' DOWNTO 'A' DO
        WRITELN ('WE ARE ON LOOP ', LETTER);

END.    { EXAMPLE_B }
```

```
WE ARE ON LOOP G
WE ARE ON LOOP F
WE ARE ON LOOP E
WE ARE ON LOOP D
WE ARE ON LOOP C
WE ARE ON LOOP B
WE ARE ON LOOP A
```

FIGURE 8-3   FOR LOOPS USING CHARACTER LOOP CONTROL VARIABLES

Because of this, the statement "I := I+1" will not increment I:

```
FOR I := 1 TO 10 DO
    I := I + 1;
```

5. Each FOR loop should have only one exit point out of the loop. The exit point should be the last statement of the loop.

The FOR statement is used to write counting loops; that is, loops where the number of executions necessary can be determined before loop repetition begins. Any FOR loop can also be written as a WHILE/DO loop. For example, the statement

```
FOR NUMBER := 1 TO 20 DO
    READLN (LETTER);
```

could be written like this using a WHILE/DO loop:

```
NUMBER := 1;
WHILE NUMBER <= 20 DO
BEGIN
    READLN (LETTER);
    NUMBER := NUMBER + 1;
END;    { WHILE }
```

The advantage of using the FOR loop is that the steps of initializing, checking, and incrementing the loop control variable are performed for the programmer. Therefore, the loop is easier to write and is more likely to be error-free.

Nested FOR Loops

As with other control statements, FOR loops can be nested inside one another. Here is an example of a nested loop:

```
WRITELN ('OUTER':8, 'INNER':8);
FOR OUTER := 1 TO 4 DO
    FOR INNER := 1 TO 3 DO
        WRITELN (OUTER:5, INNER:8);
```

The inner loop is indented to make the program more readable. Each time the outer loop is executed once, the inner loop will be executed three times. The total number of loop repetitions is 4×3, or 12. The output will be

```
OUTER    INNER
  1        1
  1        2
  1        3
  2        1
  2        2
```

```
2        3
3        1
3        2
3        3
4        1
4        2
4        3
```

■ THE REPEAT/UNTIL LOOP

The third looping statement is the REPEAT/UNTIL. This loop is similar to the WHILE/DO loop in that it is controlled by a BOOLEAN expression. An important difference is that the BOOLEAN expression in the REPEAT/UNTIL loop is evaluated *after* the loop body has been executed, not before. Therefore, the loop will always be executed at least once, unlike the FOR or WHILE/DO loop, which can be executed zero or more times. Here is a simple REPEAT/UNTIL loop:

```
NUM := 2;
REPEAT
    NUM := NUM + 1
UNTIL NUM = 4;
```

This loop will execute two times. Going into the loop the first time, the value of NUM will be two. The statement NUM := NUM+1 is executed, making the value of NUM three. The condition NUM = 4 will evaluate as false, since three is not equal to four. The loop is executed again. One more is added to NUM this time through the loop, making NUM equal to four. Since NUM = 4 is now true, the loop will not execute again. Instead, the statement following the loop will be executed.

Format For **The REPEAT/UNTIL Loop**

```
REPEAT
   statement(s)
UNTIL BOOLEAN_expression;
```

Let's write a program that will calculate the factorial of a positive integer using the REPEAT/UNTIL loop. The general formula for computing a factorial is

```
N * (N - 1) * (N - 2) * ... * 1
```

The factorial of six would be

```
6 * 5 * 4 * 3 * 2 * 1 = 720
```

The factorial of one is one. First the user should be prompted to enter the integer (NUMBER), which should be copied into a variable that will contain the factorial (FACT). NUMBER should be decreased by one, and FACT should then be multiplied by the new value of NUMBER. This process should continue until NUMBER is equal to one.

The program is shown in Figure 8–4. Let's trace through the program and see if it works properly. Suppose the integer five is used for the value of NUMBER. The values listed below are the values of NUMBER and FACT at the end of each repetition of the REPEAT/UNTIL loop:

Number of Times through the Loop	N	FACT
1	4	20
2	3	60
3	2	120
4	1	120

Why is the factorial of one not set in the loop like the other factorials? The program segment below shows what would happen in the loop if the value assigned to NUMBER were one:

```
FACT := NUMBER;                      { FACT is assigned the value of 1 }
REPEAT
    NUMBER := NUMBER - 1;            { NUMBER := 0 }
    FACT := FACT * NUMBER            { FACT := 0 }
UNTIL NUMBER = 1;
```

The last statement in the loop will assign zero to FACT. Because the factorial of one is actually one, by using the loop, the program would have obtained the incorrect result for the factorial of one.

There is another serious problem with using one for the value of NUMBER in this loop. How would the following UNTIL condition evaluate?

```
UNTIL NUMBER = 1;
```

This condition will evaluate as false because NUMBER is now equal to zero. The next time through the loop the value of NUMBER will be -1. The value of NUMBER will never be one. Instead, it will become a larger and larger negative number, creating an infinite loop.

Notice that FACT has been declared to be of data type LONGINT. This is because factorials become large numbers very quickly. For example, the factorial of eight is 40,320.

The body of a REPEAT/UNTIL loop does not need to have a BEGIN and an END no matter how many statements it contains. The boundaries of the loop are marked by the reserved words REPEAT and UNTIL.

```
PROGRAM FACTORIAL;

{ THIS PROGRAM CALCULATES THE FACTORIAL OF A POSITIVE INTEGER. }

VAR
   NUMBER, TEMP : INTEGER;
   FACT         : LONGINT;

BEGIN   { FACTORIAL }

   WRITE ('WHAT IS THE INTEGER? ');
   READLN (NUMBER);
   TEMP := NUMBER;

   { IF NUMBER = 1, FACTORIAL = 1. }
   IF NUMBER = 1
      THEN FACT := 1
      ELSE
      { LOOP TO CALCULATE FACTORIAL. }
      BEGIN
         FACT := NUMBER;
         REPEAT
            NUMBER := NUMBER - 1;
            FACT := FACT * NUMBER
         UNTIL NUMBER = 1;
      END;    { ELSE }

   WRITELN (TEMP, '! = ', FACT);

END.   { FACTORIAL }
```

```
WHAT IS THE INTEGER? 5
5! = 120
```

FIGURE 8-4   PROGRAM USING A REPEAT/UNTIL LOOP TO CALCULATE A FACTORIAL

**LEARNING
CHECK
8-2**

1. Explain how the REPEAT/UNTIL loop works.
2. Name three steps that are performed automatically for the programmer when using a FOR loop.
3. Write a FOR loop that will print the numbers from 100 down to 1.
4. How many times will the loop in the following program segment be executed? What will be the value of I at the end of the loop each time through?

```
PROGRAM EX1;

VAR
    I : INTEGER;

BEGIN

    I := 1;
    REPEAT
        I := I + 1;
        WRITELN (I)
    UNTIL I >= 10;
```

THE CASE STATEMENT

In Chapter 5, one type of decision statement, the IF statement, was introduced. Here a second decision statement, the CASE statement, will be explained. To start, let's write an IF statement that displays an appropriate message depending on the grade a student receives:

```
IF GRADE = 'A'
    THEN WRITELN ('ALL RIGHT!')
    ELSE IF GRADE = 'B'
            THEN WRITELN ('GOOD JOB.')
            ELSE IF GRADE = 'C'
                    THEN WRITELN ('NOT BAD.')
                    ELSE WRITELN ('TRY HARDER NEXT TIME.');
```

This nested IF statement could also be written as a CASE statement:

```
CASE GRADE OF
    'A' : WRITELN ('ALL RIGHT!');
    'B' : WRITELN ('GOOD JOB.');
    'C' : WRITELN ('NOT BAD.');
    'D', 'F' : WRITELN ('TRY HARDER NEXT TIME.');
END;   { CASE }
```

Only one of the statements in the CASE statement will be executed; which one depends upon the value of GRADE. The variable GRADE in the expression

```
CASE GRADE OF
```

is the CASE selector. The selector may be any expression that evaluates as an ordinal data type. The values 'A', 'B', 'C', 'D', and 'F' are labels. Labels must be constants and must be of the same data type as the case selector. If the selector evaluates as the same value as one of the labels, the statement following that label is executed. Otherwise, execution continues to the next statement within the CASE. For example, if the value of GRADE is 'B', the statement "GOOD JOB" will be output. As shown in the last statement, more than one label can be listed in a statement. Notice that although the CASE statement has an END, there is no BEGIN.

Format For The CASE Statement

```
CASE selector OF
    label1 : statement1;
    label2 : statement2;
        •
        •
        •
    last_label : last_statement;
    ELSE statement;
END;
```

Note: The ELSE clause is optional.

What if the value of GRADE were 'G' when this CASE statement was executed? Turbo Pascal allows the programmer to add an ELSE clause to be executed if the selector does not match any of the labels. We could alter this CASE statement to include an ELSE clause as shown below:

```
CASE GRADE OF
    'A' : WRITELN ('ALL RIGHT!');
    'B' : WRITELN ('GOOD JOB');
    'C' : WRITELN ('NOT BAD.');
    'D', 'F' : WRITELN ('TRY HARDER NEXT TIME.');
    ELSE WRITELN ('INVALID GRADE.');
END;    { CASE }
```

The ELSE clause allows the program to handle invalid data.

Figure 8–5 contains a CASE statement that determines the shape of a galaxy. Galaxies can have one of three basic shapes: elliptical, irregular, and spiral, which are represented by the codes E, I, and S. There are

```
PROGRAM   GALAXY;
{ THIS PROGRAM DISPLAYS A TYPE OF GALAXY, DEPENDING ON THE CODE VALUE
  ENTERED:
      E - ELLIPTICAL
      I - IRREGULAR
      S - B - BARRED SPIRAL
          N - NORMAL SPIRAL    }
USES
   CRT;
VAR
   CODE, BAR : CHAR;

BEGIN   { GALAXY }

   CLRSCR;
   GOTOXY (1,5);
   WRITELN ('E - ELLIPTICAL');
   WRITELN ('I - IRREGULAR');
   WRITELN ('S - SPIRAL');
   WRITELN;
   WRITE ('ENTER THE CODE FOR THE TYPE OF GALAXY: ');
   READLN (CODE);
   WRITELN;
   CASE CODE OF
      'E' : WRITELN ('ELLIPTICAL');
      'I' : WRITELN ('IRREGULAR');
      'S' : BEGIN
               WRITE ('IS GALAXY BARRED OR NORMAL (B OR N): ');
               READLN (BAR);
               WRITELN;
               CASE BAR OF
                  'B' : WRITELN ('BARRED SPIRAL');
                  'N' : WRITELN ('NORMAL SPIRAL');
               END;   { INNER CASE }
            END;
   END;    { OUTER CASE }
END.  { GALAXY }
```

```
E - ELLIPTICAL
I - IRREGULAR
S - SPIRAL

ENTER THE CODE FOR THE TYPE OF GALAXY: S

IS GALAXY BARRED OR NORMAL (B OR N): N

NORMAL SPIRAL
```

FIGURE 8-5   PROGRAM DEMONSTRATING THE CASE STATEMENT

two types of spiral galaxies: barred spirals and normal spirals. Therefore, if a galaxy is spiral, it must then be determined if it is barred. The
program first prompts the user to indicate the code for the type of galaxy (E, I, or S). Then, if it is E or I, an appropriate message is displayed.
If it is S, another CASE statement is used to determine whether it is
barred. This is an example of a nested CASE statement.

The CASE statement has one major drawback. Because the selector
checks for a match among a list of individual ordinal values, the conditions checked for cannot be ranges of values. Therefore, when a range
of values must be checked for, nested IF/THEN/ELSE statements are
more suitable.

---

1. Explain the purpose of the CASE selector.
2. Rewrite the CASE statement in Figure 8–5 using IF statements.
3. Write a CASE statement that outputs the corresponding color
   when the variable COLOR is equal to one of the following character codes:

Code	Color
R	Red
G	Green
B	Brown
O	Orange
W	White
P	Purple
Y	Yellow

LEARNING CHECK 8–3

▬▬▬ SUMMARY POINTS

- In counting loops, a variable is initialized to a starting value. In each
  subsequent repetition, it is incremented by one. When the variable
  reaches the ending value, loop repetition stops.
- A sentinel value can be used to indicate the end of input data. When
  this value is read, the loop stops executing.
- A BOOLEAN flag can also be used to control a loop. The value of the
  flag is checked to determine if the loop should continue
  executing.
- The FOR loop is a counting loop. The loop control variable is
  initialized to a starting value. Each time through the loop, the loop
  control variable is incremented to the next value. When the ending
  value is exceeded, the loop stops.

- The REPEAT/UNTIL loop evaluates a condition at the end of the loop. Therefore, it will always be executed at least once. A REPEAT/UNTIL loop is executed until the controlling condition evaluates as true.
- The CASE statement is used to compare a variable (the CASE selector) with a list of labels. If the selector matches one of the labels, the statement following that label is executed.

▆▆▆ VOCABULARY LIST

Counting loop   Ordinal data type
Flag   Priming read
Loop control variable (lcv)   Sentinel value

▆▆▆ CHAPTER TEST

Vocabulary

Match a term from the numbered column with the description from the lettered column that best fits the term.

1. Ordinal data type

2. Counting loop

3. Sentinel value

4. Priming read

5. Flag

6. Loop control variable

a. A READ statement placed immediately before a loop to initialize the loop control variable.

b. A data type in which each value (except the first) has a unique predecessor and each value (except the last) has a unique successor.

c. A variable incremented each time a loop is repeated; it controls how many times the loop is executed.

d. A special value used to mark the end of input.

e. A loop executed a specified number of times.

f. A BOOLEAN variable used to indicate whether a loop should be repeated.

Questions

1. How is the REPEAT/UNTIL loop different from the WHILE/DO loop?

2. What is an ordinal data type?

3. How many times will the following loop be executed? What will the value of NUM be at the end of the loop each time through?

```
PROGRAM EX2;

VAR
    NUM : INTEGER;

BEGIN
    NUM := 12;
    REPEAT
        NUM := NUM - 2;
        WRITELN (NUM)
    UNTIL NUM < 0;
```

4. How many times will the following FOR loop be executed? Explain your answer.

```
FOR I := 1 DOWNTO 10 DO
```

5. Fill in the following table for each execution of the WRITE statement.

```
                                         A       B       C
FOR A := 1 TO 2 DO
    FOR B := 1 TO 2 DO
        FOR C := 3 DOWNTO 1 DO
            WRITE (A:3, B:3, C:3);      ___     ___     ___
```

6. Rewrite the following program segment using a WHILE/DO loop instead of a REPEAT/UNTIL loop.

```
PROGRAM EXAMPLE;

VAR
    COUNT  : INTEGER;
    LETTER : CHAR;

BEGIN
    COUNT := 1;
    REPEAT
        WRITE ('ENTER A LETTER: ');
        READLN (LETTER);
        COUNT := COUNT + 1
    UNTIL COUNT >= 8;
```

7. Rewrite the program segment in Question 6 using a FOR loop.

8. Explain how the CASE statement works.

9. What is the major limitation of the CASE statement?

10. Consider the following program segment:

```
CASE KIND OF
    1   : FISH := 'B';
    2   : FISH := 'C';
    3   : FISH := 'T';
    4   : FISH := 'P';
    5,6 : FISH := 'W';
    ELSE FISH := 'Z';
END;    { CASE }

    WRITELN (FISH);
```

What will be printed for each of the values of KIND below?

a. KIND := 1 + 4;
b. KIND := 2 * 2;
c. KIND := 10 - 4;
d. KIND := 7;

▬▬▬ PROGRAMMING PROBLEMS

Level 1

1. Mickey Koth likes to go on cross-country bike trips. She needs a way to calculate the amount of time a particular bike trip will take. The distance she can travel in an hour depends on the weather conditions. They are as follows:

   E   excellent conditions: 25 miles/hour
   G   good conditions: 20 miles/hour
   P   poor conditions: 13 miles/hour

   Write a program that will allow Mickey to enter the distance in miles and then enter a code (E, G, or P) for the weather conditions. Use a CASE statement. The amount of time the trip will take should then be output in hours.

2. In Montana streams, there are four types of trout. Each type has a different daily limit on how many may be caught:

Type	Limit
Brook	8
Brown	4
Rainbow	6
Cutthroat	4

   Develop a code to allow the user to enter the type of trout caught.

Use a REPEAT/UNTIL loop to prompt the user to reenter the code until a valid one is entered. Use a procedure to assign the daily limit for this type. Output a statement telling the user how many of this type of trout may be caught in a day. Use a CASE statement to display the limit.

Level 2

3. Pat Nabel's father will only allow her to make $10 worth of long-distance phone calls a month. She would like a program to calculate the cost of each of her calls. Below is a code number for each type of call Pat makes and the cost of each per minute:

Code	Call to	Cost per Minute
1	Grandmother in Santa Clara	.17
2	Brother in Pittsburgh	.11
3	Girlfriend in St. Paul	.12
4	Boyfriend in Hamburg	.73

Use a CASE statement to read in a 1, 2, 3, or 4 and assign the appropriate charge. The cost should be output similar to the following:

The cost of the call is $2.83.

The CASE statement should include an ELSE clause to output an error message if an invalid code has been entered.

4. Write a program to display a multiplication table. The user should be asked to enter the upper and lower limits of the table. Nested FOR loops should be used to create a table similar to the following:

×	1	2	3	4
1	1	2	3	4
2	2	4	6	8
3	3	6	9	12
4	4	8	12	16

Level 3

5. Your biology project is to determine the rate of growth of a particular type of bacteria. You suspect that the bacteria population increases at the same rate as the Fibonacci numbers. In this sequence of numbers, each number is equal to the sum of its two immediate predecessors. Therefore, the first few Fibonacci numbers are

0 1 1 2 3 5 8 13 21...

Assume that your bacteria reproduce asexually once every minute. You will be starting with a single bacterium. The program should allow you to enter a given number of minutes. Then, the number of bacteria at the end of this time should be output. Use a FOR loop.

6. Write a procedure to determine the number of days in a given month. Ask the user to enter an integer representing the month. Then use a CASE statement to display the number of days. Remember that February has an extra day during leap years. Determining leap years is somewhat more complex than most people realize. If a year is evenly divisible by 4, it is a leap year unless it is evenly divisible by 100. However, years that are evenly divisible by 400 are also leap years. Therefore, 1900 was not a leap year, but 2000 will be a leap year.

CHAPTER 9

Program Style and Debugging

OBJECTIVES

After studying this chapter, you should be able to:

- Explain good program style and its importance.
- Use indentation, blank spaces, and blank lines to make programs more readable.
- Use meaningful variable names when writing programs, and explain why this is important.
- List and describe syntax, run-time, and logic errors.
- Use desk checking to locate program errors.
- Use program tracing to locate program errors.
- Define the term user-friendly and write user-friendly programs.
- Use stubs when developing programs.

OUTLINE

■■■ INTRODUCTION

The first part of this chapter will discuss program style. **Program style** is concerned with making a program as easy as possible for people to read and understand. Many of these ideas have been mentioned in earlier chapters. They are presented here to tie them together and emphasize the importance of good style in program writing.

Programs of any significant length rarely work properly the first time they are executed. The second part of this chapter will explain some proven methods of locating and correcting program errors. The techniques introduced here will help you correct programs in a logical manner.

■■■ PROGRAM STYLE

The Turbo Pascal compiler is not affected by the style of a program. It can execute a program with poor style as easily as one with good style. However, using good style makes the program easier for people to understand. A program with good style has the following characteristics:

1. It has been well documented.
2. Indentation, blank spaces, and blank lines have been used to make the program easier to read.
3. The identifiers in the program (the names of the constants, varia-

bles, procedures, and so forth) have been given descriptive names.

The importance of using descriptive identifiers has already been discussed. This is one of the best ways to make a program readable. Documentation and the use of indentation and blank spaces have also previously been mentioned. They will be discussed further here.

Documentation

Documentation consists of the comments explaining what is being done in a program. Comments must be enclosed like this:

```
(* A COMMENT *)
```

or like this:

```
{ ANOTHER COMMENT }
```

The compiler ignores anything inside these symbols. Documentation appears in two places in a program:

1. After the program (or procedure) heading (beginning documentation).
2. Within the body of the program (or procedure).

Beginning Documentation. After the program (or procedure) heading comes the documentation that explains the program as a whole. Here the purpose of the program is stated. This is where any input the program needs can be described. For example,

```
{ THE USER ENTERS AN INTEGER AT THE KEYBOARD. }
```

explains the type of data that must be entered. The output produced by the program should also be explained here. All of the input in the programs so far in this book has been read from the keyboard, and all of the output has been displayed on the monitor. Later on, this will not necessarily be true. For example, input may come from a diskette. As programs become more complex, it is important to state exactly where input comes from and where output will be going. This is very important for people who are unfamiliar with the program but want to use it.

The programs written so far have used only a few variables. As programs become more complex, it is important that the major variables be listed at the beginning of the program or procedure using them.

Documentation within the Program Body. Documentation within the body of a program (or procedure) is usually brief, not over a few lines in length. Comments should be placed before control statements to explain their purpose. The following statement tells the reader that this IF statement displays a message stating whether NUM1 is even or odd:

```
{ DISPLAY MESSAGE STATING WHETHER NUM1 IS EVEN OR ODD. }
IF NUM1 MOD 2 = 0
    THEN WRITELN (NUM1, ' is even.')
    ELSE WRITELN (NUM1, ' is odd.');
```

Comments within a program can be placed on a separate line as in the statement above or after a statement, like this:

```
READLN (NUM);    { READ NUMBER OF ITEM }
```

Using Blank Spaces and Indentation

Imagine an essay written for an English class that has no paragraphs, margins, or blank lines. The essay would be a sheet of paper filled with sentence after sentence. It would not be easy to read or understand. Certainly, it would not be enjoyable to read and would not receive a good grade.

A programmer should attempt to make a program as easy to read as a well-written English essay. Although indentation and spacing make no difference to the compiler, they can make reading a program much more pleasant for humans.

Indentation refers to blank spaces left at the beginning of program lines. Indentation is often used to set control statements apart. An IF statement could be written this way:

```
IF X <> Y THEN SUM := SUM + X ELSE WRITELN (X, ' IS A DUPLICATE.');
```

It also could be written like this:

```
IF X <> Y THEN
SUM := SUM + X
ELSE
WRITELN (X, ' IS A DUPLICATE.');
```

But in this book we have written it this way:

```
IF X <> Y
    THEN SUM := SUM + X
    ELSE WRITELN (X, ' IS A DUPLICATE.');
```

The compiler would treat all three of these examples the same way, but most people would find the last example easier to read and understand.

Blank spaces are left in statements to make them more readable. As far as the compiler is concerned, it is not necessary to leave spaces between variables and operators. This is a matter of personal preference.

Generally, leaving spaces helps to separate each part of the statement and make it more readable. Here are some examples of statements with and without spacing.

Without Spaces

```
READLN(X,Y,Z);
COST:=COST+(COST*PERCENT);
WHILE(COUNT<>100)OR(X*Y>10)DO
```

With Spaces

```
READLN (X, Y, Z);
COST := COST + (COST * PERCENT);
WHILE (COUNT <> 100) OR (X * Y > 10) DO
```

Blank lines can be used to separate different sections of the program. It is a good idea to use blank lines around major control statements such as loops. This makes it easier to see where a loop begins and ends.

1. What is meant by good program style?
2. What three characteristics will a program with good style have?
3. Why are control statements such as the IF statement indented?

LEARNING CHECK 9-1

▬▬▬ DEBUGGING

It has been estimated that professional programmers spend about 80 percent of their time testing and modifying existing programs. Even after the programmer thinks a program is working correctly, it is difficult, if not impossible, to determine if it will always work properly for all types of input. This section presents some simple techniques for locating and correcting program errors.

The Three Types of Program Errors

Program errors can be divided into three categories:

1. Syntax errors
2. Run-time errors
3. Logic errors

Syntax errors are violations of the grammatical rules of a language. These are the most common errors made by beginning programmers, but fortunately, they are usually the simplest to find and correct. Often they are due to typing mistakes. Syntax errors are discovered when the programmer attempts to compile the program. The compiler will display an error message. A program cannot be compiled and executed until all syntax errors are corrected.

Run-time errors cause the program to stop executing in the middle (this is referred to as crashing). Common run-time errors include the following:

1. Attempting to divide a number by zero.
2. Assigning a value to the wrong type of variable.
3. Using a variable in a program before assigning a value to it.
4. Incorrect passing of parameters to a procedure.

Logic errors are caused by a flaw in the program's algorithm. The program will execute, but may obtain incorrect results. The difficulty in finding and correcting logic errors is that the program may produce correct results most of the time, but occasionally produce incorrect results. Error messages will generally not appear if a logic error occurs. This makes logic errors difficult to locate and correct.

The following statement contains a logic error:

```
AVERAGE := X + Y / 2;
```

This statement is supposed to determine the average of X and Y. However, it will not work properly because parentheses need to be placed around the X and Y values:

```
AVERAGE := (X + Y) / 2;
```

This is an example of a logic error caused by the incorrect translation of a formula into Pascal. If you are getting a logic error, check all your formulas to make certain they are correctly stated.

Another common logic error is the *off-by-one* error, which has been discussed previously. This error occurs when the condition controlling loop repetition is incorrectly stated. The following loop is supposed to execute eight times:

```
LOOP := 1;
WHILE LOOP < 8 DO
BEGIN
    WRITELN ('This loop should execute 8 times.');
    WRITELN ('It really executes 7 times.');
    LOOP := LOOP + 1;
END;    { WHILE }
```

The condition controlling loop repetition should be stated

```
WHILE LOOP <= 8 DO
```

Locating and Correcting Program Errors

The various methods of testing programs for errors can be divided into two categories: static testing and run-time testing. Static testing involves studying the text of the program itself for errors. One type of static testing is called **desk checking**. When a programmer desk checks a program, he or she carefully reads through a printed copy of the program, checking for syntax and logic errors. Care should be taken to determine if there is an END for each BEGIN and that all variables have been properly declared and initialized. A few extra minutes spent at this stage of program development can save hours of debugging later.

Run-time testing involves actually executing the program. The program should be run with a wide variety of data to see if correct results are always obtained. A good strategy for locating run-time errors is to use WRITELN statements to display the values of variables. The values should be displayed at locations in the program where the programmer expects there might be a problem. This technique, which is called **program tracing**, allows you to follow the execution of a program. An example can be found in the following program segment:

```
I := 5;
LOOP := 10;
WHILE LOOP > 0 DO
BEGIN
    NUM := LOOP / I;
    LOOP := LOOP - 1;
    I := I - 1;
END;    { WHILE }
```

Before the loop terminates, the value of I will be set to zero. When I is used as a divisor, the program will crash. If this location is suspected of causing the run-time error, a WRITELN statement could be inserted in the body of the loop to check the values of I and LOOP.

Logic errors often can be detected by examining program output for accuracy. Check the program by calculating the results by hand and determining if they match the results obtained by the program. Program tracing also can be used to locate logic errors.

▬▬▬ USING STUBS TO DEVELOP PROGRAMS

One advantage of using procedures is that they allow a program to be developed one step at a time. Another advantage is that the program can be implemented using a top-down strategy. As an example, a program calculating the cost of an order at a fast-food restaurant will be developed. The program will perform four tasks:

1. Display a menu listing the available choices.
2. Calculate the bill for the food ordered.
3. Add the tax to the bill.
4. Display the total bill.

The main body of this program consists of a loop that allows the user to choose as many items as desired. The first two tasks are performed in this loop. Procedure DISPLAY_MENU performs the first task and DETERMINE_BILL, the second. The third and fourth tasks are performed only once each. Therefore they are executed after the loop. Examine the program in Figure 9–1. Notice that the body of the main program is quite short. It consists of a loop that allows the first two procedures to be called as many times as needed and then calls the last two procedures. This is an example of a **driver program** because its main purpose is simply to call or "drive" the procedures.

When writing a program, the main program is written before the procedures. All that needs to be known at this point is what tasks are to be performed by each procedure. These procedures are placed in the program by using **stubs**, which are simply empty procedures. Each stub has a procedure heading with a parameter list, a BEGIN and an END, and a WRITELN statement reporting that the procedure was called. The parameters needed by each procedure can be determined because the tasks each will perform are known. For example, DETERMINE_-BILL must have a variable parameter (called BILL) that will return the current cost of the order. At this point in the development, the program looks like the one in Figure 9–1. Now the program can be executed, and any errors can be corrected. The WRITELN statements in each of the procedures provide a trace of the procedures as they are called.

The next step is to implement each of the subprograms. In this case, it would be logical to write DISPLAY_MENU first because it simply lists the food choices. After DISPLAY_MENU is typed in, the program is run to see if the menu is properly displayed. OUTPUT_BILL could be implemented next because it will be useful in determining if DETERMINE_BILL is working properly. OUTPUT_BILL can be run and tested by substituting a constant value for the parameter BILL in the procedure call. After determining that OUTPUT_BILL is working properly, DETERMINE_BILL can be added and tested. Once the program obtains the correct total without the tax, the procedure adding on the tax (ADD_TAX) can be implemented and tested.

After the program is working correctly for valid data, procedures can be added to check for invalid user input. In this program, both the code number and the quantity need to be checked to make certain they are valid integers. In addition, the code number must fall in the range from

```
PROGRAM MEAL;

{ THIS PROGRAM CALCULATES THE COST OF A PURCHASE AT A FAST-FOOD
  RESTAURANT.  THE USER TYPES IN AN INTEGER VALUE INDICATING THE ITEM
  AND QUANTITY OF THAT ITEM TO BE PURCHASED.  THE COST OF THE ITEM IS
  THEN ADDED TO THE TOTAL BILL.  WHEN THE USER IS DONE ORDERING, A
  4% TAX IS ADDED AND THE BILL IS DISPLAYED ON THE MONITOR.

THE CODES USED TO ENTER FOOD ITEMS ARE AS FOLLOWS:

     CODE NUMBER       ITEM            COST OF ITEM
     ---------------------------------------------------
         1          HAMBURGER          $1.10
         2          CHEESEBURGER       $1.30
         3          FRENCH FRIES       $0.80
         4          FRUIT PIE          $0.90
         5          DRINK              $0.75

     ---------------------------------------------------
MAJOR VARIABLE USED:
   BILL       AMOUNT OWED
   MORE       MORE ITEMS TO BE ORDERED?  }

 USES
    CRT;

VAR
   BILL : REAL;
   MORE : CHAR;

{**********************************************************************}

PROCEDURE DISPLAY_MENU;

{ DISPLAYS THE CUSTOMER'S CHOICES. }

BEGIN   { DISPLAY_MENU }

   WRITELN ('PROCEDURE DISPLAY_MENU WAS CALLED BUT IS NOT IMPLEMENTED.'

END;    { DISPLAY_MENU }

{**********************************************************************}

PROCEDURE DETERMINE_BILL (VAR BILL : REAL);

{ PROMPTS USER TO ENTER EACH ITEM AND QUANTITY OF THAT ITEM.  RETURNS
  CURRENT BILL TO CALLING PROGRAM. }

BEGIN   { DETERMINE_BILL }

   WRITELN ('PROCEDURE DISPLAY_MENU WAS CALLED BUT IS NOT IMPLEMENTED.'

END;    { DETERMINE_BILL }
```

FIGURE 9-1 PROGRAM MEAL WITH STUBS

(Figure continued on next page)

```
{*******************************************************************}

PROCEDURE ADD_TAX (VAR BILL : REAL);

{ ADDS TAX AND RETURNS TOTAL BILL. }

BEGIN   { ADD_TAX }

   WRITELN ('PROCEDURE ADD_TAX WAS CALLED BUT IS NOT IMPLEMENTED.');

END;    { ADD_TAX }

{*******************************************************************}

PROCEDURE OUTPUT_BILL (BILL : REAL);

BEGIN   { OUTPUT_BILL }

   WRITELN ('PROCEDURE OUTPUT_BILL WAS CALLED BUT IS NOT IMPLEMENTED.')

END;    { OUTPUT_BILL }

{*******************************************************************}

BEGIN   { MAIN }

   BILL := 0.0;

   { LOOP TO ALLOW CUSTOMER TO CHOOSE AS MANY ITEMS AS DESIRED. }
   REPEAT
      DISPLAY_MENU;
      DETERMINE_BILL (BILL);
      WRITELN;
      WRITE ('DO YOU WANT TO CHOOSE MORE ITEMS (Y OR N): ');
      READLN (MORE)
   UNTIL (MORE = 'N') OR (MORE = 'n');

   ADD_TAX (BILL);
   OUTPUT_BILL (BILL);

END.    { MAIN }
```

FIGURE 9–1 PROGRAM MEAL WITH STUBS (Cont.)

1 through 5. Because both of these values are entered in procedure DETERMINE_BILL, the procedures to check their validity can be nested in this procedure. Error-handling routines are always added last, after the program is working properly for valid data. The final program appears in Figure 9–2.

```
PROGRAM MEAL;

{ THIS PROGRAM CALCULATES THE COST OF A PURCHASE AT A FAST-FOOD
  RESTAURANT.  THE USER ENTERS AN INTEGER VALUE INDICATING THE ITEM
  AND QUANTITY OF THAT ITEM TO BE PURCHASED.  THE COST OF THE ITEM IS
  THEN ADDED TO THE TOTAL BILL.  WHEN THE USER IS DONE ORDERING, A
  4% TAX IS ADDED AND THE BILL IS DISPLAYED ON THE MONITOR.

THE CODES USED TO ENTER FOOD ITEMS ARE AS FOLLOWS:

      CODE NUMBER        ITEM                COST OF ITEM
      -----------------------------------------------------------
         1               HAMBURGER           $1.10
         2               CHEESEBURGER        $1.30
         3               FRENCH FRIES        $0.80
         4               FRUIT PIE           $0.90
         5               DRINK               $0.75


      -----------------------------------------------------------

MAJOR VARIABLES USED:
    BILL       AMOUNT OWED
    MORE       MORE ITEMS TO BE ORDERED?  }

USES
    CRT;

VAR
   BILL : REAL;
   MORE : CHAR;

{******************************************************************}

PROCEDURE DISPLAY_MENU;

{ DISPLAYS THE CUSTOMER'S CHOICES. }

BEGIN   { DISPLAY_MENU }

   CLRSCR;
   GOTOXY (1,6);
   WRITELN ('1.  HAMBURGER     $1.10');
   WRITELN ('2.  CHEESEBURGER  $1.30');
   WRITELN ('3.  FRENCH FRIES  $0.80');
   WRITELN ('4.  FRUIT PIE     $0.90');
   WRITELN ('5.  DRINK         $0.75');
   WRITELN;
   WRITELN;

END;    { DISPLAY_MENU }

{******************************************************************}
```

FIGURE 9-2 COMPLETED PROGRAM MEAL

(Figure continued on next page)

```
PROCEDURE DETERMINE_BILL (VAR BILL : REAL);

{ PROMPTS USER TO ENTER EACH ITEM AND QUANTITY OF THAT ITEM.   RETURNS
  CURRENT BILL TO CALLING PROGRAM.

MAJOR VARIABLES USED:
    CODE            INTEGER CODE FOR EACH TYPE OF FOOD
    QUANTITY      AMOUNT OF A PARTICULAR ITEM NEEDED   }

CONST
    HAMBURGER      = 1.10;
    CHEESEBURGER = 1.30;
    FRENCH_FRIES = 0.80;
    FRUIT_PIE      = 0.90;
    DRINK          = 0.75;

VAR
    STR_CODE, STR_QUAN : CHAR;
    CODE, QUANTITY      : INTEGER;

{* * * * * * * * * * * * * * * * * * * * * * * * * * * * * * * * * * *}

PROCEDURE CHECK_CODE (STR_CODE : STRING; VAR CODE : INTEGER);

{ DETERMINES WHETHER USER HAS ENTERED AN INTEGER FROM 1 THROUGH 5.
  THE VALUE OF THE INTEGER IS RETURNED IN THE VARIABLE CODE. }

VAR
    ERROR : INTEGER;

BEGIN    { CHECK_CODE }

    VAL (STR_CODE, CODE, ERROR);
    WHILE (ERROR <> 0) OR (STR_CODE < '1') OR (STR_CODE > '5') DO
    BEGIN
        WRITELN;
        WRITELN ('PLEASE REENTER YOUR ORDER.');
        WRITE ('USING THE CORRESPONDING CODE NUMBER (1-5): ');
        READLN (STR_CODE);
        VAL (STR_CODE, CODE, ERROR);
    END;    { WHILE }

END;    { CHECK_CODE }


{* * * * * * * * * * * * * * * * * * * * * * * * * * * * * * * * * * *}

PROCEDURE CHECK_QUANTITY (STR_QUAN : STRING; VAR QUANTITY : INTEGER);

{ DETERMINES WHETHER USER HAS ENTERED A VALID INTEGER.   IF VALID,
  THE INTEGER VALUE IS RETURNED IN QUANTITY. }

VAR
    ERROR : INTEGER;
```

FIGURE 9–2 COMPLETED PROGRAM MEAL (Cont.)   *(Figure continued on next page)*

```
BEGIN    { CHECK_QUANTITY }

    VAL (STR_QUAN, QUANTITY, ERROR);
    WHILE (ERROR <> 0) DO
    BEGIN
        WRITELN;
        WRITELN ('PLEASE REENTER THE QUANTITY YOU WISH TO PURCHASE: ');
        READLN (STR_QUAN);
        VAL (STR_QUAN, QUANTITY, ERROR);
        WHILE (ERROR <> 0) DO
        BEGIN
            WRITELN;
            WRITE ('PLEASE REENTER THE QUANTITY YOU WISH TO PURCHASE: ');
            READLN (STR_QUAN);
            VAL (STR_QUAN, QUANTITY, ERROR);
        END;    { INNER WHILE }
    END;    { OUTER WHILE }

END;    { CHECK_QUANTITY }

{* * * * * * * * * * * * * * * * * * * * * * * * * * * * * * * * *}

BEGIN    { DETERMINE_BILL }

    { GET CODE NUMBER OF ITEM. }
    WRITE ('PLEASE ENTER YOUR ORDER USING THE CODE NUMBER: ');
    READLN (STR_CODE);
    { DETERMINE IF A VALID CODE WAS ENTERED. }
    CHECK_CODE (STR_CODE, CODE);

    { DETERMINE QUANTITY OF ITEM. }
    WRITELN;
    WRITE ('HOW MANY OF THIS ITEM DO YOU WISH TO PURCHASE: ');
    READLN (STR_QUAN);
    { DETERMINE IF VALID INTEGER HAS BEEN ENTERED FOR QUANTITY. }
    CHECK_QUANTITY (STR_QUAN, QUANTITY);

    { ADD COST OF THIS ITEM TO TOTAL BILL. }
    CASE CODE OF
        1 : BILL := BILL + (1.10 * QUANTITY);
        2 : BILL := BILL + (1.30 * QUANTITY);
        3 : BILL := BILL + (0.80 * QUANTITY);
        4 : BILL := BILL + (0.90 * QUANTITY);
        5 : BILL := BILL + (0.75 * QUANTITY);
    END;    { CASE }

END;    { DETERMINE_BILL }

{*********************************************************************}
```

FIGURE 9-2 COMPLETED PROGRAM MEAL (Cont.)   *(Figure continued on next page)*

```
PROCEDURE ADD_TAX (VAR BILL : REAL);

{ ADDS TAX AND RETURNS TOTAL BILL. }

CONST
   TAX_RATE = 0.04;

BEGIN   { ADD_TAX }

   BILL := BILL + BILL * TAX_RATE;

END;    { ADD_ TAX }

{*********************************************************************}

PROCEDURE OUTPUT_BILL (BILL : REAL);

{ DISPLAYS TOTAL AMOUNT OWED. }

BEGIN   { OUTPUT_BILL }

   GOTOXY (5, 24);
   WRITELN ('TOTAL BILL:    $', BILL:6:2);

END;    { OUTPUT_BILL }

{*********************************************************************}

BEGIN   { MAIN }

   BILL := 0.0;

   { LOOP TO ALLOW CUSTOMER TO CHOOSE AS MANY ITEMS AS DESIRED. }
   REPEAT
      DISPLAY_MENU;
      DETERMINE_BILL (BILL);
      WRITELN;
      WRITE ('DO YOU WANT TO CHOOSE MORE ITEMS (Y OR N): ');
      READLN (MORE)
   UNTIL (MORE = 'N') OR (MORE = 'n');

   { ADD THE TAX TO THE COST AND DISPLAY TOTAL BILL. }
   ADD_TAX (BILL);
   OUTPUT_BILL (BILL);

END.    { MAIN }
```

FIGURE 9–2 COMPLETED PROGRAM MEAL (Cont.)   *(Figure continued on next page)*

```
1.  HAMBURGER      $1.10
2.  CHEESEBURGER   $1.30
3.  FRENCH FRIES   $0.80
4.  FRUIT PIE      $0.90
5.  DRINK          $0.75


PLEASE ENTER YOUR ORDER USING THE CODE NUMBER:  6

PLEASE REENTER YOUR ORDER.
USING THE CORRESPONDING CODE NUMBER (1-5):  a

PLEASE REENETER YOUR ORDER.
USING THE CORRESPONDING CODE NUMBER (1-5):  2

HOW MANY OF THIS ITEM DO YOU WISH TO PURCHASE:  3

DO YOU WANT TO CHOOSE MORE ITEMS (Y OR N):  N
     TOTAL BILL:     $  4.06
```

FIGURE 9–2 COMPLETED PROGRAM MEAL (Cont.)

WRITING USER-FRIENDLY PROGRAMS

The term **user-friendly** is often heard in the world of programming. A user-friendly program is written so as to make it as easy and enjoyable as possible for people to use. User-friendly programs have the following characteristics:

- The prompts are easy to understand and are written to make it as easy as possible for the user to enter responses. For example, if the user is directed to respond to a prompt with an uppercase Y (for YES), a well-written program might also allow the user to enter a lowercase y.
- If the user has a number of options to choose from, a clearly stated menu should list all of these options and the codes necessary for choosing them.
- The program should be able to handle invalid input and respond with a polite error message. The program should then prompt the user to reenter the data.

Examine the program in Figure 9–2. Notice that it starts by displaying a menu allowing the user to enter a choice. To make a selection, the user merely enters the corresponding integer value. Notice that the code value entered by the user is assigned to a string variable. This is done to prevent the program from "crashing" if the user accidentally enters a noninteger value. Next, procedure CHECK_CODE is called to see if a valid code has been entered. The VAL procedure determines if STR_CODE contains an integer. If it does, the compiler will assign the integer to the variable CODE and set ERROR to zero. If it does not, CODE will be undefined, and ERROR will indicate the position of the first noninteger character. Examine the condition controlling the execution of the WHILE/DO loop:

```
WHILE (ERROR <> 0) OR ((STR_CODE < '1') OR (STR_CODE > '5')) DO
```

This WHILE/DO loop will only be executed if the user enters a noninteger value (indicated by ERROR not being a zero) or an integer outside of the allowable range of 1 through 5. The loop will continue executing as long as the value entered is invalid. Procedure CHECK_QUANTITY is similar to CHECK_CODE except that it does not check to see if the integer is inside any range, simply that it is a valid integer.

This type of error checking is called "defensive programming." We are defending the program from user errors. If an invalid value is entered, the user is prompted to reenter the number. After each selection, the user is asked if more items are to be purchased. Any word that starts with a "Y" or a "y" will be seen as a yes answer.

LEARNING CHECK 9–2

1. What kind of error does the following statement contain?

   ```
   WRITLN ('TODAY IS WEDNESDAY.');
   ```

2. Why was the variable STR_CODE in Figure 9–2 declared to be of type CHAR?
3. How are stubs used in developing programs in a top-down fashion? What are some advantages of using this method?
4. Explain how desk checking can be used to locate program errors.

■ SUMMARY POINTS

- Using good programming style means making a program as easy as possible for people to read and understand. Programs that have good style are well documented and use indentation and blank spaces to make the programs easier to follow. Meaningful names are used to identify variables.

■ Documentation should be used both at the beginning and within the body of a program. The documentation at the beginning should contain a general description of the program and the major variables used. The documentation inside the program should be used to explain specific sections of the program.

■ The three types of program errors are syntax, run-time, and logic errors. Syntax errors are violations of the grammatical rules of the language. Run-time errors often cause a program to crash before it is through executing. When a program has a logic error, it executes but obtains incorrect results at least part of the time.

■ User-friendly programs make it as easy as possible for people to use and enjoy them. Prompts are clearly worded, and it is easy to enter data.

■ Stubs can be used to implement a program in a top-down fashion. The main program is written first. When it is running properly, procedures are gradually added and tested. This allows a program to be developed in a structured way.

VOCABULARY LIST

Desk checking
Driver program
Logic errors
Program style
Program tracing

Run-time errors
Stubs
Syntax errors
User-friendly

CHAPTER TEST

Vocabulary

Match a term from the numbered column with the description from the lettered column that best fits the term.

1. Program tracing

2. User-friendly

3. Desk check

a. Tracing through a program by hand attempting to locate any errors.

b. An error caused by not following the grammatical rules of a language.

c. A way of writing a program to make it easier for humans to understand.

4. Run-time error

   d. A procedure declaration that contains only a heading, a BEGIN-END pair, and possibly a WRITELN statement indicating that the procedure was called.

5. Syntax error

   e. Printing the values of variables at various points in a program in order to locate program errors.

6. Program style

   f. A flaw in a program's algorithm.

7. Stub

   g. A term applied to a program that is written in such a way as to make it as easy and enjoyable as possible for people to use.

8. Logic error

   h. An error that causes abnormal program behavior during execution.

9. Driver program

   i. A program whose main purpose is to call procedures.

Questions

1. Why should programmers use good program style?
2. Rewrite the following statements, using blank spaces to make them more readable.

   a. `WRITELN('THE SUM OF ',X,Y,Z,' IS ',SUM);`
   b. `PERCENT:=(NUM1+NUM2+NUM3)/TOTAL;`
   c. `SCORE:=10*12+50*10;`

3. What is meant by using meaningful variable names? Give three examples of meaningful variable names.
4. What are the three types of program errors? Give an example of each.
5. Why are logic errors often difficult to locate and correct?
6. What is the most common cause of syntax errors? How can it be avoided?
7. Use desk checking to find the eight syntax errors in this procedure:

```
PROCEDURE SUPPLIES (AVE_USE, GONE, LEFT : REAL; PEOPLE : INTEGER);

   IF PEOPLE > 20
     THEN GONE := PEOPLE * AVE_USE;
      ELSE GONE := PEOPLE * AVE_USE * 0.75;
   LEFT = LEFT - GONE
   WRITELN (THERE ARE '; LEFT:8:2, ' QUARTS LEFT.');

   END.   { SUPPLIES
```

8. Explain how program tracing can be used to locate run-time errors.
9. What is meant by the term user-friendly? What are some characteristics of a user-friendly program?

▆▆▆▆▆ PROGRAMMING PROBLEMS

Level 1

1. Rewrite the following program segment so that it is protected from user input of zero or negative numbers. Assume that all of the variables have been declared as type REAL.

```
WRITE ('PLEASE ENTER YOUR DEPOSIT: ');
READLN (DEPOSIT);
NEWBALANCE := OLDBALANCE + DEPOSIT;
WRITELN ('YOUR NEW BALANCE IS ', NEWBALANCE);
```

2. Find the run-time error in this program segment:

```
VAR
    X, Y : INTEGER;

BEGIN
    X := 5;
    WHILE X > 0 DO
    BEGIN
        TOTAL := X + Y;
        X := X - 1;
    END;    { WHILE }
```

Level 2

3. The Tuesday evening bowling league would like a program to calculate the average bowling score of each of its members. The program should read each bowler's name and the scores of her last five games. The average of these five scores should then be calculated. The output should be similar to

```
SALLY DOE HAS AN AVERAGE SCORE OF 173.5
```

The program should be well documented and use meaningful variable names.

4. Write a well-documented program that will decode messages using the following code: A vowel is decoded as the vowel that follows it, and a consonant is decoded as the consonant that follows it. The last vowel, "u," is decoded as "a" and the last consonant, "z," is decoded as "b." Develop your own data to test this program.

5. Student employees at Bromfield University are categorized into three job classifications according to their pay: C1, $3.60 per hour; C2, $3.85 per hour; C3, $4.10 per hour. Write a well-documented procedure that calculates an employee's gross pay. Variables representing the employee's job classification, hours worked, and gross pay should be passed to the procedure and returned to the calling program.

CHAPTER 10

Functions, Enumerated Data Types, and Subrange Data Types

OBJECTIVES

After studying this chapter, you should be able to:

- Define a function.
- Use standard arithmetic functions correctly.
- Use the functions PRED, SUCC, ORD, and CHR correctly.
- Explain how the EOLN function works.
- Explain how the string functions work and use them correctly.
- Write user-defined functions when appropriate.
- Define and use enumerated data types.
- Define and use subrange data types.

OUTLINE

■■■ INTRODUCTION

Procedures were introduced in Chapter 7. A procedure is generally designed to perform a specific task. **Functions** are another type of subprogram. They are similar to procedures, but have a more limited purpose. Whereas a procedure can return many values to the calling program and is often used to perform tasks other than returning values, a function is used to compute a single value to be returned to the calling program. For example, a function could be used to calculate and return the square root of a positive number. Another difference between functions and procedures is that the function name represents the returned value. Like procedures, functions can be either standard or user defined. Some standard functions will be discussed first.

■■■ STANDARD FUNCTIONS

Many small tasks that programmers need to perform are done over and over again. Rounding off a real number to the nearest integer is an example. Because of this, the Turbo Pascal compiler contains standard functions that perform these tasks. Like standard procedures, these functions are "built in" to the compiler. Many of these functions perform arithmetic operations; others manipulate character and string values. The ones that perform arithmetic will be presented first.

ARITHMETIC FUNCTIONS

A function is executed by using a **function designator**, which is an expression containing the name of the function and one or more arguments or actual parameters. These arguments are used by functions in the same way that procedures use them. Each of the standard functions discussed here has only a single argument. Later, functions with many arguments will be discussed. The argument used with these standard functions may be an expression, a variable, or a constant as long as the argument has the data type appropriate for that function.

The ROUND function is an example of a standard function. It rounds a real number to the nearest integer. For example, the statement

```
NEAREST := ROUND (10.86);
```

will result in 11 being assigned to NEAREST. Notice that the syntax for a function designator is different from that for a procedure call. A procedure call simply contains the name of the procedure and its parameters. The function designator uses the value of the function just as if it were any other variable or expression. Here is another example of a function designator:

```
WRITELN (ROUND (10.86));
```

When this statement is executed, the following will be displayed:

```
11
```

The argument does not have to be a constant. It can be any expression or variable as long as it evaluates as the correct data type for the function being called. In the first function designator below, the argument is a variable, whereas in the second it is an expression:

```
I := 10.86;
WRITELN (ROUND (I));
WRITELN (ROUND (I + 1.4));
```

The BOOLEAN function ODD returns a value of true if the argument is an odd integer; otherwise it returns a value of false. When the following statement is executed, ODD_STATUS (which must be of type BOOLEAN) will be assigned the value of false:

```
ODD_STATUS := ODD (234);
```

Program DEMO in Figure 10–1 demonstrates the use of several standard functions. Note that the absolute value of NUMBER is stored in ABS_VALUE. Then the square root of ABS_VALUE is found. Because attempting to find the square root of a negative value will generate an error when the program is run, getting the number's absolute value before determining the square root is a good way of avoiding this problem.

```
PROGRAM DEMO;

{ THIS PROGRAM DEMONSTRATES THE USE OF SEVERAL STANDARD FUNCTIONS. }

VAR
   NUMBER, ABS_VALUE : REAL;
   INT1, INT2        : INTEGER;

BEGIN   { DEMO }

   NUMBER := -417.635;
   INT1 := TRUNC (NUMBER);
   WRITELN (NUMBER:8:3, ' TRUNCATED IS ', INT1:4);
   INT2 := ROUND (NUMBER);
   WRITELN (NUMBER:8:3, ' ROUNDED IS ', INT2:4);
   ABS_VALUE := ABS (NUMBER);
   WRITELN ('THE ABSOLUTE VALUE OF ', NUMBER:8:3, ' IS ', ABS_VALUE:8:3);
   INT2 := SQR (INT1);
   WRITELN ('THE SQUARE OF ', INT1:4, ' IS ', INT2:4);
   NUMBER := SQRT (ABS_VALUE);
   WRITELN ('THE SQUARE ROOT OF ', ABS_VALUE:8:3, ' IS ', NUMBER:8:3);

END.   { DEMO }
```

```
-417.635 TRUNCATED IS -417
-417.635 ROUNDED IS -418
THE ABSOLUTE VALUE OF -417.635 IS  417.635
THE SQUARE OF -417 IS -22719
THE SQUARE ROOT OF  417.635 IS   20.436
```

FIGURE 10-1 PROGRAM DEMONSTRATING SEVERAL STANDARD ARITHMETIC FUNCTIONS

The functions SQR and SQRT calculate the square and the square root of a number, respectively. We will write a program using SQR and SQRT to calculate the hypotenuse of a right triangle. The Pythagorean theorem can be used to determine the length of the hypotenuse:

Hypotenuse^2 = (side 1)^2 + (side 2)^2

The following Pascal statement can be used to calculate the square of the hypotenuse:

```
SQUARE_OF_HYPOTENUSE := SQR (SIDE1) + SQR (SIDE2);
```

Once this is done, the hypotenuse can be determined by finding the square root of the previous result:

```
HYPOTENUSE := SQRT (SQUARE_OF_HYPOTENUSE);
```

These two statements can be combined into a single statement like this:

```
HYPOTENUSE := SQRT (SQR (SIDE1) + SQR (SIDE2));
```

Figure 10–2 contains the complete program.

Some commonly used arithmetic functions are listed in the following table:

Name	Data Type of Argument	Data Type of Result	Value Returned
ABS (X)	INTEGER/REAL	Same as argument	Absolute value of X
ARCTAN (X)	INTEGER/REAL	REAL	Arctangent of X (X in radians)
COS (X)	INTEGER/REAL	INTEGER/REAL	Cosine of X (X in radians)
EXP (X)	INTEGER/REAL	REAL	e to the X power
INT (X)	REAL	REAL	Returns the integer portion of a real number
LN (X)	INTEGER/REAL	REAL	Natural logarithm of X
ODD (X)	INTEGER	BOOLEAN	True if X is odd False if X is even
PI	None	REAL	Value of pi
ROUND (X)	REAL	LONGINT	Rounds X to the nearest integer
SIN (X)	INTEGER/REAL	REAL	Sine of X (X in radians)
SQR (X)	REAL/INTEGER	Same as X	Square of X
SQRT (X)	REAL/INTEGER (positive)	REAL	Square root of X
TRUNC (X)	REAL	LONGINT	Cuts off a real number at the decimal point

The Functions PRED, SUCC, ORD, and CHR

As previously discussed, the data types INTEGER, CHAR, and BOOLEAN are ordinal data types. Each value in these types has a unique predecessor (except the first) and a unique successor (except the last). These ordinal values can be regarded as a list of values with a beginning and an end. The functions SUCC, PRED, ORD, and CHR are used only with ordinal data types.

```
PROGRAM FIND_HYPOTENUSE;

{ DETERMINES THE LENGTH OF THE HYPOTENUSE OF A RIGHT TRIANGLE. }

VAR
   HYPOTENUSE, SQUARE_OF_HYPOTENUSE, SIDE1, SIDE2 : REAL;

BEGIN   { FIND_HYPOTENUSE }

   WRITE ('ENTER THE LENGTHS OF THE OTHER TWO SIDES: ');
   READLN (SIDE1, SIDE2);
   SQUARE_OF_HYPOTENUSE := SQR (SIDE1) + SQR (SIDE2);
   HYPOTENUSE := SQRT (SQUARE_OF_HYPOTENUSE);
   WRITELN ('THE LENGTH OF THE HYPOTENUSE IS ', HYPOTENUSE:8:2);

END.   { FIND_HYPOTENUSE }
```

```
ENTER THE LENGTHS OF THE OTHER TWO SIDES: 4.5  5.2
THE LENGTH OF THE HYPOTENUSE IS      6.88
```

FIGURE 10-2 PROGRAM FIND_HYPOTENUSE

The standard function PRED returns the value immediately before a given ordinal value. The statement

```
PREVIOUS := PRED (2);
```

will result in PREVIOUS (which must be of type INTEGER) being assigned the value 1. The standard function SUCC returns the successor of a given ordinal value. When the following statement is executed

```
NEXT_LETTER := SUCC ('M');
```

the value N is assigned to NEXT_LETTER, which must be of type CHAR. The ORD function returns the ordinal position of the argument. When the data is of type INTEGER, the value is the same as the argument. This statement

```
WRITELN (ORD (750));
```

results in the integer 750 being displayed. The order of the BOOLEAN values is false and true. This means that the successor of false is true, but false has no predecessor. Conversely, the predecessor of true is false, but true has no successor. When used with data of type BOOLEAN, the ordinal value of false is zero and true is one. When the following program segment is executed

```
SWITCH := FALSE;
WRITELN (ORD (SWITCH));
```

the number zero will be output. When ORD is used with data of type CHAR, the value returned is the ASCII value of the character. After this statement is executed

```
POSITION := ORD ('q');
```

the variable POSITION will contain the value 113. If you refer to Appendix E, which lists the ASCII codes, you can verify that this is correct. Remember from Chapter 5 that the ASCII code is the internal ordering that the computer assigns to the characters it can recognize. The CHR function works in the opposite manner. Assuming POSITION has a value of 113, the statement

```
SYMBOL := CHR (POSITION);
```

results in SYMBOL being assigned the value "q." If no corresponding character exists for the integer listed as the argument in the CHR function, the value of CHR is undefined. The following program segment uses the CHR function to display the uppercase letters of the alphabet:

```
POSITION := 65;
WHILE POSITION <= 90 DO
BEGIN
    WRITELN (CHR (POSITION));
    POSITION := SUCC (POSITION);
END;    { WHILE }
```

Figure 10–3 demonstrates how these four functions can be used with data of type CHAR.

```
PROGRAM ORDER;

{ DEMONSTRATES THE FOUR FUNCTIONS PRED, SUCC, ORD, AND CHR.  }

VAR
    LETTER, AFTER, BEFORE, VALUE : CHAR;
    PLACE                        : INTEGER;

BEGIN  { ORDER }

    WRITE ('TYPE IN A LETTER: ');
    READLN (LETTER);
    AFTER := SUCC (LETTER);
    WRITELN ('THE SUCCESSOR OF ', LETTER, ' IS ', AFTER);
    BEFORE := PRED (LETTER);
    WRITELN ('THE PREDECESSOR OF ', LETTER, ' IS ', BEFORE);
    PLACE := ORD (LETTER);
    WRITELN ('THE ASCII VALUE OF ', LETTER, ' IS ', PLACE);
    VALUE := CHR (PLACE);
    WRITELN ('THE LETTER WITH AN ASCII VALUE OF ', PLACE, ' IS ', VALUE);

END.   { ORDER }
```

```
TYPE IN A LETTER: G
THE SUCCESSOR OF G IS H
THE PREDECESSOR OF G IS F
THE ASCII VALUE OF G IS 71
THE LETTER WITH AN ASCII VALUE OF 71 IS G
```

FIGURE 10-3 PROGRAM DEMONSTRATING THE PRED, SUCC, ORD, AND CHR FUNCTIONS

1. Explain the difference between a procedure and a function.
2. State the results of each of the following:

    a. ROUND (250.35);
    b. TRUNC (250.35);
    c. ABS (250.35);
    d. SQR (16);
    e. SQRT (16);

3. Tell whether each of the following is a function designator or a procedure call.

    a. IF EVEN (NUM)
        THEN TOTAL := TOTAL + NUM;
    b. COST := TOTAL_BILL (BILL, TAX, TIP);
    c. IF GRADE = 'A'
        THEN HONOR_ROLL (NAME, GPA);
    d. PR_TABLE;

4. Evaluate the following:

    a. PRED ('Z');
    b. ORD (14);
    c. ORD ('m');
    d. PRED (14 + 18);
    e. CHR (68);

The EOLN Function

When the user is entering data at the keyboard and presses the Enter key, a special character called the end-of-line character or <eoln> is inserted at that point. When the computer reads this input, the <eoln> character can be checked for by using the BOOLEAN function EOLN. When <eoln> is encountered, EOLN becomes true; until then, it is false. In the following segment, a list of integers is read until the end of the input line is reached:

```
NUMBER := 0;
TOTAL  := 0;
WHILE NOT EOLN DO
BEGIN
    READ (AGE);
    TOTAL := TOTAL + AGE;
END;   { WHILE }
WRITELN (TOTAL);
```

In this program segment, EOLN is used to control repetition of the WHILE/DO loop. As long as "NOT EOLN" is true, the loop will execute.

String Functions

Turbo Pascal contains several functions used to manipulate strings. Here are some commonly used ones:

- **CONCAT** Joins together a series of strings. For instance, after this program segment is executed

```
FIRST := 'JANE ';
MIDDLE := 'M ';
LAST := 'FOLEY';
FULL_NAME := CONCAT (FIRST, MIDDLE, LAST);
```

the value of FULL_NAME will be JANE M FOLEY.

- **COPY** Returns a sequence of characters from a string, starting at a specified position and continuing for a specified length. Assume the value of NAME in the statement below is A. B. Miller:

```
LAST_NAME := COPY (NAME, 7, 6);
```

The value assigned to LAST_NAME will be Miller. The middle initial could be assigned to MIDDLE_INIT by the following statement:

```
MIDDLE_INT := COPY (NAME, 4, 2);
```

- **LENGTH** Returns the length of a string as an integer value. For example, if STRING1 contains "1919 Mockingbird Lane", then the statement

```
LONG := LENGTH (STRING1);
```

assigns the value 21 to LONG.

- **POS** Returns an integer value representing the starting position of a specified substring. In the following statement, assume that STATE has the value MISSISSIPPI:

```
SUB_STRING := POS ('ISSI',STATE);
```

The variable SUB_STRING will be assigned the value two. If the specified substring is not located, the value returned is zero.

Additional Standard Functions

Turbo Pascal has many additional standard functions. A few of the more useful ones are presented here.

Turbo Pascal has two RANDOM functions. The first is called like this:

```
N := RANDOM;
```

It returns a random number greater than or equal to zero and less than one. No arguments are used, and the result is of type REAL. The second random number function can be called like this:

```
N := RANDOM (NUMBER);
```

It returns a random number greater than or equal to zero and less than the argument NUMBER. The argument and the result must both be integers. Figure 10–4 shows a program allowing the user to play a guessing game. Examine the first statement of this program:

```
RANDOMIZE;
```

This is a call to the procedure RANDOMIZE, which causes the Turbo system to generate a different random number each time the program is executed. The statement

```
ANSWER := RANDOM (100);
```

assigns a number from 0 to 100 to ANSWER. The player is prompted to guess the number and is told whether the guess is higher or lower than ANSWER. The player continues guessing until a correct guess is entered. Each time this game is played, a different random number will be generated.

The UPCASE function returns the uppercase value of the argument. For example,

```
WRITELN (UPCASE ('a'));
```

causes the letter A to be displayed.

The KEYPRESSED function returns a value of true if a key has been pressed and false if no key has been pressed. The function does not have an argument. Here is a program segment using KEYPRESSED:

```
REPEAT
    WRITELN ('Continue');
UNTIL KEYPRESSED;
```

The word "Continue" will be printed over and over on the screen until the user presses any key.

The KEYPRESSED function is contained in the CRT unit. Therefore the following statement must be placed at the beginning of the program:

```
USES
    CRT;
```

The READKEY function reads a single character that has been entered at the keyboard. The value can be assigned to a variable of type

```
PROGRAM GUESSING_GAME;

{ PROMPTS THE PLAYER TO GUESS AN INTEGER VALUE FROM 0 TO 100.   WHEN
  THE PLAYER ENTERS THE CORRECT VALUE, THE GAME STOPS. }

USES
   CRT;

VAR
  GUESS, ANSWER : INTEGER;

BEGIN    { GUESSING_GAME }

  RANDOMIZE;
  ANSWER := RANDOM (100);
  CLRSCR;
  WRITE ('THIS IS A GUESSING GAME.');
  WRITELN;
  WRITELN ('TRY TO GUESS THE NUMBER BETWEEN 0 AND 100.');
  REPEAT
     WRITE ('ENTER YOUR GUESS: ');
     READLN (GUESS);
     IF GUESS = ANSWER
        THEN WRITELN ('CORRECT!!!! YOU ARE A WINNER!')
        ELSE IF GUESS > ANSWER
                THEN WRITELN ('WRONG ANSWER - YOUR GUESS IS TOO HIGH.')
                ELSE WRITELN ('WRONG ANSWER - YOUR GUESS IS TOO LOW.')
  UNTIL GUESS = ANSWER;

END.    { GUESSING_GAME }
```

```
THIS IS A GUESSING GAME.
TRY TO GUESS THE NUMBER BETWEEN 0 AND 100.
ENTER YOUR GUESS: 50
WRONG ANSWER - YOUR GUESS IS TOO HIGH.
ENTER YOUR GUESS: 25
WRONG ANSWER - YOUR GUESS IS TOO HIGH.
ENTER YOUR GUESS: 10
WRONG ANSWER - YOUR GUESS IS TOO LOW.
ENTER YOUR GUESS: 17
CORRECT!!!! YOU ARE A WINNER!
```

FIGURE 10-4 PROGRAM USING THE RANDOM FUNCTION

CHAR. Below is an example of a program segment that uses READKEY (assume ANSWER is of type CHAR):

```
WRITE ('Do you want to continue (Y/N)? ');
ANSWER := READKEY;
WRITELN (ANSWER);
```

The user enters a character, but does not press the Return key. The READKEY function does not echo the user's response to the monitor screen. Therefore, if the programmer wants the user's response to be displayed, a WRITELN statement must be used. Like KEYPRESSED, READKEY is contained in the CRT unit.

DIFFERENCES FOR VERSION 3 USERS

There is no READKEY function in Version 3. The device name KBD (short for keyboard) can be used to enter single-character input like this:

READ (KBD, ANSWER);

This reads a single character entered by the user. The user does not press the Return key, and the value entered is not displayed on the monitor screen.

DIFFERENCES FOR MACINTOSH USERS

READCHAR is used in place of READKEY. No USES statement is used with KEYPRESSED or READCHAR.

If you are using Version 1.1 of Turbo Pascal for the Macintosh, you can use the RANDOM function and the RANDOMIZE procedure by inserting the following USES statement at the beginning of your program:

USES
MEMTYPES, QUICKDRAW, OSINTF, TOOLINTF, COMPAT;

The folder named "Compat Unit" should be on the disk containing the Turbo Pascal compiler.

▬▬ USER-DEFINED FUNCTIONS

The syntax of a user-defined function is similar to that of a procedure. The function starts with a function heading containing the name of the function and the formal parameters. There is one major difference, however: because the function itself is assigned a value, it must be assigned a data type. Below is the function heading for a function to convert a temperature from Celsius to Fahrenheit:

```
FUNCTION F_TEMP (C_TEMP : REAL) : REAL;
```

The single parameter, C_TEMP, will be used to pass the Celsius temperature to the function. The Fahrenheit temperature will be returned in F_TEMP.

Format For **Function**

```
FUNCTION function_name (formal parameter list) : data_type;

local declaration section
BEGIN
   statement1;
         •
         •
         •
   last_statement;
END;
```

Notice that the data type of the function is placed immediately after the formal parameter list. Function F_TEMP is of type REAL. The complete function to perform the conversion could be written like this:

```
FUNCTION F_TEMP (C_TEMP : REAL) : REAL;

BEGIN    { F_TEMP }

   F_TEMP := 1.8 * C_TEMP + 32.0;

END;    { F_TEMP }
```

The body of a function must contain at least one statement assigning a value to this function.

Each of the following function designators will cause F_TEMP to be called:

```
FAHREN := F_TEMP (48.5);
WRITELN (F_TEMP (100 - 6));
FAHREN := F_TEMP (CELSIUS);
```

A function designator is placed in the calling program at the point at which the function is to be called. Figure 10–5 contains the complete program that performs the temperature conversion problem. Figure 10–6 demonstrates how the value of the actual parameter will be passed to the function and how the value of the function will be returned to the calling program.

Because the purpose of a function is to determine a single value, variable parameters should not be used with functions. If more than one value needs to be returned to the calling program, use a procedure instead of a function.

---

1. What will be displayed by each of the following?

    a. WRITELN (LENGTH ('WEEG CENTER'));
    b. WRITELN (CONCAT ('BOZEMAN' + 'MONTANA'));
    c. WRITELN (POS ('BOZE', 'BOZEMAN'));
    d. WRITELN (POS ('BOZE', 'MONTANA'));
    e. WRITELN (COPY ('BOZEMAN', 4, 2));

2. Write a function that will calculate the area of a triangle and return this value to the calling program. The formula for calculating the area of a triangle is ½(base × height).
3. How is a function heading different from a procedure heading?
4. Explain how the COPY function works.

ENUMERATED DATA TYPES

One of the useful features of Pascal is that it allows the programmer to define new data types. They are called **enumerated data types**. Here is an example of such a definition:

```
TYPE
    COLOR = (RED, YELLOW, GREEN, BLUE);
```

When an enumerated data type is defined, each possible value of that type must be listed. Now variables can be declared of type COLOR:

```
VAR
    TINT, SHADE : COLOR;
```

TINT and SHADE are now variables of type COLOR. They can have the value of RED, YELLOW, GREEN, or BLUE.

```
PROGRAM CONVERSION;

{ READS A CELSIUS TEMPERATURE AND OUTPUTS THE CORRESPONDING
  FAHRENHEIT TEMPERATURE. }

VAR
  C_TEMP, FAHRENHEIT : REAL;

{*******************************************************************}

FUNCTION F_TEMP (C_TEMP : REAL) : REAL;

{ RECEIVES A CELSIUS TEMPERATURE AND RETURNS THE CORRESPONDING
  FAHRENHEIT TEMPERATURE. }

BEGIN   { F_TEMP }

   F_TEMP := 1.8 * C_TEMP + 32.0;

END;    { F_TEMP }

{*******************************************************************}

BEGIN   { MAIN }

   WRITE ('ENTER THE CELSIUS TEMPERATURE: ');
   READLN (C_TEMP);
   FAHRENHEIT := F_TEMP (C_TEMP);
   WRITELN ('THE FAHRENHEIT TEMPERATURE IS ', FAHRENHEIT:8:2);

END.    { MAIN }
```

```
ENTER THE CELSIUS TEMPERATURE: 100
THE FAHRENHEIT TEMPERATURE IS   212.00
```

FIGURE 10–5 PROGRAM CONTAINING A USER-DEFINED FUNCTION

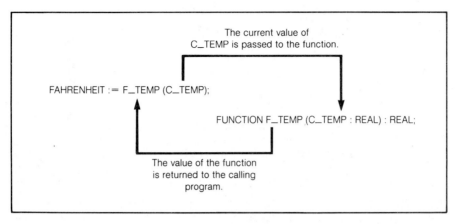

FIGURE 10–6 SUBSTITUTING ACTUAL PARAMETERS FOR FORMAL PARAMETERS

Format For **Enumerated Data Type**

TYPE
    type_name = (value1, value2, . . . value*n*);
VAR
    variable_name : type_name;

The compiler assigns an order to these values according to the order in which they are listed in the TYPE definition. RED has an ordinal value of 0, YELLOW has a value of 1, GREEN has a value of 2, and BLUE has a value of 3. Because these values have an order, the following expressions all evaluate as true:

```
RED < GREEN
BLUE <> YELLOW
PRED (GREEN) = YELLOW
SUCC (GREEN) = BLUE
```

The functions ORD, PRED, and SUCC can be used with enumerated data types. ORD will return the ordinal position of a particular value in an enumerated type. The value of POSITION in the following statement will be three (POSITION must be declared as type INTEGER):

```
POSITION := ORD (BLUE);
```

Unlike standard data types, enumerated data types cannot be directly read or written using READ and WRITE statements. A code can be used to allow the values to be entered. The following program segment reads a color code (COLOR_CODE) and uses nested IF statements to assign the appropriate value to the variable TINT. COLOR_CODE is declared to be of type INTEGER.

```
READ (COLOR_CODE);
IF COLOR_CODE = 0
   THEN TINT := RED
   ELSE IF COLOR_CODE = 1
           THEN TINT := YELLOW
           ELSE IF COLOR_CODE = 2
                   THEN TINT := GREEN
                   ELSE IF COLOR_CODE = 3
                           THEN TINT := BLUE
                           ELSE WRITELN('INVALID VALUE FOR COLOR.');
```

This same task can be performed by using a CASE statement. In the following program segment, a CASE statement is used to display the color depending on the current value of TINT:

```
CASE TINT OF
   RED    : WRITELN ('RED');
   YELLOW : WRITELN ('YELLOW');
   GREEN  : WRITELN ('GREEN');
   BLUE   : WRITELN ('BLUE');
   ELSE WRITELN ('INVALID COLOR CODE.');
END;   { CASE }
```

The values used in enumerated data types must be unique. This means that they cannot be members of an already existing data type. For example, integer values are already members of type INTEGER. Therefore, the following type definition is invalid:

```
TYPE
   MODEL = (20, 35, 40, 45, 50);
```

Also, the same value cannot appear in two different enumerated data types. The value FISH appears in both type definitions below, making them invalid:

```
TYPE
   PETS = (CAT, DOG, FISH, SNAKE, BIRD, LIZARD);
   OCEAN = (SHELLS, FISH, PLANTS, WATER, MINERALS);
```

▬▬▬ SUBRANGE DATA TYPES

A **subrange data type** is a data type that contains a portion of a predefined or user-defined data type. Every subrange has a *base type*. This base type is the data type from which the subrange is taken. The base type of a subrange must be an ordinal data type (it cannot be of type REAL).

Format For **Subrange Data Type**

```
TYPE
   subrange_type = first_value..last_value;
VAR
   subrange_variable : subrange_type;
```

Subranges are used to specify a range of allowable values. Below are several examples of subrange definitions:

```
TYPE
    PASSING = 'A'..'D';
    MINOR   = 1..20;

VAR
    GRADE : PASSING;
    AGE   : MINOR;
```

When a subrange is defined, the first and the last values are listed. Notice that there are two (not three) dots between the first and last values. These two values and all values between them are included in the subrange. The allowable values for the variable GRADE are A, B, C, and D. The allowable values for the variable AGE are the integers 1 through 20.

Consider the following program segment:

```
PROGRAM CHECK_AGE;

TYPE
    MINOR = 1..20;

VAR
    AGE : MINOR;

BEGIN
   WRITE ('Enter your age: ');
   READLN (AGE);
```

You may be wondering what would happen if you typed in an age of 21. This is outside the range of the variable AGE. However, the compiler will not indicate an error. This is because the "range-checking" capability of the compiler is ordinarily turned off. You can turn it on by placing the following statement at the beginning of this program:

```
{$R+}
PROGRAM CHECK_AGE;
```

```
TYPE
   MINOR = 1..20;

VAR
   AGE : MINOR;

BEGIN

   WRITE ('Enter your age: ');
   READLN (AGE);
```

Now, if you attempted to assign the value 21 to AGE, the program would stop running, and an error message would be displayed.

It is also possible to define subranges of enumerated data types as shown below:

```
TYPE
   MONTHS = (JAN, FEB, MAR, APR, MAY, JUN, JUL, AUG, SEP, OCT, NOV, DEC);
   SUMMER = JUN..AUG;
```

```
VAR
   VACATION : SUMMER;
```

The variable VACATION is a subrange of the type MONTHS. It can contain the values JUN, JUL, and AUG.

LEARNING CHECK 10-3

1. Define an enumerated data type named DAYS that contains the days of the week. Then define a subrange of this type that contains the schooldays.
2. How is a subrange data type different from an enumerated data type?
3. Given the following TYPE definition, determine whether the expressions in parts a–e evaluate as true or false.

```
TYPE
   GELATIN = (STRAWBERRY, LIME, ORANGE, CHERRY, GRAPE);
```

```
   a. PRED (CHERRY) = ORANGE
   b. LIME <> SUCC (STRAWBERRY)
   c. CHERRY < STRAWBERRY
   d. ORD (LIME) - 1
   e. ORD (STRAWBERRY) + ORD (GRAPE) = 4
```

4. Define a subrange of data type GELATIN (from problem 3) containing the values ORANGE, CHERRY, and GRAPE.

▬ SUMMARY POINTS

- Functions are subprograms that return a single value to the calling program. The value is returned in the function. Functions can be either standard or user defined.
- Standard functions are part of the compiler. Some standard arithmetic functions are ROUND, TRUNC, ABS, SQR, and SQRT.
- PRED returns the predecessor of an ordinal value whereas SUCC returns its successor. ORD returns its ordinal position. CHR returns the character value that has a specific ASCII value.
- The EOLN function becomes true when the end of an input line is reached; otherwise it is false.
- User-defined functions are written by the programmer to determine and return a specific value to the calling program. The syntax of a function is similar to that of a procedure except that a function has a data type. The function designator is used to call functions.
- Enumerated data types are ordinal data types that are defined by the programmer to meet the needs of a specific program. All possible values of that data type must be listed in the definition.
- Subranges are defined as being a portion of a particular ordinal data type. Subranges are useful when a value should fall within a given range.

▬ VOCABULARY LIST

Enumerated data types	Function designator
Functions	Subrange data type

▬ CHAPTER TEST

Vocabulary

Match a term from the numbered column with the description from the lettered column that best fits the term.

1. Function designator

   a. A user-defined data type that contains a portion of an ordinal data type.

2. Enumerated data type

   b. A subprogram designed to return a single value to the calling program.

3. Subrange data type

   c. An expression used to call a function.

4. Function

d. An ordinal data type that has been defined by the programmer. Every possible value of that type must be listed in the definition.

Questions

1. Which of the following are valid function calls for this function heading? Why or why not?

```
FUNCTION GRADE (TEST1, TEST2 : REAL; PROG1, PROG2 : CHAR) : CHAR;

    a. WRITELN (GRADE (34.5, 37, 'a', 'B'));
    b. LETTER := GRADE (39, 37, 35, 'B', 'C');
    c. GRADE (40, 37.4, 38, 'A');
    d. IF GPA > 3.5
         THEN WRITELN (GRADE (36.5, 34, 'A', 'A'));
```

2. Explain the difference between a standard function and a user-defined function.
3. How is the ROUND function different from the TRUNC function?
4. Explain how the KEYPRESSED function works.
5. Write a function call that would be valid for each of the following function headings.

```
    a. FUNCTION LETTER (CODE1, CODE2, CODE3, : CHAR) : CHAR;
    b. FUNCTION PAYCHECK (HOURS, RATE, TAX : REAL) : REAL;
    c. FUNCTION SIZE (OUNCES : REAL) : INTEGER;
```

6. What is an enumerated data type?
7. After execution of the following program, what values will variables A, B, C, D, E, F, and G have?

```
PROGRAM RESULT;

TYPE
    FLAVOR = (GRAPE, ORANGE, STRAWBERRY);

VAR
    I, A, C, D, E, F : INTEGER;
    LET1, B : CHAR;
    X : REAL;
    POP, G : FLAVOR;
```

```
BEGIN    { RESULT }

    I := 5;
    LET1 := SUCC ('J');
    X := -173.55;
    POP := GRAPE;
    A := SUCC (SUCC (I + 1));
    B := PRED (LET1);
    C := ABS (SQR (I));
    D := ABS (TRUNC (X));
    E := ABS (ROUND (X));
    F := ORD (POP);
    G := SUCC (POP );

END.  { RESULT }
```

8. Explain how the functions LENGTH, POS, COPY, and CONCAT work.

9. Use a TYPE definition to define a subrange of the characters J through O. Then declare a variable to be of this type. List all the values included in this subrange.

■■■■■■ PROGRAMMING PROBLEMS

Level 1

1. Write a program that will perform the following calculations:
   a. Read two real numbers entered at the keyboard.
   b. Add the numbers together.
   c. Find the absolute value of this sum.
   d. Find the square root of this result.
   e. Round off the result to two decimal places.
   f. Display this result on the monitor.

2. Refer to the program that calculates the hypotenuse of a right triangle (Figure 10–2). Rewrite the program so that a user-defined function is used to perform the calculation. The lengths of the two sides should be passed to the function. The function should return the length of the hypotenuse.

Level 2

3. Refer to the program in Figure 10–5. Rewrite this program so that a Fahrenheit temperature is converted to Celsius. Use a function to perform the actual conversion and return the Celsius temperature.

4. Write a program to read a student's name and then a number representing the class of the student:

   1: Freshman
   2: Sophomore
   3: Junior
   4: Senior

   Define a user-defined data type called CLASS that looks like this:

   ```
   TYPE
        CLASS = (FRESHMAN, SOPHOMORE, JUNIOR, SENIOR);
   ```

   A CASE statement can be used to assign the appropriate class to its corresponding number. Then use this user-defined data type to

   a. Determine if the student is an underclassman or an upperclassman.
   b. Determine the year the student will graduate. The output should be similar to this:

   ```
   SARAH WILLIAMS IS AN UPPERCLASSMAN
   AND WILL GRADUATE IN 1990.
   ```

5. Write a function that will have a letter passed to it. If the letter is uppercase, the function should return the corresponding lowercase letter. If the letter is lowercase, the function should return the corresponding uppercase letter. If the character is not a letter of the alphabet, a value of zero should be returned in the function.

Level 3

6. Write a program that calls a function to determine the distance a car has traveled. Assume that the car starts at rest. The user should be prompted to enter the acceleration and amount of elapsed time. A function should be called to calculate the distance based on the following formula:

   $$\text{Distance} = \tfrac{1}{2}\text{acceleration} \times \text{time}^2$$

   A second function should then be called to calculate the velocity:

   $$\text{Velocity} = \text{acceleration} \times \text{time}$$

   The main program should then display both of these values with appropriate labels.

7. The constant pi can be approximated by the following formula:

   $$\frac{\text{pi}^2}{6} = 1 + \frac{1}{2^2} + \frac{1}{3^2} + \frac{1}{4^2} + \frac{1}{5^2} \cdots$$

   Write a function that will perform this calculation for 200 values and print the resulting value of pi.

CHAPTER 11

Arrays

OBJECTIVES

After studying this chapter, you should be able to:

- Explain the purpose of using arrays.
- Declare and use one-dimensional arrays.
- Explain how array subscripts are used to access array elements.
- Describe a two-dimensional array.
- Declare and use two-dimensional arrays in programs.
- Explain how the bubble sort works.
- Write programs to sort arrays using the bubble sort.

OUTLINE

INTRODUCTION

In the programming problems written so far in this textbook, values have been read to a variable one at a time, and any processing has been done before another value is read to that variable. If a number is read to the variable SCORE:

```
READLN (SCORE);
```

and then another number is read to SCORE:

```
READLN (SCORE);
```

the first value is lost. It is impossible to go back and do any processing with this first value. The second value has replaced the first. To avoid this problem, a variable could be declared for each of the scores:

```
VAR
   SCORE1, SCORE2 : REAL;

BEGIN
   READLN (SCORE1);
   READLN (SCORE2);
```

This way SCORE1 and SCORE2 can be referred to anywhere in the program. But suppose it were necessary to read and process 50 scores. It would be very time-consuming to declare 50 variables. You would need 50 READ statements to read them all.

A much easier way of doing this is to use an **array.** An array is an ordered set of related data items. This chapter will explain how to declare arrays and use them in programs. It will also discuss how to arrange the values in an array in a specific order, such as alphabetizing a list of names.

▬▬ DECLARING ARRAYS

An array may be thought of as a table of values, all of the same data type. Arrays may be declared in two ways. First, arrays may be defined under the TYPE definitions. Here is an example of an array TYPE definition:

```
TYPE
    CORRECT = ARRAY[1..10] OF REAL;
```

Then one or more variables may be declared of this type under the variable declarations:

```
VAR
    SCORE : CORRECT;
```

The second method of declaring an array is to declare it under the variable declarations with no TYPE definition:

```
VAR
    SCORE : ARRAY[1..10] OF REAL;
```

The first method will be used in this book. With this method, declaring as many variables of the same array type as are needed is simple. For example, there could be a number of variables of type CORRECT:

```
VAR
    SCORE    : CORRECT;
    HI_SCORE : CORRECT;
    LO_SCORE : CORRECT;
```

This method also allows arrays to be passed as parameters to subprograms.

Format For **Array Declaration: Method 1**

TYPE
    Array_type = ARRAY[first_sub..last_sub] OF element_type;

VAR
    Array_name : Array_type

> Format For **Array Declaration: Method 2**
>
> VAR
>   Array_name : ARRAY[first_sub..last_sub] OF element_type;

The declaration for array SCORE sets up an array containing up to 10 **elements**. An array element is an individual value stored in an array. In the array SCORE, each element will be of type REAL. Figure 11–1 shows how SCORE could be represented in storage. There are 10 storage locations, each of which can be assigned a real number. Arrays may be of any data type, including user-defined data types.

■■■■ ARRAY SUBSCRIPTS

Subscripts are used to refer to a particular array element. In an array definition, the largest and smallest subscripts are stated. The array SCORE may have up to 10 elements. The following expression could be used to reference the third element of SCORE:

`SCORE[3]`

The array name is followed by the position of the element, which is placed in brackets. Any subscript from 1 through 10 could be used to access the elements in SCORE. Subscripts may be of the data types CHAR, BOOLEAN, user-defined, or a subrange of any ordinal data type. The subscripts of array SCORE are a subrange of type INTEGER (that is, the integers 1 through 10). Below is an example of an array of integers:

```
TYPE
    LETTER_ARRAY = ARRAY[CHAR] OF INTEGER;

VAR
    LETTERS : LETTER_ARRAY;
```

SCORE[1]	SCORE[2]	SCORE[3]	SCORE[4]	SCORE[5]	SCORE[6]	SCORE[7]	SCORE[8]	SCORE[9]	SCORE[10]

FIGURE 11–1 TABLE REPRESENTING ARRAY SCORE

Each element of LETTERS would be an integer. The subscript could be any character. The following statements would assign values to elements in this array:

```
LETTERS['x'] := 101;
LETTERS['$'] := 280;
LETTERS['P'] := 92;
```

Notice that the characters must be in quotation marks. Examine the following declarations:

```
TYPE
    NUM_STUDENTS = 1..14;
    GRADE_RANGE = 'A'..'F';
    CLASS_ARRAY = ARRAY[NUM_STUDENTS] OF GRADE_RANGE;

VAR
    CLASS : CLASS_ARRAY;
```

Each element in array CLASS contains one of the letters from A through F. There are 14 elements, each representing the grade of one student. In this example, both the subscript type and the element type are subranges. NUM_STUDENTS is a subrange of integers (1 through 14), and GRADE_RANGE is a subrange of characters (A through F). This array could also be declared as shown below:

```
TYPE
    CLASS_ARRAY = ARRAY[1..14] OF 'A'..'F';

VAR
    CLASS : CLASS_ARRAY;
```

However, defining the subranges separately can make the logic of the program easier to follow. These subranges are also often useful for other purposes in the program.

The compiler will not allow you to define an array this way:

```
TYPE
    CORRECT = ARRAY[INTEGER] OF REAL;
```

The number of possible integers is too large. The compiler will not allow you to set aside this amount of storage space for an array. Therefore, when you wish to use integer subscripts, use a subrange of integer values. The integer subrange does not have to start with one. The following will declare an array that can hold up to 10 elements of type REAL:

```
TYPE
    REAL_ARRAY = ARRAY[15..24] OF REAL;

VAR
    REAL_NUMBER : REAL_ARRAY;
```

The first element can be accessed by the expression REAL_-NUMBERS[15] and the last by the expression REAL_NUMBERS[24].

Array subscripts may be any valid expression evaluating as the data type of the subscript. The following examples use arithmetic expressions.

```
SCORE[1+6] := 133.18;
SCORE[3*3] := 0.98;
SCORE[8-2] := 77.50;
```

Given the following declarations,

```
TYPE
    QUANTITY = ARRAY['A'..'K'] OF INTEGER;

VAR
    NUM_ITEMS : QUANTITY;
```

these assignment statements are valid:

```
NUM_ITEMS['C'] := 108 - 10;

NUM_ITEMS[PRED('J')] := 1108;

NUM_ITEMS['E'] := 240 * 3;

NUM_ITEMS[SUCC('A')] := 15 + 4 + 23;
```

After these statements are executed, array NUM_ITEMS will appear as shown in Figure 11–2.

The elements of an array can be of type STRING. The following array will hold the names of the members of the drama club:

```
TYPE
    CLUB_SIZE    = 1..40;
    CLUB_MEMBERS = ARRAY[CLUB_SIZE] OF STRING;

VAR
    MEMBERS : CLUB_MEMBERS;
```

The subscripts are of data type CLUB_SIZE, which is a subrange of integers. This array may contain a maximum of 40 names.

FIGURE 11–2 ARRAY NUM_ITEMS PARTIALLY FILLED WITH VALUES

1. What is an array?
2. Use the following declarations to answer parts a–d.

```
TYPE
    CLASS_SIZE = ARRAY['G'..'P'] OF INTEGER;

VAR
    NUM_STUDENTS = CLASS_SIZE;
```

   a. What is the name of the array declared above?
   b. Of what data type are the elements of this array?
   c. Of what data type are the subscripts of this array?
   d. How many elements does this array have?

3. Fill in the table below using the following program segment:

```
PROGRAM COST;

TYPE
    ALL = ARRAY[1..5] OF REAL;

VAR
    TOTAL : ALL;

BEGIN
    TOTAL[3]   := 31.89;
    TOTAL[5-4] := 21.85;
    TOTAL[4]   := 45/66;
    TOTAL[2*1] := 14.67;
```


TOTAL[1]   TOTAL[2]   TOTAL[3]   TOTAL[4]   TOTAL[5]

READING AND WRITING ARRAYS

An easy way to read values to an array is by using a FOR loop:

```
FOR COUNT := 1 TO 10 DO
    READ (SCORE[COUNT]);
```

This statement reads 10 numbers entered at the keyboard. Each number is assigned to an element of SCORE. The first number is assigned to SCORE[1], the tenth number to SCORE[10]. The array does not have to be filled.

```
FOR COUNT := 1 TO 8 DO
    READ (SCORE[COUNT]);
```

reads values to array elements 1 through 8. The contents of SCORE[9] and SCORE[10] are unknown. When using FOR loops to read values to arrays, the loop control variable must be of the same data type as the array subscripts. In this example, the subscripts are integer values. Therefore, COUNT must be declared as type INTEGER or a subrange of type INTEGER.

Below is an example of an array whose subscripts are an enumerated type:

```
TYPE
    ANIMAL_TYPE = (PONY, ZEBRA, HORSE, DONKEY, MULE);
    ANIMAL_ARRAY = ARRAY[ANIMAL_TYPE] OF INTEGER;

VAR
    ANIMALS : ANIMAL_ARRAY;
    COUNT   : ANIMAL_TYPE;
```

Each array element will contain an integer value indicating the number of that type of animal in the city zoo. The following program segment reads values to this array:

```
FOR COUNT := PONY TO MULE DO
    READLN (ANIMALS[COUNT]);
```

The loop control variable is of type ANIMAL_TYPE. The first number read will be placed in ANIMALS[PONY], the second in ANIMALS-[ZEBRA], and so forth through ANIMALS[MULE].

Arrays can be written in the same way that they are read. The following program segment reads the contents of array SCORE. (Assume COUNT is of type INTEGER.)

```
FOR COUNT := 1 TO 10 DO
    WRITE (SCORE[COUNT]:10);
```

Notice that each integer will be output in a field 10 characters long. Remember that enumerated data types cannot be directly written. Therefore, the contents of array ANIMALS could not be displayed using this method.

A PROGRAM USING ONE-DIMENSIONAL ARRAYS

The marching band needs a program to keep track of its magazine sales. The program should allow the user to enter each band member's name and sales amount. At the end of the program, this information should be displayed in table form. The following summary information should be output below the table: total sales, average sales per student, and the name of the student with the most sales along with the amount that student sold.

This program must perform two basic tasks: reading the data and displaying the sales results. The total sales and the high salesperson can be determined while the data is being read. Two arrays will be needed to hold the data: one for the students' names and the other for the amount each has sold.

The completed program is in Figure 11–3. Notice that it has two procedures, READ_DATA and DISPLAY_RESULTS. The program also uses two arrays: one with the students' names (NAME) and one with the amount of sales (SALES) that each student makes. These two arrays are "parallel"; array element AMOUNT[3] contains the sales of the student whose name is in NAME[3]. While data is being read to the arrays, the total of all sales (TOTAL_SALES) is being tabulated. The program is also keeping track of the student with the current high sales. The array position of this student is kept in the variable HIGH.

After the data is read to the arrays, the average sales amount is determined by dividing total sales by the number of students:

```
AVERAGE_SALES := TOTAL_SALES / NUM;
```

Procedure DISPLAY_RESULTS is called to output the table and the summary information.

---

1. Why are FOR loops useful in reading data to arrays?
2. Write a FOR loop that will read data entered at the keyboard to the array declared below. Write another FOR loop that will display the data on the monitor.

   ```
   TYPE
       SIZE = ARRAY['B'..'F'] OF CHAR;

   VAR
       CODE : SIZE;
   ```

3. Find two errors in the following program segment:

LEARNING CHECK 11–2

```
PROGRAM READ_VALUES;

TYPE
    NUM = 1..15;
    VALUE_TYPE = ARRAY['D'..'G'] OF NUM;

VAR
    VALUES : VALUE_TYPE;
    POSITION : NUM;

BEGIN    { READ_VALUES }

    FOR POSITION := 1 TO 15 DO
        READ (VALUE_TYPE[POSITION]);
```

▬▬ TWO-DIMENSIONAL ARRAYS

So far, the arrays discussed in this chapter have been one-dimensional arrays. One-dimensional arrays can be represented by a single row of values:

1	2	3	4	5	6

This one-dimensional array can contain up to six values.

An array may have more than one dimension, however. A two-dimensional array may be visualized as a table with both rows and columns. Here is an array with five rows and four columns:

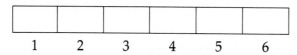

The subscripts in this array are subranges of data type CHAR and data

```
PROGRAM MAGAZINES;

{ THIS PROGRAM READS MAGAZINE SALES FOR A HIGH SCHOOL BAND.  IT
  DETERMINES WHICH STUDENT MADE THE MOST MONEY IN SALES, THE
  AVERAGE AMOUNT OF SALES BY ALL STUDENTS, AND THE TOTAL AMOUNT
  OF SALES.  A TABLE IS DISPLAYED GIVING EACH STUDENT'S NAME AND
  SALES.  SUMMARY INFORMATION IS GIVEN AT THE END OF THE TABLE. }

CONST
   NUM = 12;

TYPE
   STUDENT = ARRAY[1..NUM] OF STRING;
   AMOUNT  = ARRAY[1..NUM] OF REAL;

VAR
   NAME          : STUDENT;
   SALES         : AMOUNT;
   TOTAL_SALES   : REAL;
   AVERAGE_SALES : REAL;
   HIGH          : INTEGER;

{************************************************************************}

PROCEDURE READ_DATA (VAR NAME : STUDENT; VAR SALES : AMOUNT;
                     VAR TOTAL_SALES : REAL; VAR HIGH : INTEGER);

   { THIS PROCEDURE READS EACH STUDENT'S NAME AND SALES, DETERMINES
     STUDENT WITH HIGHEST SALES AND TOTAL SALES BY ALL STUDENTS. }

VAR
   HIGHEST_SALES : REAL;
   COUNT         : INTEGER;

BEGIN   { READ_DATA }

   HIGHEST_SALES := 0.0;
   TOTAL_SALES   := 0.0;

   FOR COUNT := 1 TO NUM DO
   BEGIN
      WRITE ('ENTER NAME OF THE STUDENT: ');
      READLN (NAME[COUNT]);
      WRITE ('ENTER AMOUNT SOLD BY THE STUDENT IN DOLLARS: ');
      READLN (SALES[COUNT]);
      TOTAL_SALES := TOTAL_SALES + SALES[COUNT];

      { SEE IF CURRENT STUDENT'S SALES ARE GREATER THAN CURRENT
        HIGH STUDENT.  IF THEY ARE, SAVE THE ARRAY SUBSCRIPT OF
        THIS STUDENT IN HIGH. }
```

FIGURE 11-3 PROGRAM MAGAZINES

(Figure continued on next page)

```
      IF SALES[COUNT] > HIGHEST_SALES
      THEN
      BEGIN
         HIGHEST_SALES := SALES[COUNT];
         HIGH := COUNT;
      END;    { THEN }
END;    { FOR }

END;    { READ_DATA }


{*********************************************************************}

PROCEDURE DISPLAY_RESULTS (NAME : STUDENT; SALES : AMOUNT;
                          HIGH : INTEGER);

{ THIS PROCEDURE DISPLAYS EACH STUDENT'S SALES IN TABLE FORM.
  THE TOTAL SALES AND THE PERSON WITH THE HIGHEST SALES ARE OUTPUT
  AT THE BOTTOM OF THE TABLE. }

VAR
   COUNT : INTEGER;

BEGIN    { DISPLAY_RESULTS }

   WRITELN;
   WRITELN ('SALES REPORT');
   WRITELN ('_____');
   WRITELN;
   FOR COUNT := 1 TO NUM DO
      WRITELN (NAME[COUNT]:25, SALES[COUNT]:8:2);
   WRITELN ('_____');
   WRITELN;
   WRITELN ('THE TOTAL SALES WERE: $', TOTAL_SALES:7:2);
   WRITELN ('THE AVERAGE SALES PER STUDENT WERE: $', AVERAGE_SALES:7:2);
   WRITELN ('THE HIGHEST SALES WERE MADE BY: ', NAME[HIGH]);
   WRITELN ('THE HIGHEST AMOUNT SOLD WAS: $', SALES[HIGH]:7:2);

END;    { DISPLAY_RESULTS }

{*********************************************************************}

BEGIN    { MAIN }

   { READ INFORMATION ON EACH STUDENT AND DETERMINE THE STUDENT
     WITH HIGHEST SALES. }

   READ_DATA (NAME, SALES, TOTAL_SALES, HIGH);

   { CALCULATE AVERAGE SALES PER STUDENT. }
   AVERAGE_SALES := TOTAL_SALES / NUM;

   { OUTPUT THE RESULTS. }
   DISPLAY_RESULTS (NAME, SALES, HIGH);

END.    { MAIN }
```

FIGURE 11–3 PROGRAM MAGAZINES (Cont.)

(Figure continued on next page)

```
ENTER NAME OF THE STUDENT: Maurice
ENTER AMOUNT SOLD BY THE STUDENT IN DOLLARS: 19.95
ENTER NAME OF THE STUDENT: Georgia
ENTER AMOUNT SOLD BY THE STUDENT IN DOLLARS: 56.60
ENTER NAME OF THE STUDENT: Patrick
ENTER AMOUNT SOLD BY THE STUDENT IN DOLLARS: 40.00
ENTER NAME OF THE STUDENT: Mary
ENTER AMOUNT SOLD BY THE STUDENT IN DOLLARS: 0.00
ENTER NAME OF THE STUDENT: Bernice
ENTER AMOUNT SOLD BY THE STUDENT IN DOLLARS: 89.90
ENTER NAME OF THE STUDENT: Paul
ENTER AMOUNT SOLD BY THE STUDENT IN DOLLARS: 104.56
ENTER NAME OF THE STUDENT: Matthew
ENTER AMOUNT SOLD BY THE STUDENT IN DOLLARS: 10.75
ENTER NAME OF THE STUDENT: Jonathan
ENTER AMOUNT SOLD BY THE STUDENT IN DOLLARS: 42.25
ENTER NAME OF THE STUDENT: Naomi
ENTER AMOUNT SOLD BY THE STUDENT IN DOLLARS: 35.50
ENTER NAME OF THE STUDENT: Val
ENTER AMOUNT SOLD BY THE STUDENT IN DOLLARS: 18.85
ENTER NAME OF THE STUDENT: Eric
ENTER AMOUNT SOLD BY THE STUDENT IN DOLLARS: 0.00
ENTER NAME OF THE STUDENT: Peter
ENTER AMOUNT SOLD BY THE STUDENT IN DOLLARS: 25.99


SALES REPORT
═══════════════════════════════════

            Maurice   19.95
            Georgia   56.60
            Patrick   40.00
               Mary    0.00
            Bernice   89.90
               Paul  104.56
            Matthew   10.75
           Jonathan   42.25
              Naomi   35.50
                Val   18.85
               Eric    0.00
              Peter   25.99

═══════════════════════════════════

THE TOTAL SALES WERE: $ 444.35
THE AVERAGE SALES PER STUDENT WERE: $  37.03
THE HIGHEST SALES WERE MADE BY: Paul
THE HIGHEST AMOUNT SOLD WAS: $ 104.56
```

FIGURE 11-3 PROGRAM MAGAZINES (Cont.)

type INTEGER. This two-dimensional array could be declared this way:

```
TYPE
    FEET = ARRAY['A'..'E',1..4] OF REAL;

VAR
    SIZE : FEET;
```

The first dimension listed gives the number of rows. The subscripts for the rows will be A through E. The second dimension gives the subscripts for the columns, which can be 1 through 4. This array can contain a maximum of 20 (5 × 4) real numbers. This statement

```
SIZE['B',3] := 10.35;
```

will assign the value 10.35 to the second row, third column of array SIZE. Look at the assignment statements and the table in Figure 11–4. Make certain that you understand how these assignment statements work.

A PROGRAM USING A TWO-DIMENSIONAL ARRAY

Now consider writing a program to create a pricing table for a small store selling only 10 different items. Each item is assigned a number from 1 through 10. The program should allow a price for each item to be entered at the keyboard. Discounts are given for buying items in quantity as follows:

- 1 to 4:   no discount
- 5 to 9:   8.5 percent discount
- 10 to 19:   12.7 percent discount
- 20 or more: 15.0 percent discount

After the price of each item is read to an array, the program should display a table listing prices according to the item and the quantity purchased. Basically, this program has only two tasks:

1. To read the price of each item and calculate the cost depending on quantity purchased.
2. To print the price table.

Figure 11–5 shows the program for creating the price table. A 10 × 4 array named PRICE is used. Each of the 10 rows contains the price of one item. The four columns list that item's price depending on the quantity bought. Procedure READ_PRICES uses a FOR loop to read

```
SIZE[PRED('B'),2] := 12.23;
SIZE['D',1+2] := 10.85;
SIZE[SUCC('D'), 2*2] := 15.25;
SIZE['A',4] := 23.15;
```

Columns

	1	2	3	4
A		12.23		23.15
B				
C				
D			10.85	
E				15.25

Rows

FIGURE 11–4 A TWO-DIMENSIONAL ARRAY

each price and calculate the quantity discounts. The loop control variable is used for the row subscript whereas columns 1–4 represent the four quantities. In procedure DISPLAY_TABLE, nested FOR loops are used to output the price table. The inside FOR loop prints each row of prices. The outside FOR loop prints the correct number of rows.

◼ SORTING AN ARRAY

Sorting means arranging data items in a particular order. An example would be putting a list of names in alphabetical order or putting numbers in order from the smallest to the largest. Many different algorithms have been developed for sorting. The one explained here is the bubble sort. Bubble sorts are simple to write but use more computer time than some other sorting algorithms. For the small amount of data being sorted here, this is not important. But when you are dealing with large amounts of data, the time factor can be critical.

The bubble sort starts at one end of the array and compares each adjacent element exchanging the elements if they are out of order; this is

```
PROGRAM PRICE_TABLE;

{ THIS PROGRAM PRINTS A TABLE GIVING THE PRICE OF AN ITEM DEPENDING
  ON THE QUANTITY BEING BOUGHT.  EACH ITEM IS ASSIGNED A NUMBER,
  1 - 10.   THE PRICE OF A PARTICULAR ITEM IS ENTERED AT THE KEY-
  BOARD.   QUANTITY DISCOUNTS ARE GIVEN AS FOLLOWS:
       1-4            NO DISCOUNT
       5-9            8.5% DISCOUNT
       10-19          12.7% DISCOUNT
       20 OR MORE     15% DISCOUNT  }

CONST
   NUM = 10;

TYPE
   AMOUNT = ARRAY[1..NUM,1..4] OF REAL;

VAR
   PRICE : AMOUNT;

{*********************************************************************}

PROCEDURE READ_PRICES (VAR PRICE : AMOUNT);

{ READS THE COST OF EACH ITEM AND CALCULATES THE VOLUME DISCOUNTS. }

VAR
   I    : INTEGER;
   COST : REAL;

BEGIN   { READ_PRICES }

   FOR I := 1 TO NUM DO
   BEGIN
      WRITE ('TYPE IN REGULAR PRICE OF ITEM NUMBER ', I, ': ');
      READLN (COST);
      PRICE[I,1] := COST;
      PRICE[I,2] := COST - (COST * 0.085);
      PRICE[I,3] := COST - (COST * 0.127);
      PRICE[I,4] := COST - (COST * 0.15);
   END;    { FOR }

END;   { READ_PRICES }

{*********************************************************************}

PROCEDURE DISPLAY_TABLE (PRICE : AMOUNT);

{ DISPLAYS THE TABLE SHOWING PRICE OF EACH ITEM DEPENDING ON QUANTITY
  PURCHASED. }

VAR
   I, J : INTEGER;
```

FIGURE 11-5 PROGRAM PRICE_TABLE

(Figure continued on next page)

```
BEGIN   { DISPLAY_TABLE }

   { DISPLAY TABLE HEADINGS. }
   WRITELN;
   WRITELN ('PRICE TABLE':30);
   WRITELN ('-------------------------------------------------------------------');
   WRITELN;
   WRITELN ('ITEM NUMBER', '1-4':16, '5-9':10, '10-19':12, '20 OR MORE':14);
   WRITELN ('-------------------------------------------------------------------');
   WRITELN;

   { DISPLAY THE TABLE. }
   FOR I := 1 TO NUM DO
   BEGIN
      WRITE (I:7,' ':11);
      FOR J := 1 TO 4 DO
         WRITE (PRICE[I,J]:10:2);
      WRITELN;
   END;    { FOR }

END;   { DISPLAY_TABLE }
{***********************************************************************}

BEGIN   { MAIN }

   READ_PRICES (PRICE);
   DISPLAY_TABLE (PRICE);

END.    { MAIN }
```

```
TYPE IN REGULAR PRICE OF ITEM NUMBER 1: 18.75
TYPE IN REGULAR PRICE OF ITEM NUMBER 2: 4.50
TYPE IN REGULAR PRICE OF ITEM NUMBER 3: 76.00
TYPE IN REGULAR PRICE OF ITEM NUMBER 4: 19.99
TYPE IN REGULAR PRICE OF ITEM NUMBER 5: 63.25
TYPE IN REGULAR PRICE OF ITEM NUMBER 6: 25.45
TYPE IN REGULAR PRICE OF ITEM NUMBER 7: 183.00
TYPE IN REGULAR PRICE OF ITEM NUMBER 8: 104.59
TYPE IN REGULAR PRICE OF ITEM NUMBER 9: 23.45
TYPE IN REGULAR PRICE OF ITEM NUMBER 10: 89.99
```

```
                        PRICE TABLE
-------------------------------------------------------------------

ITEM NUMBER              1-4       5-9      10-19    20 OR MORE
-------------------------------------------------------------------

        1              18.75     17.16     16.37      15.94
        2               4.50      4.12      3.93       3.83
        3              76.00     69.54     66.35      64.60
        4              19.99     18.29     17.45      16.99
        5              63.25     57.87     55.22      53.76
        6              25.45     23.29     22.22      21.63
        7             183.00    167.45    159.76     155.55
        8             104.59     95.70     91.31      88.90
        9              23.45     21.46     20.47      19.93
       10              89.99     82.34     78.56      76.49
```

FIGURE 11-5 PROGRAM PRICE_TABLE (Cont.)

referred to as a *pass*. The bubble sort continues to make passes through the array until a pass is made in which no changes take place. This signals that the array is sorted.

Let's determine how the bubble sort can be used to sort five integers. The starting array contains five elements:

| 32 | 12 | 44 | 0 | 18 |

The first two array elements are compared and exchanged because they are out of order:

| 12 | 32 | 44 | 0 | 18 |

Next, the second and third elements are compared, but are not exchanged because 32 is less than 44.

| 12 | 32 | 44 | 0 | 18 |

Elements 3 and 4 are compared and exchanged.

| 12 | 32 | 0 | 44 | 18 |

Finally, the fourth and fifth elements are compared and exchanged.

| 12 | 32 | 0 | 18 | 44 |

One pass is now completed. The last array element is now in its correct place. This is why it is shaded.

Now the bubble sort will go back to the beginning of the array. During this pass through the array, only elements 1 through 4 will be compared because 5 is already in its correct place. At the end of the second pass through the array, the elements will be in this order:

| 12 | 0 | 18 | 32 | 44 |

Notice that the last two elements are now in their correct positions. After the third pass through the array, the elements will look like this:

0	12	18	32	44

On the last pass through, the first two elements will be compared, and no exchange will be made because they are already in order:

0	12	18	32	44

The sorting is completed. This may seem like a very time-consuming way of sorting a list, but remember that the computer is able to do each of these steps very quickly.

Figure 11–6 shows a program that sorts an array of cities. First, procedure READ_CITIES is called to fill the array. Procedure SORT_LIST performs the actual sorting process. A REPEAT loop is executed until all the names are in order. Notice the condition at the end of the loop:

```
UNTIL SWITCH = FALSE;
```

The BOOLEAN variable SWITCH determines whether the loop will be executed. If any names are exchanged during the loop's repetition, SWITCH is set to TRUE, and the loop is repeated. If no exchanges are made, SWITCH will remain FALSE, and the loop will stop executing. When SWITCH is FALSE, the sorting process is completed. Inside the REPEAT loop is a FOR loop. This loop goes through the array, exchanging adjacent array elements that are out of order. After each execution of the FOR loop, the value of NUMPASS is decremented by one:

```
NUMPASS := NUMPASS - 1;
```

Each time the FOR loop is executed, one more element at the end of the array is in its correct position. Therefore, that element need not be examined again, and NUMPASS can be decreased by one.

---

1. In a two-dimensional array, the first subscript refers to the _____, and the second subscript refers to the _____.
2. What is the maximum number of elements each of the following array types may contain?

   a. POSITION = ARRAY['D'..'N'] OF INTEGER;
   b. CLASS = ARRAY[1..6,5..10] OF CHAR;
   c. TAX = ARRAY['A'..'E',1..9] OF REAL;
   d. MINUTES = ARRAY[1..5,1..8] OF REAL;

3. Look at program SORT_CITY in Figure 11–6. Can you change it so the cities will be arranged in reverse alphabetical order?

LEARNING CHECK 11–3

```
PROGRAM SORT_CITY;

{ THIS PROGRAM SORTS A LIST OF 20 CITIES IN ALPHABETICAL ORDER. }

CONST
   NUM = 20;

TYPE
  CITIES = ARRAY[1..20] OF STRING;

VAR
   CITY : CITIES;

{*****************************************************************}

PROCEDURE READ_CITIES (VAR CITY : CITIES);

{ READS THE LIST OF CITIES TO BE SORTED. }

VAR
   POSITION : INTEGER;

BEGIN    { READ_CITIES }

   WRITELN ('ENTER NAMES OF ', NUM, ' CITIES, EACH ON A SEPARATE LINE.');
   FOR POSITION := 1 TO NUM DO
      READLN (CITY[POSITION]);

END;    { READ_CITIES }

{*****************************************************************}

PROCEDURE SORT_LIST (VAR CITY : CITIES);

{ USES A BUBBLE SORT TO SORT THE NAMES ALPHABETICALLY. }

VAR
   POSITION, NUMPASS : INTEGER;
   TEMP              : STRING[15];
   SWITCH            : BOOLEAN;

BEGIN    { SORT_LIST }

   NUMPASS := NUM - 1;

   { SORT UNTIL NO MORE CHANGES NEED TO BE MADE. }
   REPEAT
      SWITCH := FALSE;
      FOR POSITION := 1 TO NUMPASS DO
         IF CITY[POSITION] > CITY[POSITION+1]
```

FIGURE 11-6 PROGRAM SORT_CITY

(Figure continued on next page)

```
                THEN
                BEGIN
                    TEMP := CITY[POSITION];
                    CITY[POSITION] := CITY[POSITION+1];
                    CITY[POSITION+1] := TEMP;
                    SWITCH := TRUE;
                END;    { THEN }

                { DECREMENT THE NUMBER OF PASSES MADE BY 1. }
                NUMPASS := NUMPASS - 1
            UNTIL SWITCH = FALSE;

END;    { SORT_LIST }

{************************************************************}

PROCEDURE DISPLAY_LIST (CITY : CITIES);

{ OUTPUTS THE LIST OF SORTED NAMES. }

VAR
    POSITION : INTEGER;

BEGIN    { DISPLAY_LIST }

    WRITELN;
    WRITELN ('SORTED LIST OF CITIES:':30);
    WRITELN ('---------------------':30);

    FOR POSITION := 1 TO NUM DO
        WRITELN (CITY[POSITION]:25);

END;    { DISPLAY_LIST }

{************************************************************}

BEGIN    { MAIN }

    READ_CITIES (CITY);
    SORT_LIST (CITY);
    DISPLAY_LIST (CITY);

END.    { MAIN }
```

FIGURE 11–6 PROGRAM SORT_CITY (Cont.)

(Figure continued on next page)

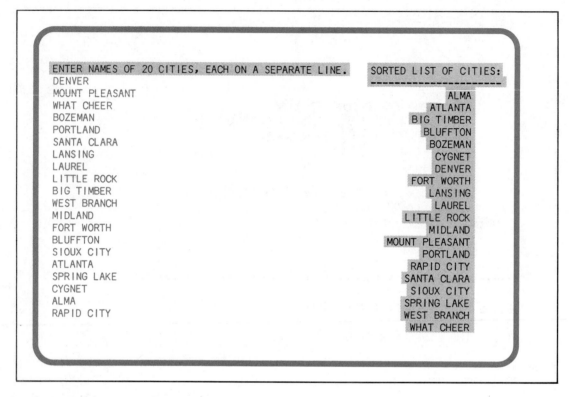

FIGURE 11-6 PROGRAM SORT_CITY (Cont.)

▬ SUMMARY POINTS

- Arrays allow for a number of related data items, all of the same data type, to be stored under a single variable name. Individual array elements can be referred to by using the array name with a subscript.
- FOR loops can be used to easily read values to an array and display the contents of an array.
- A one-dimensional array can be viewed as a row of values, whereas a two-dimensional array can be pictured as a table with both rows and columns. Two-dimensional arrays have two subscripts. The first refers to the rows and the second to the columns.
- One way to put data in an array in order is to use a bubble sort. The bubble sort compares adjacent elements of the array and exchanges them if they are out of order. Repeated passes through the array are made until no changes occur.

◼◼◼ VOCABULARY LIST

Array	Sorting
Elements	Subscripts

◼◼◼ CHAPTER TEST

Vocabulary

Match a term from the numbered column with the description from the lettered column that best fits the term.

1. Sort	a. An individual value in an array.
2. Array	b. To arrange a list of values in a particular order.
3. Element	c. An ordered set of related data items, all of the same data type.
4. Subscript	d. A value enclosed in brackets, used to refer to a particular array element.

Questions

1. Why are arrays so useful?
2. Write type definitions and variable declarations for the arrays in parts a–d.

    a. An array called PERCENT of type REAL that may contain up to 15 values.
    b. An array called WEEKDAYS of data type STRING that may contain up to seven values.
    c. An array called LETTERS of data type CHAR that may contain up to three values.
    d. A BOOLEAN array called FOUND, the subscripts of which may be from 'A' through 'Z.'

3. Use the following program segment to fill in the table below:

```
PROGRAM ASSIGN;

TYPE
   EMPLOYEE = ARRAY[1..5,1..4] OF STRING;

VAR
   I, J : INTEGER;
   WORKER : EMPLOYEE;
```

```
BEGIN    { ASSIGN }

    I := 2;
    J := 3;
    WORKER[I,J]    := 'SAMPSON';
    WORKER[I*2,4]  := 'MOSES';
    WORKER[1,1+1]  := 'AARON';
    WORKER[1+3,J]  := 'MICAH';
    WORKER[4,J-1]  := 'JONATHAN';
    WORKER[3*1,1]  := 'SOLOMON';

END.    { ASSIGN }
```

Columns

Rows	1	2	3	4
1				
2				
3				
4				
5				

4. What is the difference between a two-dimensional array and a one-dimensional array?

5. Explain how nested FOR loops can be used to display the contents of a two-dimensional array.

6. Use the following TYPE and VAR declarations to write the code for parts a–d.

```
TYPE
    INCHES = ARRAY[1..12,1..10] OF REAL;

VAR
    HEIGHT : INCHES;
```

   a. Assign −172.04 to HEIGHT[6,4].
   b. Assign 14.82 to the second column, fifth row of array HEIGHT.
   c. Assign 189.90 to the third row, tenth column of array HEIGHT.
   d. Assign the value of HEIGHT[6,4] to HEIGHT[7,10].

7. Explain how the bubble sort works.

8. Explain the purpose of the BOOLEAN variable SWITCH in the bubble sort in Figure 11–6.

9. The following program contains several logic errors. Type the pro-

gram into your computer and run it once. Then use program tracing
and hand-simulation techniques to find and correct the logic errors.

```
PROGRAM VACATION;

{ THIS PROGRAM READS THE NAMES OF CITIES OR VACATION SPOTS AND
  THE DISTANCES BETWEEN EACH CITY.  A LIST OF THE VACATION PLAN
  IS PRINTED WITH NAME, DISTANCE, AND TRAVEL TIME LISTED.  }

VAR
    CITIES    : ARRAY[1..4] OF STRING;     { ARRAY OF VACATION SPOTS }
    CITY      : STRING;                    { NAME OF VACATION SPOT }
    HOUR      : REAL;                      { TRAVEL TIME }
    HOURS     : ARRAY[1..4] OF REAL;       { ARRAY OF TRAVEL TIMES }
    I         : INTEGER;                   { LOOP AND ARRAY COUNTERS }
    MILES     : REAL;                      { NUMBER OF MILES TRAVELED }
    TMILES    : ARRAY[1..4] OF REAL;       { LOG OF MILES TRAVELED }

BEGIN   { VACATION }

    WRITELN ('THIS PROGRAM WILL HELP YOU PLAN A TRIP TO 4 CITIES OR');
    WRITELN ('VACATION SPOTS.  THINK OF 4 PLACES YOU WOULD LIKE');
    WRITELN ('TO VISIT, THE ORDER IN WHICH YOU WANT TO VISIT THEM,');
    WRITELN ('AND THE DISTANCE BETWEEN EACH PLACE.');
    WRITELN;

    { CITIES AND DISTANCES READ. }
    FOR I := 1 TO 4 DO
    BEGIN
       WRITE ('CITY OR PLACE ', I, ' IS: ');
       READLN (CITY);
       CITIES[I] := CITY;

       IF I = 1                     { FIRST CITY READ }
       THEN
       BEGIN
          WRITE ('DISTANCE TO ', CITIES[I], ' :');
          READLN (MILES);
          TMILES[I] := MILES    { DISTANCE CALCULATED }
       END    { THEN }
       ELSE
       BEGIN
          WRITE ('DISTANCE TO ', CITIES[1], ' FROM ', CITIES[I],
             ': ');
          READLN (MILES);
          TMILES[I] := MILES    { DISTANCE CALCULATED }
       END;    { ELSE }

       HOURS[I] := MILES * 55;     { TRAVEL TIME CALCULATED }
    END;    { FOR }
```

```
{ VACATION PLAN PRINTED -- PLACE, DISTANCE BETWEEN
  SPOTS, AND TIME. }
WRITELN;
WRITELN ('YOUR VACATION PLAN':32);
WRITELN ('PLACE':12, 'DISTANCE':18, 'TRAVEL TIME':18);
WRITELN;

FOR I := 1 TO 4 DO
   WRITELN (CITIES[I]:14, TMILES[I]:15:2, HOURS[I]:18:2);

END.   { VACATION }
```

PROGRAMMING PROBLEMS

Level 1

1. Read 15 numbers to array A and 15 numbers to array B. Compute the product of each pair of numbers and place the results in array PRODUCT. Print a table similar to the one below at the end of your program.

A	B	PRODUCT
5	6	30
2	8	16
.	.	.
.	.	.
.	.	.

2. Write a program to alphabetize the last names of the students in your class. Write it so that the names will be alphabetized in ascending order (A, B, C . . .). Then change it so that the names will be alphabetized in descending order (Z, Y, X . . .).

Level 2

3. Write a program that will read your last name and display it backwards as in the following example:

        INPUT   OUTPUT
        SCHWARTZ   ZTRAWHCS

4. Ask 50 students the name of their favorite NFL team. Write a program that reads the name of each team and the number of students voting for that team. Sort the teams so that the most popular is first

and the least popular is last. Display this list on the monitor screen. Here is an example of possible output:

NAME	NUMBER OF VOTES
STEELERS	12
COWBOYS	10
RAMS	7
.	.
.	.
.	.

5. Below is a list of schools and the number of wins each school had in four different sports. Write a program to read the name of the school and its wins in each of the four sports. Use a two-dimensional array. Put the results in a table like the one shown here:

SPORT

	BASE-BALL	BASKET-BALL	FOOT-BALL	GOLF
LAKEVIEW	2	10	5	4
KIRKLAND	9	3	4	7
CAMBRIDGE	14	7	5	3
JEFFERSON	7	9	8	5

Level 3

6. Write a program that reads a string of up to 10 characters representing a Roman numeral. Print the Roman numeral and the equivalent base 10 number. Use the following table to help in making the conversion:

M = 1000
D = 500
C = 100
L = 50
X = 10
V = 5
I = 1

Use a user-defined data type for the Roman numerals. Remember that if a smaller Roman numeral precedes a larger one, the smaller one is subtracted from the larger one (for example, IV is 4).

7. One method of converting a base 10 number to base 2 is by using

the division remainder method. In the following example, the base 10 number 14 is converted:

Step a	Step b	Step c	Step d

$$
\begin{array}{r} 7 \\ 2\overline{)\,14} \\ 14 \\ \hline \end{array}
\qquad
\begin{array}{r} 3 \\ 2\overline{)\,7} \\ 6 \\ \hline \end{array}
\qquad
\begin{array}{r} 1 \\ 2\overline{)\,3} \\ 2 \\ \hline \end{array}
\qquad
\begin{array}{r} 0 \\ 2\overline{)\,1} \\ 0 \\ \hline \end{array}
$$

remainder   0   remainder   1   remainder   1   remainder   1

The remainders of the repeated division process are 0111. In order to obtain the correct base 2 value, the digits must be reversed to 1110. Write a program that will allow the user to enter a positive base 10 integer. Use the MOD and DIV operators to divide the number continually. Each of the remainders should be placed in a successive element of an array. The array should then be output in reverse order to obtain the base 2 number.

CHAPTER 12

Records and Sets

OBJECTIVES

After studying this chapter, you should be able to:

- Explain what is meant by a structured data type.
- Declare and use records in programs.
- Refer to the individual fields of a record.
- Use the WITH statement in working with records.
- Copy entire records.
- Search an array of records for a particular record.
- Use the following set operators: $+$, $*$, $-$.
- Use the following set relational operators: $=$, $>=$, $<=$, $<>$.

OUTLINE

▬▬▬ INTRODUCTION

Chapter 11 discussed one **structured data type**: the array. In this chapter, two more structured data types will be covered: **records** and **sets**. These are called structured data types because they can be used to store many individual values. These individual values can then be referred to as a single unit. For example, a single variable name can be used to refer to an entire array. Individual array elements, however, can be accessed by using a subscript with the array name. The format of each structured data type has strict rules, and each has situations in which it is useful.

The values in an array must all be of the same data type. An array cannot be declared having some elements of data type STRING and others of data type INTEGER. There are many situations in which it might be desirable to keep data of different types in a single unit. For example, think of the data a school might have on a student:

- Name
- Birth date
- Sex
- Grade
- Grade point average

266   A record would be ideal for storing this information. A record is a group

of related data items, not necessarily of the same data type, gathered together as a single unit.

Sets will also be covered in this chapter. A set consists of a collection of items classed together. All of the items in a set must be of the same type.

RECORDS

Declaring Records

A student record containing the information previously listed could be defined as follows:

```
TYPE
    STUDENT_RECORD = RECORD
                        NAME        : STRING;
                        BIRTH_DATE  : STRING;
                        SEX         : CHAR;
                        GRADE       : INTEGER;
                        GPA         : REAL;
                    END;    { STUDENT_RECORD }
```

Notice that the first line of the record

```
STUDENT_RECORD = RECORD
```

is not followed by a semicolon. Also, there is no BEGIN even though there is an END. This record type is named STUDENT_RECORD. Each data item that is a part of the record is called a **field**. STUDENT_RECORD has five fields: NAME, BIRTH_DATE, SEX, GRADE, and GPA. The fields can be of any data type. To use this record type in a program, one or more variables must be declared as type STUDENT_RECORD:

```
VAR
    STUDENT : STUDENT_RECORD;
```

Figure 12–1 shows how this record could be represented in storage.

FIGURE 12–1 STUDENT RECORD IN STORAGE

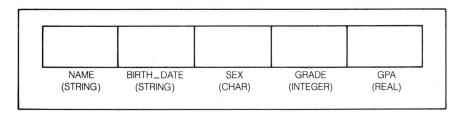

| NAME | BIRTH_DATE | SEX | GRADE | GPA |
| (STRING) | (STRING) | (CHAR) | (INTEGER) | (REAL) |

Format For Record Declaration

TYPE
  Record_type = RECORD
    Field_Name1 : data_type;
    Field_Name2 : data_type;
        •
        •
        •

    Field_Name*n* : data_type;
  END;

VAR
    Record_name : Record_type;

Referring to Individual Fields

There are two ways of referring to a field in a record. The first is to place a period between the name of the record and the field name. The general format for this is

  record_name.field_name

The NAME field of record STUDENT could be assigned a value this way:

```
STUDENT.NAME := 'JONES, VIOLA';
```

Even if there are other records with a NAME field, the compiler knows that this statement refers to the NAME field of STUDENT. The other fields in this record could also be assigned values in the same way:

```
STUDENT.BIRTH_DATE := '08/05/71';
STUDENT.SEX := 'F';
STUDENT.GRADE := 12;
STUDENT.GPA := 3.2;
```

Figure 12–2 demonstrates how this record could now be represented in storage. A second way of referring to the fields of a record is to use a WITH statement. The general format of the WITH statement is

WITH record_name DO
BEGIN
  •
  •
  •
END;

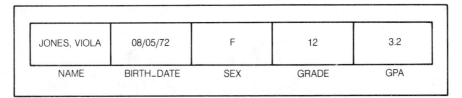

NAME	BIRTH_DATE	SEX	GRADE	GPA
JONES, VIOLA	08/05/72	F	12	3.2

FIGURE 12-2 STUDENT RECORD CONTAINING DATA

The WITH statement could be used to assign values to record STUDENT this way:

```
WITH STUDENT DO
BEGIN
    NAME := 'JONES, VIOLA';
    BIRTH_DATE := '08/05/72';
    SEX := 'F';
    GRADE := 12;
    GPA := 3.2;
END;   { WITH }
```

When the WITH statement is used, it is no longer necessary to state the record name each time a field is referenced.

Copying an Entire Record

A complete record may be copied to another record if both are of the same record type. Suppose two variables are declared as type STUDENT_RECORD:

```
VAR
    CENTRAL_STUDENT : STUDENT_RECORD;
    SOUTH_STUDENT   : STUDENT_RECORD;
```

Let's assume that a CENTRAL_STUDENT record has been filled with data, and we wish to assign this same data to a SOUTH_STUDENT record. This can be done by using an assignment statement:

```
SOUTH_STUDENT := CENTRAL_STUDENT;
```

Now every field of these two records will be the same.

Arrays of Records

Records are most commonly used in groups. For example, a school would want to be able to place all of the students' records together. This can be done by declaring an array of records. An array of records of type STUDENT_RECORD could be defined like this:

```
TYPE
   STUDENT_RECORD = RECORD
                       NAME        :  STRING;
                       BIRTH_DATE  :  STRING;
                       SEX         :  CHAR;
                       GRADE       :  INTEGER;
                       GPA         :  REAL;
                    END;    { STUDENT_RECORD }

   STUDENT_ARRAY = ARRAY[1..100] OF STUDENT_RECORD;

VAR
   STUDENTS : STUDENT_ARRAY;
```

Figure 12–3 illustrates how each array element contains a complete record. This declaration statement will set up an array holding up to 100 records. The fourth record in this array can be referred to by using a subscript:

```
STUDENTS[4]
```

Individual fields in this record can be referred to in the same way as fields in individual records. The only difference is an array subscript must be used to determine which array element is being referenced. The GRADE field of the fourth record in array STUDENTS could be assigned a value this way:

```
STUDENTS[4].GRADE := 'A';
```

FIGURE 12–3 AN ARRAY OF RECORDS

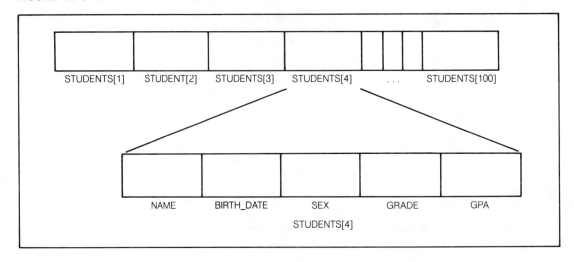

This field could also be referred to by using a WITH statement:

```
WITH STUDENTS[4] DO
    GRADE := 'A';
```

Notice that no BEGIN or END is needed if the WITH statement is not a compound statement.

A Program Using an Array of Records

Eric needs a program to keep track of odd jobs he does in the neighborhood. He would like the following information on each job:

1. Name of person the job was done for.
2. Type of job (rake, mow, garden, or babysit).
3. Time spent on the job.
4. Amount customer owes.

The program should be written so that Eric can enter the first three items at the keyboard. The amount to be charged for the job will be computed by the program. The program can be divided into two tasks:

1. Get information on each job.
2. Display the listing of all bills.

The program is shown in Figure 12–4. An array of records named CUSTOMERS is used. Each record is of type BILL and contains the needed data fields. Examine the body of the program. If the user wants to enter any data, procedure READ_JOBS is called. It contains a WHILE/DO loop that executes as long as there are more jobs to be entered. A WITH statement is used to allow the customer's name, the job type, and the amount of time to be entered to each consecutive record in the array CUSTOMERS. Nested IF/THEN/ELSE statements are used to calculate the cost of the job. When the user has finished entering jobs, program control returns to the main program, and procedure DISPLAY_TABLE is called. This procedure uses a FOR loop to output all of the customer records.

Searching an Array

What if a particular record in the array CUSTOMERS in program ODD_JOBS is needed? The process of attempting to locate a *target* value in a list of values is called searching. Searching, like sorting, is a process that computers are very good at performing. One way of locating the target would be to start at the beginning of the array and examine each record until the specified one was found or the end of the list

```
PROGRAM ODD_JOBS;

{ THIS PROGRAM READS A CUSTOMER'S NAME, THE TYPE OF JOB DONE FOR THE
  CUSTOMER, AND THE NUMBER OF HOURS SPENT ON THAT JOB.  THE AMOUNT OWED
  BY THE CUSTOMER IS THEN CALCULATED.  UP TO TWENTY JOBS CAN BE ENTERED
  AT A TIME.  THE COST OF THE FOLLOWING JOBS CAN BE CALCULATED:
          MOW      $4.50 / HOUR
          RAKE     $3.50 / HOUR
          GARDEN   $4.00 / HOUR
          BABYSIT  $2.00 / HOUR
  AT THE END OF THE PROGRAM A TABLE LISTING ALL JOBS PERFORMED IS
  DISPLAYED. }

USES
   CRT;

CONST
   MOW_RATE      = 4.50;
   RAKE_RATE     = 3.50;
   GARDEN_RATE   = 4.00;
   BABYSIT_RATE  = 2.00;

TYPE
   BILL = RECORD
             NAME : STRING;
             JOB  : STRING;
             TIME : REAL;
             COST : REAL;
          END;    { RECORD }

   CUSTOMER_LIST = ARRAY[1..20] OF BILL;

VAR
   CUSTOMERS        : CUSTOMER_LIST;
   ANSWER           : CHAR;
   POSITION, COUNT  : INTEGER;

{********************************************************************}

PROCEDURE READ_JOBS (VAR COUNT : INTEGER;
                     VAR CUSTOMERS : CUSTOMER_LIST);

{ THIS PROCEDURE ALLOWS THE USER TO ENTER INFORMATION ON A MAXIMUM OF
  20 DIFFERENT JOBS.  THE USER IS PROMPTED TO ENTER THE CUSTOMER'S
  NAME, TYPE OF JOB, AND TIME SPENT ON THE JOB.  THE AMOUNT OWED IS
  THEN CALCULATED. }
```

FIGURE 12-4 PROGRAM ODD_JOBS

(Figure continued on next page)

```
BEGIN   { READ_JOBS }

    WHILE ANSWER = 'Y' DO
    BEGIN
        COUNT := COUNT + 1;
        WITH CUSTOMERS[COUNT] DO
        BEGIN
            WRITE ('ENTER CUSTOMER''S NAME: ');
            READLN (NAME);
            WRITE ('ENTER THE JOB: ');
            READLN (JOB);
            WRITE ('ENTER THE TIME SPENT ON THE JOB: ');
            READLN (TIME);
            { CALCULATE COST OF THE JOB. }
            IF JOB = 'MOW'
                THEN COST := MOW_RATE * TIME
                ELSE IF JOB = 'RAKE'
                    THEN COST := RAKE_RATE * TIME
                    ELSE IF JOB = 'GARDEN'
                        THEN COST := GARDEN_RATE * TIME
                        ELSE COST := BABYSIT_RATE * TIME;
        END;   { WITH }

        WRITELN ('DO YOU WANT TO ENTER ANOTHER JOB?');
        WRITE ('IF YES, ENTER Y, IF NO, ENTER N: ');
        ANSWER := READKEY;
        WRITELN (ANSWER);
    END;   { WHILE }

END;   { READ_JOBS }

{*********************************************************************}

PROCEDURE DISPLAY_TABLE (COUNT : INTEGER; CUSTOMERS : CUSTOMER_LIST);

{ THIS PROCEDURE DISPLAYS A LIST OF CUSTOMERS THAT OWE MONEY ALONG
  WITH THE AMOUNT OWED. }

VAR
    POSITION : INTEGER;

BEGIN   { DISPLAY_TABLE }

    WRITELN;
    WRITELN ('NAME':20, 'JOB':20, 'TIME':10, 'AMOUNT DUE':12);
    FOR POSITION := 1 TO 66 DO
        WRITE ('-');
    WRITELN;
    FOR POSITION := 1 TO COUNT DO
        WITH CUSTOMERS[POSITION] DO
            WRITELN (NAME:20, JOB:20, TIME:10:2, COST:10:2);

END;   { DISPLAY_TABLE }
```

FIGURE 12-4 PROGRAM ODD_JOBS (Cont.)

(Figure continued on next page)

```
{*********************************************************************}

BEGIN    { MAIN }

    COUNT := 0;

    { SEE IF DATA IS TO BE ENTERED. }
    WRITELN ('DO YOU WANT TO ENTER A JOB?');
    WRITE ('IF YES, ENTER Y, IF NO, ENTER N: ');
    ANSWER := READKEY;
    WRITELN (ANSWER);
    IF ANSWER = 'Y'
        THEN READ_JOBS (COUNT, CUSTOMERS);

    { OUTPUT LIST OF BILLS DUE. }
    DISPLAY_TABLE (COUNT, CUSTOMERS);

END.    { MAIN }
```

```
DO YOU WANT TO ENTER A JOB?
IF YES, ENTER Y, IF NO, ENTER N: Y
ENTER CUSTOMER'S NAME: ALBERTSON
ENTER THE JOB: RAKE
ENTER THE TIME SPENT ON THE JOB: 2.5
DO YOU WANT TO ENTER ANOTHER JOB?
IF YES, ENTER Y, IF NO, ENTER N: Y
ENTER CUSTOMER'S NAME: JACKMAN
ENTER THE JOB: MOW
ENTER THE TIME SPENT ON THE JOB: 3.75
DO YOU WANT TO ENTER ANOTHER JOB?
IF YES, ENTER Y, IF NO, ENTER N: Y
ENTER CUSTOMER'S NAME: HALL
ENTER THE JOB: BABYSIT
ENTER THE TIME SPENT ON THE JOB: 4.0
DO YOU WANT TO ENTER ANOTHER JOB?
IF YES, ENTER Y, IF NO, ENTER N: N
```

NAME	JOB	TIME	AMOUNT DUE
ALBERTSON	RAKE	2.50	8.75
JACKMAN	MOW	3.75	16.88
HALL	BABYSIT	4.00	8.00

FIGURE 12-4 PROGRAM ODD_JOBS (Cont.)

was reached (signifying that the target was not in the list). This is called **sequential searching**.

A procedure for performing a sequential search could easily be added to program ODD_JOBS. Imagine that Eric wants to be able to enter a customer's name and have that customer's record displayed on the screen. If no customer with that name is in the array, he would like a message displayed saying that the record was not found. An efficient way of doing this is to create a BOOLEAN variable that will indicate whether or not the target has been found. An appropriate name for this variable might be FOUND. This variable should remain false until the record is located.

Figure 12–5 shows procedure FIND_RECORD, which performs a sequential search of the array CUSTOMERS. The variable FOUND is set to FALSE at the beginning of the procedure. The WHILE/DO loop that examines each array element is only executed as long as FOUND is false. As soon as the target is found, the variable FOUND is set to TRUE. The loop will not be executed again. The desired record is then displayed. If the entire array has been examined without finding the target, the following message is displayed:

THE CUSTOMER'S RECORD WAS NOT IN THE LIST.

LEARNING CHECK 12–1

1. What is a record?
2. Declare a record named PLAYER. This record will be used for baseball players on a team. The record should have the following fields:

NAME   (name of the player)
AGE   (age of the player)
BAT_AVE   (batting average of the player)
POSITION   (position played by the player)

Each field should be assigned an appropriate data type.
3. Use the following program segment to answer parts a–b.

```
PROGRAM GOLF;

TYPE
   PLAYER = RECORD
              NAME    : STRING;
              AVERAGE : REAL;
          END;    { PLAYER }
```

a. Declare an array of type PLAYER that can hold up to six records.
b. Write a loop to read six names, and assign the names to the NAME field of each of the records in the array declared above. Be sure to write a prompt to tell the user when the name should be entered.

```
PROCEDURE FIND_RECORD (CUSTOMERS : CUSTOMER_LIST; COUNT : INTEGER);

{  THIS PROCEDURE PROMPTS THE USER TO ENTER A CUSTOMER'S NAME. THE
   LIST IS THEN SEARCHED FOR THAT CUSTOMER'S RECORD WHICH IS DISPLAY-
   ED WHEN IT IS FOUND.  IF IT IS NOT FOUND, AN APPROPRIATE MESSAGE
   IS DISPLAYED.  }

VAR
   TARGET : STRING;
   FOUND  : BOOLEAN;

BEGIN   { FIND_RECORD }

   WRITELN;
   WRITELN;
   { PROMPT USER TO ENTER NAME TO BE LOCATED. }
   WRITE ('ENTER THE NAME OF THE CUSTOMER WHOSE RECORD YOU WANT TO SEE: ');
   READLN (TARGET);

   FOUND := FALSE;
   POSITION := 1;
   { SEARCH LIST UNTIL TARGET IS FOUND OR END OF LIST IS REACHED. }
   WHILE (POSITION <= COUNT) AND (NOT FOUND) DO
       IF CUSTOMERS[POSITION].NAME = TARGET
          THEN FOUND := TRUE
          ELSE POSITION := POSITION + 1;

   IF FOUND
       { IF RECORD WAS FOUND, DISPLAY IT. }
       THEN
       BEGIN
           WRITELN;
           WRITELN ('NAME':20, 'JOB':20, 'TIME':10, 'AMOUNT DUE':12);
           WRITELN;
           WRITELN (CUSTOMERS[POSITION].NAME:20, CUSTOMERS[POSITION].JOB:20,
                   CUSTOMERS[POSITION].TIME:10:2,
                   CUSTOMERS[POSITION].COST:10:2);
       END   { THEN }
       { IF RECORD WAS NOT FOUND, DISPLAY "NOT IN LIST" MESSAGE. }
       ELSE WRITELN ('THE CUSTOMER''S RECORD WAS NOT IN THE LIST.');

END;   { FIND_RECORD }
```

FIGURE 12-5 PROCEDURE TO PERFORM A SEQUENTIAL SEARCH

SETS

Pascal was the first general-purpose programming language to include sets as a structured data type. A set is a collection of items that are classed together. Sets can be very useful in writing programs.

Declaring Sets

In mathematics a set containing the integers 1 through 7 could be written this way:

{1, 2, 3, 4, 5, 6, 7}

In Pascal, a set type may be defined as follows:

```
TYPE
    SMALLNUM = SET OF 1..7;
```

Variables may then be declared of type SMALLNUM:

```
VAR
    LITTLE : SMALLNUM;
```

LITTLE is now a set that may contain any of the integers from 1 through 7. Here are a few examples of how the set LITTLE might look:

[2, 6, 7]
[5, 3, 1]   (Set elements do not have to be in order.)
[ ]

The last example is called the empty set. It is useful when a set needs to be initialized to nothing. The following would *not* be sets of LITTLE:

[1, 8]   (No number can be larger than 7.)
[−2, 3, 6]   (No number can be smaller than 1.)

The elements of a set must all be of the same type. In set LITTLE above, the values are all of the data type INTEGER. A set may be of any ordinal type or a subrange of an ordinal type.

Format For **Set Declaration**

TYPE
  Set_type = SET OF data_type;
VAR
  Set_name : Set_type;

Note: Sets must be ordinal data types or subranges of ordinal types.

Assigning Values to Sets

Values are assigned to a set by using the assignment operator (:=):

```
LITTLE := [1, 3, 4];
LITTLE := [6];
LITTLE := [ ];
```

All of the values to be assigned to a set must be separated by commas and enclosed in brackets.

Sets may also be user-defined data types:

```
TYPE
    MONTH = (JAN, FEB, MAR, APR, MAY, JUN, JUL, AUG, SEP, OCT, NOV, DEC);
    MONTHS = SET OF MONTH;

VAR
    FALL_SEMESTER, SPRING_SEMESTER : MONTHS;
```

The following assignment statements are valid for these declarations:

```
FALL_SEMESTER   := [SEP, DEC];
SPRING_SEMESTER := [JAN..MAY];
```

Set Operators

Three operators can be used with a set:

- Union (+)
- Intersection (*)
- Difference (−)

They will be discussed individually.

Union. The plus sign (+) is the operator that indicates the union of two sets. The union of two sets is a set containing all the elements that are in either or both sets. Here are a few examples:

['A', 'B', 'Z'] + ['A', 'D', 'M'] results in ['A', 'B', 'D', 'M', 'Z']
[2, 4, 12] + [6, 4, 8, 10, 12] results in [2, 4, 6, 8, 10, 12]

Intersection. The intersection of two sets consists of a set containing only those values common to both sets. The asterisk (*) is the operator for set intersection. Below are several examples:

['A', 'B', 'Z'] * ['A', 'D', 'M'] results in ['A']
[2, 4, 12] * [6, 4, 8, 10, 12] results in [4, 12]

Difference. The difference between two sets consists of all the values present in the first set, but not the second. The minus sign ($-$) is used to represent set difference. Two examples are shown below:

['A', 'B', 'Z'] $-$ ['A', 'B', 'M'] results in ['Z']
[2, 4, 1] $-$ [6, 4, 8, 10, 12] results in [2, 1]

In determining the difference between two sets, the order of the sets (but not the order of the set elements) affects the results. If the order of the first example above were changed, the result would be different:

['A', 'B', 'M'] $-$ ['A', 'B', 'Z'] results in ['M']

In set union and intersection, the order of the sets does not make a difference. Here are some more examples using the three operators:

Expression	Results in
[2, 3, 8] + [1, 3]	[1, 2, 3, 8]
[2, 3, 8] * [1, 3]	[3]
[2, 3, 8] $-$ [1, 3]	[2, 8]
['A', 'D'] $-$ ['C']	['A', 'D']
['B', 'E', 'F'] + ['D']	['B', 'E', 'F', 'D']

Using Relational Operators with Sets

The following relational operators may be used to compare two sets:

A = B	Set A is equal to set B.
A <> B	Set A is not equal to set B.
A >= B	Set A is a *superset* of set B.
A <= B	Set A is a *subset* of set B.

Both operands must be of the same type. The order in which elements appear within the set is not important, but as a convention elements are generally listed from smallest to largest.

The relational set operators = and <> are used to determine if two sets contain the same elements. Here are some examples:

Expression	Evaluates as
[2, 4] = [2, 4]	True
[2, 4] = [4, 2]	True
[2, 4] <> [4, 2]	False
[2, 4, 5] <> [4, 2]	True
[1, 8, 9] = [9, 1]	False

The operator <= determines if the first set is a subset of the second.

Set A is a subset of set B if every element of set A is also an element of set B. For example,

Expression	Evaluates as
[1, 4] <= [1, 2, 3, 4, 5]	True
[1, 4] <= [1, 4]	True
[1, 2, 3] <= [1, 2]	False
[ ] <= [1, 3]	True

The empty set is a subset of every set.

The operator >= determines if the first set is a superset of the second. Set A is a superset of set B if every element of B is also an element of A. For example,

Expression	Evaluates as
[1, 2, 3] >= [1, 2]	True
[1, 2] >= [1, 2, 3, 4]	False
[1, 2] >= [1, 2]	True
[1, 2] >= [ ]	True

The final set operator, IN, is used to determine whether a given value is an element of a particular set. This is called the set membership test. The value being tested for set membership must be of the same data type as the set. Some examples are listed below:

Expression	Evaluates as
2 IN [1, 2, 3, 4, 5]	True
6 IN [1, 2, 3, 4, 5]	False
'd' IN ['b', 'c', 'd']	True

One common use for sets is to determine if program input is valid. The following program segment is supposed to read an integer between 1 and 7:

```
REPEAT
   WRITE ('ENTER A NUMBER BETWEEN 1 AND 7: ');
   READLN (NUMBER)
UNTIL NUMBER IN [1..7];
```

If the number entered is not in the set [1 . . 7], the user will be prompted to enter the number again.

Reading and Writing Sets

Sets cannot be used directly in READ or WRITE statements. Each element must be processed individually. Consequently, in order to read data to be placed in a set, a value must first be read and tested to make certain that it is valid. The new set element may then be combined with the other elements of the set by using set operators. The same method must be used in reverse when the contents of a set are to be written.

Suppose that a set is defined like this:

```
TYPE
    VEGGIE = (CARROT, POTATO, BROCCOLI, SQUASH);
    VEGSET = SET OF VEGGIE;

VAR
    A : VEGSET;
```

Assume that the user will enter the values to be added to this set by using an integer code. For example, if the user wanted to add CARROT, the value 1 would be entered; if the user wanted to add SQUASH, the value 4 would be entered. Then a CASE statement could be used to add the corresponding element to A:

```
CASE CODE OF
    1 : A := A + [CARROT];
    2 : A := A + [POTATO];
    3 : A := A + [BROCCOLI];
    4 : A := A + [SQUASH];
END;    { CASE }
```

A similar process can be used to write the contents of the set. The following program segment demonstrates how the contents of A could be output:

```
FOR B := CARROT TO SQUASH DO
    IF B IN A
        THEN
        CASE B OF
            CARROT   : WRITELN ('CARROT');
            POTATO   : WRITELN ('POTATO');
            BROCCOLI : WRITELN ('BROCCOLI');
            SQUASH   : WRITELN ('SQUASH');
        END;    { CASE }
```

The variable B must be declared as type VEGGIE. The FOR loop will allow each possible value of A to be checked. The IF statement determines if the current value of B is in set A. If it is, the name of that vegetable will be displayed. If it is not, the loop will evaluate the next possible vegetable.

A Program Demonstrating Sets

Sets are useful when a program needs to determine whether or not a given item is contained in a group of items. For example, program ACTIVITIES in Figure 12–6 reads an individual's name and three of that person's hobbies. The hobbies are entered by using an integer code.

```
PROGRAM ACTIVITIES;

{ THIS PROGRAM READS 10 INDIVIDUAL'S NAMES AND A LIST OF EACH
  PERSON'S HOBBIES.  EACH PERSON CHOOSES  THREE FAVORITE
  HOBBIES FROM THE LIST BELOW.  THE HOBBIES ARE ENTERED USING
  THE CORRESPONDING CODE NUMBER:
      1     BASKETBALL
      2     RACKETBALL
      3     READING
      4     TENNIS
      5     BASEBALL
      6     FOOTBALL
      7     JOGGING
      8     SEWING
AFTER ALL THE DATA IS ENTERED, THE NAMES OF PEOPLE WHO ENJOY BOTH
BASKETBALL AND TENNIS ARE DISPLAYED ON THE MONITOR.  ALSO PRINTED ARE
THE NAMES OF PEOPLE WHO DID NOT PICK JOGGING. }


TYPE
    ACTIVITY = SET OF 1..8;

    PERSON = RECORD
                 NAME     : STRING;
                 HOBBIES : ACTIVITY;
             END;    { RECORD }

    ARRAY_TYPE = ARRAY[1..10] OF PERSON;

VAR
    PEOPLE  : ARRAY_TYPE;
    COUNT   : INTEGER;
    A, B, C : INTEGER;

{*******************************************************************}

PROCEDURE GET_DATA (VAR PEOPLE : ARRAY_TYPE);

{ ALLOWS THE DATA ON THE 10 PEOPLE TO BE READ. }

BEGIN    { GET_DATA }

    FOR COUNT := 1 TO 10 DO
        WITH PEOPLE[COUNT] DO
        BEGIN
            WRITE ('ENTER NAME: ');
            READLN (NAME);
            WRITE ('ENTER THREE HOBBIES USING INTEGER CODE: ');
            READLN (A, B, C);
            HOBBIES := [A, B, C];
        END;    { WITH }

END;    { GET_DATA }
```

FIGURE 12–6 PROGRAM ACTIVITIES

(Figure continued on next page)

```
{*******************************************************************}

PROCEDURE BASKETBALL_AND_TENNIS (PEOPLE : ARRAY_TYPE);

{ DISPLAYS THE NAMES OF PEOPLE WHO CHOSE BOTH BASKETBALL AND TENNIS. }

BEGIN    { BASKETBALL_AND_TENNIS }

    WRITELN;
    WRITELN ('THE FOLLOWING PEOPLE ENJOY BOTH BASKETBALL AND TENNIS:');
    FOR COUNT := 1 TO 10 DO
        WITH PEOPLE [COUNT] DO
            IF HOBBIES >= [1,4]
                THEN WRITELN (NAME);

END;    { BASKETBALL_AND_TENNIS }

{*******************************************************************}

PROCEDURE NO_JOGGING (PEOPLE : ARRAY_TYPE);

{ DISPLAYS THE NAMES OF THE PEOPLE WHO DID NOT PICK JOGGING. }

BEGIN    { NO_JOGGING }

    WRITELN;
    WRITELN ('THE FOLLOWING PEOPLE DID NOT PICK JOGGING:');
    FOR COUNT := 1 TO 10 DO
        WITH PEOPLE[COUNT] DO
            IF HOBBIES * [7] <> [7]
                THEN WRITELN (NAME);

END;    { NO_JOGGING }

{*******************************************************************}

BEGIN    { MAIN }

    GET_DATA (PEOPLE);
    BASKETBALL_AND_TENNIS (PEOPLE);
    NO_JOGGING (PEOPLE);

END.    { MAIN }
```

FIGURE 12-6 PROGRAM ACTIVITIES (Cont.)   *(Figure continued on next page)*

This list of hobbies is placed in a set. It is then easy to determine whether or not a person is interested in a given hobby. In the program this expression

```
IF HOBBIES >= [1, 4]
```

```
ENTER NAME: JACKSON
ENTER THREE HOBBIES USING INTEGER CODE: 2  4  5
ENTER NAME: SCHWARTZ
ENTER THREE HOBBIES USING INTEGER CODE: 1  4  7
ENTER NAME: FORSE
ENTER THREE HOBBIES USING INTEGER CODE: 2  7  3
ENTER NAME: LING
ENTER THREE HOBBIES USING INTEGER CODE: 2  5  6
ENTER NAME: PATTERSON
ENTER THREE HOBBIES USING INTEGER CODE: 6  1  4
ENTER NAME: FRIEDRICK
ENTER THREE HOBBIES USING INTEGER CODE: 1  3  6
ENTER NAME: HALL
ENTER THREE HOBBIES USING INTEGER CODE: 2  5  6
ENTER NAME: TRIGGER
ENTER THREE HOBBIES USING INTEGER CODE: 4  5  7
ENTER NAME: SAMPSON
ENTER THREE HOBBIES USING INTEGER CODE: 3  4  5
ENTER NAME: APPLEBAUM
ENTER THREE HOBBIES USING INTEGER CODE: 3  6  5


THE FOLLOWING PEOPLE ENJOY BOTH BASKETBALL AND TENNIS:
SCHWARTZ
PATTERSON

THE FOLLOWING PEOPLE DID NOT PICK JOGGING:
JACKSON
LING
PATTERSON
FRIEDRICK
HALL
SAMPSON
APPLEBAUM
```

FIGURE 12-6 PROGRAM ACTIVITIES (Cont.)

checks to see which people are interested in basketball and tennis. Only those people who list both basketball and tennis as hobbies will have their names printed. The expression

```
IF HOBBIES * [7] <> [7]
```

will evaluate as true only if jogging is not listed as a hobby. It would be easy to add more statements to this program to check for other hobbies.

1. What is a set?
2. Answer questions a–c below using the following TYPE definitions:

   TYPE
   ```
       DAYS  = SET OF 1..7;
       WHOLE = SET OF 1..20;
   ```

   a. Declare a variable WEEKDAYS to be of type DAYS. Assign the values 1, 2, 3, 4, and 5 to variable WEEKDAYS.
   b. Declare a variable ODD of type WHOLE and assign all of the odd values that are contained in set WHOLE to this variable.
   c. Declare a variable MULTTWO of type WHOLE. Assign to it all the multiples of 2 up to 20 (2, 4, 6, . . .).

3. Given the following program segment, answer questions a–d below.

   ```
   TYPE
       ALPHA = SET OF 'A'..'Z';

   VAR
       VOWELS, SMALPHA, COMBINE, TOGETHER, DIFF, FINAL : ALPHA;

   BEGIN

       VOWELS  := ['A', 'E', 'I', 'O', 'U'];
       SMALPHA := ['A', 'B', 'C', 'D', 'E'];
   ```

   a. What is the value of COMBINE?

      ```
      COMBINE := VOWELS + ['Y', 'W'];
      ```

   b. What is the value of TOGETHER?

      ```
      TOGETHER := VOWELS * SMALPHA;
      ```

   c. What is the value of DIFF?

      ```
      DIFF := ['B', 'C', 'F', 'G'] - SMALPHA;
      ```

   d. What is the value of FINAL?

      ```
      FINAL := ['B', 'C', 'F', 'G'] * SMALPHA;
      ```

4. Write a program segment to ask the user to enter a vowel. A message then should be displayed stating whether or not the letter entered is actually a vowel. If it is not, the user should be prompted to reenter the vowel. Use the SET data type to determine if the letter is valid.

■■■ SUMMARY POINTS

■ Two structured data types were introduced in this chapter: the record and the set. Structured data types are made up of components. An array is also an example of a structured data type.

■ A record is a group of related data items that are gathered together as a single unit. These items need not be of the same data type. Each item within a record is a field. A record may have any number of fields.

■ Records are very useful whenever a number of facts need to be kept together. An example would be a record containing information about a student in a school.

■ Record fields may be referenced by using the WITH statement or by using the format "record_name . field_name."

■ Arrays of records allow a group of records of the same type to be stored together.

■ A sequential search may be used to locate a specific value in a list of values. The sequential search starts at the beginning of the list, and examines each item until the target item is located or the end of the list is reached.

■ A set is a collection of items classed together. All of the values in a set must be of the same type. Three set operators may be used in Pascal: union ($+$), intersection ($*$), and difference ($-$). The following relational operators may also be used: $=$, $>=$, $<=$, $<>$, and IN.

■■■ VOCABULARY LIST

Field	Sets
Records	Structured data type
Sequential searching	

■■■ CHAPTER TEST

Vocabulary

Match a term from the numbered column with the description from the lettered column that best fits the term.

1. Set

    a. The process of locating a target item within a list of items by starting at the beginning of the list and examining each item until the target is found or the end of the list is reached.

2. Record

b. A structured data type consisting of a collection of values that are classed together.

3. Structured data type

c. A data item that is part of a record.

4. Field

d. A data type that is made up of many components.

5. Sequential search

e. A structured data type containing a group of related data items (fields) not necessarily of the same data type, that are gathered together in a single unit.

Questions

1. How and where are records defined in a program?
2. What is a record field? What data types may be assigned to fields?
3. Describe the purpose of using the WITH statement. What is its advantage?
4. Use the following program segment to answer parts a–c below.

```
TYPE
    AUTO = RECORD
        MAKE  : STRING;
        YEAR  : INTEGER;
        COLOR : STRING;
    END;   { AUTO }

VAR
    CAR     : AUTO;
    CLUNKER : AUTO;
```

a. Use the WITH statement to assign these values to the following fields of record CAR:

MAKE = CHEVROLET
YEAR = 1984
COLOR = BLUE

b. Assign the values listed in part a to record CAR, using this format:

record_name.field_name

c. Copy record CAR into record CLUNKER.

5. Look at the program segment below. Determine whether the expressions in parts a–e evaluate as true or false.

```
TYPE
    NUM = SET OF 1..20;

VAR
    POINTS1, POINTS2 : NUM;

BEGIN

POINTS1 := [2, 4, 10, 18];
POINTS2 := [4, 8, 11, 20]
```

a. POINTS1 >= POINTS2
b. [ ] <= POINTS1
c. POINTS2 >= [4, 8, 11, 19, 20]
d. POINTS2 <> [4, 8, 11, 19, 20]
e. [4, 10, 18] >= POINTS1

6. How is the empty set used when performing set operations?
7. Explain how the subset and superset operators work.
8. Explain the purpose of the set operator IN.

▆▆▆ PROGRAMMING PROBLEMS

Level 1

1. Write a program that allows data to be read to an array of records described as follows:

   Name of city
   Population
   State

   The array has a maximum of 20 records. Once all the data is entered, go through the array and output only those cities with populations over 100,000.
2. Write a program that will print a list of the students who are eligible for driver's education. To be eligible for driver's education at City High, a student must be at least 15 years old and have a grade point average of 2.5 or better. Each student's record looks like this:

```
STUDENTREC = RECORD
    NAME : STRING;
    AGE  : INTEGER;
    GPA  : REAL;
END;    { STUDENTREC }
```

Use the following data to test this program.

Name	Age	GPA
Morrison, Sam	17	2.0
Jefferson, Jane	15	3.6
Adams, Sarah	14	3.2
Ross, Betsy	16	3.0
Paine, Tom	15	2.5

Level 2

3. Survey your class to see which of the following toppings people like on their hamburgers. Have each student pick three favorite toppings from the following list:

   Cheese: 1
   Catsup: 2
   Mustard: 3
   Onions: 4
   Pickles: 5
   Tomatoes: 6
   Lettuce: 7
   Bananas: 8

   Use a set to hold the code numbers of the toppings. Enter each student's name and the set of toppings to a record. After all the data is entered, print the following headings along with the names of the students fitting into each category:

   a. THE FOLLOWING STUDENTS DIDN'T CHOOSE CATSUP AS A FAVORITE TOPPING:
   b. THE FOLLOWING STUDENTS LIKE ONIONS AND TOMATOES:
   c. THE FOLLOWING STUDENTS CHOSE CHEESE AS ONE OF THEIR FAVORITE TOPPINGS:

4. Write a program to determine whether a particular senior's choice of classes meets the minimum requirements at Bowsher High School. Each student must take five courses with at least one course in each of the areas listed below:

Course Number	Area	Course
11	English	English Literature
12		Contemporary Literature
13		Drama
14		Film Making
31	Math	Algebra II
32		Trigonometry
33		Calculus
34		Statistics
41	Science	Geology
42		Physics
43		Chemistry

Have the user enter the numbers of the five courses being taken.

Level 3

5. Write a program that will remove all punctuation from a string of characters. Use the following character strings to test your program:
   He said, "We'll go to the park tomorrow, when it's not raining!"
   "Why don't we go today?"
6. Ms. Walsh needs a program to calculate the average score on two physics tests. An array of records should be used to hold the information. Each student's record should hold the following information:

Name	(student's name)
Test1	(score on the first test)
Test2	(score on the second test)
Average	(student's average on the two tests)
Difference	(student's difference from the class average)

   The first three items will be entered at the keyboard. The student's average should be computed at this point. In addition, the class average should be determined. The program should then go back to the beginning of the array and calculate the difference between each student's average and the class average. The output should be similar to this:

Name	Test1	Test2	Average	Difference from Class Average
Morris	77.0	83.0	80.0	3.5
Stephens	72.0	70.0	71.0	−5.5

CHAPTER 13

Files

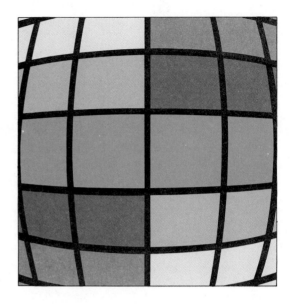

OBJECTIVES

After studying this chapter, you should be able to:

- Define the term file.
- List the advantages and disadvantages of using files.
- Write programs using text files.
- Use the EOF and EOLN functions when reading files.
- Write programs using nontext files.

OUTLINE

INTRODUCTION

So far in this text, the structured data types arrays, records, and sets have been discussed. This chapter will present another structured data type: the file. Unlike arrays, files are kept in secondary storage rather than in main memory. When using Turbo Pascal, files are commonly stored on disk. The disk can be either a floppy diskette or an internal hard disk.

A **file** consists of a sequence of components, all of the same data type. The components of a file are stored sequentially, one following the other. These components may be of any data type. Figure 13–1 shows how a file of integers might be visually represented in storage. In this file each component consists of a single integer.

FIGURE 13–1 A FILE OF INTEGERS

−17	2	184	0	−79	241	93

ADVANTAGES AND DISADVANTAGES OF USING FILES

Files allow data to be stored permanently on secondary storage such as a diskette. These files may be used again later. For example, an alphabetized list of 50 names stored in a file called NAME_FILE could then be used later as input to a different program that uses the list of names for another purpose. The ability to store data permanently so that it may be used by other programs at a later time is an important advantage of files.

If the amount of space needed to store the data for a program is greater than that available in main memory, this data must be stored externally in files. But, because files are kept in secondary storage, it takes longer to access them than it does to access an array that is stored in the computer's main memory. Also, new components must be added to the end of a file; they cannot be inserted into the middle of the file. However, Turbo Pascal does allow the programmer to access and update a file component that already exists.

The length of a file is the number of components in the file. For example, the length of the file in Figure 13–1 is 7. The length of a file does not have to be stated when the file is declared and can vary during program execution. A file might be empty before program execution begins but have several hundred values stored in it by the time the program has been executed. This is a distinct advantage over arrays. When using arrays, the maximum length of the array must be stated when it is declared. This memory space is "set aside" during program execution, regardless of how much is actually used. Files, on the other hand, will use only the amount of storage space actually needed at any given time.

Files may be passed as parameters to procedures and functions, but they must always be passed as variable parameters, not as value parameters. This is true even if the subprogram does not alter the contents of the file.

DECLARING FILES

A program may use any number of files. In Pascal, files are a type of variable and must be declared in the variable declaration section of the program. A file name may be any valid identifier but should be descriptive. These variables are somewhat different from other types of variables because the files they create continue to exist after program execution is completed. Many versions of Pascal require the names of the files used by a program to be listed in the program heading, as in the following example:

```
PROGRAM READ_LIST (FIRST_FILE, NEXT_FILE, LAST_FILE);
PROGRAM IDENTIFY (ID_NUM);
PROGRAM ROCK_GROUP (SONGS, HITS);
```

The first program heading indicates that the program will access three files named FIRST_FILE, NEXT_FILE, and LAST_FILE. The second heading indicates that the file ID_NUM will be used by the program IDENTIFY. Turbo Pascal does not require file names to be listed in the program heading. However, this is an easy way of telling people what files are used by a particular program.

The files used by a program must be declared in the variable declaration section. Each file must be given a type. In Turbo Pascal, a file may be one of three types: a text file, a typed file, or an untyped file. In this chapter text and typed files will be discussed. Untyped files are used in more advanced programming than that covered in this text. A file named INTEGER_LIST could be declared like this:

```
TYPE
    INTEGER_FILE = FILE OF INTEGER;

VAR
    INTEGER_LIST : INTEGER_FILE;
```

This is an example of a typed file. Its components are of type INTEGER. The following program segment contains four file declarations:

```
PROGRAM EXAMPLE_FILES (LENGTH, WIDTH, ID_NUM, NAME_FILE);
```

```
TYPE
    R_NUM = FILE OF REAL;
    I_NUM = FILE OF INTEGER;
    NAMES = FILE OF STRING;

VAR
    LENGTH, WIDTH : R_NUM;
    ID_NUM : I_NUM;
    NAME_FILE : NAMES;
```

Each of the files is listed in the program heading. Look at the last file that has been declared, NAME_FILE. Each component of this file consists of a character string.

As mentioned earlier, files are technically considered variables. But they cannot be given values in assignment statements, nor can they be manipulated by arithmetic operations. For this reason, it is best to consider files separately as a "special type" of variable.

Format For **File Declaration**

TYPE
   file_type = FILE OF data_type;
 	
VAR
   file_variable : file_type;

---

1. What is a file?
2. Name a disadvantage of using files.
3. Name several advantages of using files.
4. How is the length of a file determined?

**LEARNING
CHECK
13-1**

▄▄▄▄ TEXT FILES

Pascal has a standard (or predefined) type of file, the text file. Each component of a text file is of type CHAR and may be any character recognized by the computer system being used. The programmer may simply declare a file variable to be of type TEXT like this:

```
VAR
    SONG : TEXT;
```

Any number of text files may be declared and used in a single program. Two files named FIRST_FILE and NEXT_FILE can be declared to be of type TEXT like this:

```
VAR
    FIRST_FILE, NEXT_FILE : TEXT;
```

The components of text files are always represented as characters. These characters may include the end-of-line marker <eoln>, which is used to indicate how the characters should be divided into lines, and the end-of-file marker <eof>, which is used to mark the end of a particular file. As already discussed, <eoln> is inserted whenever the user presses the Return (or Enter) key. The <eof> marker is inserted automatically whenever a file is saved on disk. The programmer does not have to worry about entering the <eof> marker.

Reading a Text File

Consider the problem of writing a program to read a text file. A text file can be created using the same method used to enter Pascal programs. Type in the following text exactly as shown:

```
many a
times
```

Now save this file on a disk under the name TEXT_IN.P. The characters ".P" are used to indicate that this file is used by a Pascal program. This is referred to as an *extension*. This file will now appear as shown in Figure 13–2. It contains two <eoln> markers. These markers were entered when the Return key was pressed. There is also one <eof> marker. The computer automatically inserted this marker at the end of the file when it was saved on disk. Remember that the computer stores files as a continuous series of characters, not in the separate lines seen on the screen.

Before a program can access a file, the ASSIGN statement must be used to link the file variable with a disk file. The format of this statement is

ASSIGN (file_name, disk_name);

The following statement

```
ASSIGN (TEXT_IN, 'TEXT_IN.P');
```

will assign the file name TEXT_IN to the disk file name TEXT_IN.P. Therefore, whenever the name TEXT_IN is used in the program, the file stored under TEXT_IN.P in the directory will actually be referenced. TEXT_IN.P is the name given to the file previously created. It is also possible to specify the disk drive on which the file is located. For example, the following statement indicates that TEXT_IN.P is on the disk in drive B:

```
ASSIGN (TEXT_IN, 'B:TEXT_IN.P');
```

FIGURE 13–2   REPRESENTATION OF A TEXT FILE

| m | a | n | y | ∅ | a | <eoln> | t | i | m | e | s | <eoln> | <eof> |

Next, the RESET procedure must be used to prepare the file to be read. File TEXT_IN is reset like this:

```
RESET (TEXT_IN);
```

A file must always be reset before its contents can be read. This process sets up a **file pointer**, which is an imaginary pointer that indicates which file component is currently being accessed.

After the file is reset, the first character of TEXT_IN is read like this:

```
READ (TEXT_IN, LETTER);
```

In this READ statement, the file name must be stated first, followed by the name of the variable to which the first character is to be assigned. LETTER must be declared to be of type CHAR because it will contain a single character value. After this statement is executed, LETTER will contain the value 'm,' the first letter in TEXT_IN.

An entire line of TEXT_IN could be read by using a WHILE/DO loop and the EOLN function. Remember that the EOLN function is false until the end of a line is reached; then it becomes true. The following WHILE/DO loop will read the first line of TEXT_IN:

```
WHILE NOT EOLN (TEXT_IN) DO
    READ (TEXT_IN, LETTER);
```

However, the entire TEXT_IN file needs to be read. Therefore, a way of detecting the end of the file is needed. This can be done by using the EOF function, which is similar to EOLN. EOF checks for the <eof> marker. When the file pointer reaches this marker, EOF becomes true; until then it is false. To read the entire file TEXT_IN, line by line, two WHILE/DO loops can be nested within one another. The outer one will check for the end of the file, the inner one for the end of each line:

```
WHILE NOT EOF (TEXT_IN) DO
    WHILE NOT EOLN (TEXT_IN) DO
        READ (TEXT_IN, LETTER);
```

A common mistake among beginning programmers is forgetting to list the file name in the READ statement:

```
READ (LETTER);
```

This will cause the program to attempt to read a character entered at the keyboard rather than from the file TEXT_IN.

DIFFERENCES FOR MACINTOSH USERS

The ASSIGN statement is not used in the Macintosh version of Turbo Pascal. Instead, the disk file name is specified in the RESET or REWRITE statement. The general format of these statements is:

RESET (file_name, 'disk_name');
REWRITE (file_name, 'disk_name');

To change the program in Figure 13–4 so that it will run on the Macintosh, leave the two ASSIGN statements out and alter the RESET and REWRITE statements as follows:

```
RESET (TEXT_IN, 'TEXT_IN.P');
REWRITE (TEXT_OUT, 'TEXT_OUT.P');
```

Writing to a Text File

The standard procedure REWRITE is used to prepare a file so that data may be written to it. Let's assume we want to write some data to a file named TEXT_OUT. The following statement can prepare this file to be written to

```
REWRITE (TEXT_OUT);
```

If a file already exists with the specified name, its contents will be lost. Therefore, be careful to use REWRITE only when an empty file is to be used for output.

Once this is done, data values may be written to this file by using a WRITE statement:

```
WRITE (TEXT_OUT, LETTER);
```

Variable LETTER must be of type CHAR. If we forget to specify the file name and simply write the statement as follows:

```
WRITE (LETTER);
```

the value of LETTER will be displayed on the monitor screen. Figure 13–3 explains some procedures and functions that can be used with files.

Copying a Text File

As you may remember, one array may be copied to another by using a single assignment statement; however, this is not possible when

ASSIGN (File_name, Disk_file);	Links a program file with a disk file.
RESET (File_name);	Prepares an input file to be read.
REWRITE (File_name);	Prepares an output file to be written to.
READ (variable);	Reads a value entered at the keyboard to a variable.
READ (File_name, variable);	Reads a single file component to the variable.
WRITE (output);	Writes the stated output to the monitor screen.
WRITE (File_name, output);	Writes the stated output to a file.
CLOSE (File_name);	Saves the file permanently on disk.

FIGURE 13–3 PROCEDURES AND FUNCTIONS USED WITH FILES

using files. Given two text files, TEXT_IN, and TEXT_OUT, the following statement could not be used to copy TEXT_IN to TEXT_OUT:

```
TEXT_OUT := TEXT_IN;
```

Files must be copied one component at a time. Therefore, it is necessary to read each component of the input file and write this value to the corresponding position in the output file.

Figure 13–4 contains a program that reads a text file named TEXT_IN and writes its contents to file TEXT_OUT. This program will be traced to show how it works.

The first thing the program does is assign the program file names to disk files. Then the program resets TEXT_IN and rewrites TEXT_OUT. Examine Figure 13–5. Part A shows where the file pointers are at this time. Notice that TEXT_OUT is currently empty. The file pointer indicates where anything read to this file will be placed.

Next, the program evaluates the condition controlling the outer WHILE/DO loop to determine if TEXT_IN is empty:

```
WHILE NOT EOF (TEXT_IN) DO
```

This test is made before the loop is ever entered. If TEXT_IN is empty, this loop will not be executed. However, in this case the file contains data and EOF is false, so the condition controlling the inner WHILE/DO loop is tested:

```
WHILE NOT EOLN (TEXT_IN) DO
```

EOLN also is false, so the body of the inner loop is executed, causing the first character of the file TEXT_IN to be written to the first position in TEXT_OUT. The file pointers will now be as they appear in part B of Figure 13–5.

The inner loop will continue to read each character individually (including any blanks) until the first <eoln> marker is encountered. At

```
PROGRAM COPY_TEXT (TEXT_IN, TEXT_OUT);

{  THIS PROGRAM COPIES THE TEXT CONTAINED IN FILE TEXT_IN TO FILE
   TEXT_OUT. }

VAR
   TEXT_IN, TEXT_OUT : TEXT;
   LETTER            : CHAR;

BEGIN   { COPY_TEXT }

   ASSIGN (TEXT_IN, 'TEXT_IN.P');
   ASSIGN (TEXT_OUT, 'TEXT_OUT.P');
   RESET (TEXT_IN);
   REWRITE (TEXT_OUT);

   { READ UNTIL AT END OF THE FILE. }
   WHILE NOT EOF (TEXT_IN) DO
   BEGIN
      { READ UNTIL AT END OF THE LINE. }
      WHILE NOT EOLN (TEXT_IN) DO
      BEGIN
         READ (TEXT_IN, LETTER);
         WRITE (TEXT_OUT, LETTER);
      END;   { INNER WHILE }
      READLN (TEXT_IN);
      WRITELN (TEXT_OUT);
   END;    { OUTER WHILE }

   CLOSE (TEXT_IN);
   CLOSE (TEXT_OUT);

END.   { COPY_TEXT }
```

Contents of File TEXT_IN

```
many a
times
```

Contents of File TEXT_OUT

```
many a
times
```

FIGURE 13-4   PROGRAM TO COPY A TEXT FILE

this point, program execution will skip to the two statements following the inner loop:

```
READLN (TEXT_IN);
WRITELN (TEXT_OUT);
```

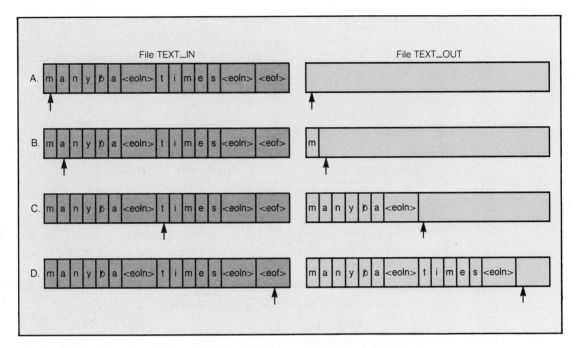

FIGURE 13-5   TRACING THROUGH A PROGRAM THAT COPIES A TEXT FILE

The first statement causes the <eoln> marker in the input file TEXT_IN to be skipped over. The second statement causes an <eoln> marker to be inserted at this point in file TEXT_OUT. Therefore, when TEXT_OUT is printed, it will be identical to TEXT_IN. Part C of Figure 13-5 shows where the file pointers are at this point.

The condition controlling the outer loop is tested again; the next file component will be examined to see if it is <eof>. It isn't, so the inner loop is executed again until the next <eoln> marker is encountered. When the second <eoln> marker is found, EOLN will again become true, and program control will skip to the READLN and WRITELN statements. After these two statements are executed, the file pointers will be as shown in part D of Figure 13-5. The condition controlling the outer loop is now tested and found to be true because <eof> is the next file component. Therefore, the outer loop will not be executed again, and the program is completed.

Notice the last two statements in Figure 13-4:

```
CLOSE (TEXT_IN);
CLOSE (TEXT_OUT);
```

These statements close the two files used in this program. Closing a file permanently saves its contents on disk so that the file can be accessed again. Now that the program has finished creating TEXT_OUT, the system will automatically insert an <eof> marker at its end.

Numeric Data in Text Files

It is possible to store numbers in text files. For example, with these declarations

```
VAR
     TEXT_OUT : TEXT;
     NUMBER   : INTEGER;
```

the following program segment could be used to read a number entered at the keyboard and to copy that number to TEXT_OUT:

```
READ (NUMBER);
WRITE (TEXT_OUT, NUMBER);
```

The Turbo Pascal compiler is able to write a numeric value to a text file by converting the number to its character equivalent (that is, the ASCII value of the character representing the number 1). This process may also be performed in reverse. The compiler can read a number from a text file and assign it to an INTEGER variable.

LEARNING CHECK 13-2

1. What is a text file?
2. Write a program segment to declare a text file named CITIES and prepare it to be read. Assign the file to a disk file named CITIES.P.
3. Assume that POEM1 and POEM2 are both files of type TEXT. What is wrong with the following statement?
   POEM1 := POEM2;
4. What is the purpose of the EOLN function?

▬▬▬ NONTEXT FILES

Suppose a file containing only the results of student final exam grades is being created. It would be possible to place them into a text file, which means that they would be converted to their corresponding ASCII values before they were stored in the file. Before the numbers in the file could be read to INTEGER variables, they would have to be converted back to numeric values. This conversion process is performed automatically by the compiler. To save the time involved in this conversion process, a file could be declared to be of type INTEGER:

```
TYPE
    I_FILE = FILE OF INTEGER;

VAR
    INTEGER_FILE : I_FILE;
```

This means that INTEGER_FILE can contain only integer values. These nontext files are referred to as "typed" files; each of their components is of a specific data type, such as real, integer, array, or record. File components can be of any data type. However, only text files are divided into lines; other types of files are simply strings of components. This means that the EOLN function can only be used with text files. However, the EOF function can be used to check for the end of any type of file.

A File of Records

Assume a file is needed to store information on students at City High. It would be logical to create a file of records for this purpose. The declaration section of this program might look like this:

```
PROGRAM CREATE_FILE (STUDENT_FILE);

TYPE
   STUDENT_RECORD = RECORD
                    NAME        : STRING;
                    BIRTH_DATE  : STRING;
                    SEX         : CHAR;
                    GRADE       : INTEGER;
                    GPA         : REAL;
                END;    { STUDENT_RECORD }

   STUDENTS  = FILE OF STUDENT_RECORD;

VAR
   STUDENT_FILE : STUDENTS;
```

Each component of the file STUDENT_FILE will be an entire record of type STUDENT_RECORD.

The program needs to prompt the user to enter each of the fields of the record. The data on each student should be entered at the keyboard. A loop should allow the user to continue entering data as long as needed.

The program to create STUDENT_FILE is shown in Figure 13–6. The ASSIGN and REWRITE statements prepare the file to accept data. A WHILE/DO loop prompts the user to enter the data for each field of a record. When the record is filled, a single WRITE statement writes the record to STUDENT_FILE:

```
WRITE (STUDENT_FILE, STUDENT);
```

The loop continues to execute as long as there is more data to be entered. When the user has finished entering records, the loop is exited and STUDENT_FILE is closed.

```
PROGRAM CREATE_FILE (STUDENT_FILE);

{  THIS PROGRAM CREATES A FILE OF STUDENT RECORDS.  EACH RECORD
   CONTAINS THE STUDENT'S NAME, BIRTH DATE, SEX, GRADE, AND GRADE
   POINT AVERAGE. }

USES
   CRT;

TYPE
   STUDENT_RECORD = RECORD
                      NAME       : STRING;
                      BIRTH_DATE : STRING;
                      SEX        : CHAR;
                      GRADE      : INTEGER;
                      GPA        : REAL;
                    END;    { STUDENT_RECORD }

   STUDENTS = FILE OF STUDENT_RECORD;

VAR
   STUDENT_FILE : STUDENTS;
   STUDENT      : STUDENT_RECORD;
   ANSWER       : CHAR;

{****************************************************************}

PROCEDURE GET_DATA (VAR STUDENT : STUDENT_RECORD);

{  PROMPTS USER TO ENTER DATA TO THE FIELDS OF A STUDENT RECORD.
   THIS RECORD IS THEN RETURNED TO THE CALLING PROGRAM. }

BEGIN    { GET_DATA }

   WRITELN;
   WRITELN;
   { PROMPT USER TO ENTER INFORMATION ON EACH STUDENT. }
   WITH STUDENT DO
   BEGIN
      WRITE ('ENTER THE STUDENT''S NAME: ');
      READLN (NAME);
      WRITE ('ENTER THE BIRTH DATE (XX/XX/XX): ');
      READLN (BIRTH_DATE);
      WRITE ('ENTER THE STUDENT''S SEX: ');
      READLN (SEX);
      WRITE ('ENTER THE STUDENT''S GRADE: ');
      READLN (GRADE);
      WRITE ('ENTER THE STUDENT''S GRADE POINT: ');
      READLN (GPA);
   END;    { WITH }

END;    { GET_DATA }
```

FIGURE 13-6   PROGRAM CREATE_FILE

(Figure continued on next page)

```
{***************************************************************}

BEGIN   { MAIN }

   { PREPARE THE FILE STUDENT_FILE TO ACCEPT INPUT. }
   ASSIGN (STUDENT_FILE, 'STUDENT_F.P');
   REWRITE (STUDENT_FILE);

   { LOOP TO ALLOW USER TO ENTER AS MANY RECORDS AS NEEDED. }
   REPEAT
      { GET DATA FOR ONE RECORD. }
      GET_DATA (STUDENT);
      { WRITE THE ENTIRE RECORD TO THE FILE. }
      WRITE (STUDENT_FILE, STUDENT);
      { SEE IF THERE ARE MORE RECORDS TO BE ENTERED. }
      WRITE ('DO YOU WANT TO ADD MORE RECORDS (Y OR N): ');
      ANSWER := READKEY;
      WRITELN (ANSWER)
   UNTIL ANSWER IN ['N', 'n'];

   CLOSE (STUDENT_FILE);

END.   { MAIN }
```

```
ENTER THE STUDENT'S NAME: James Forse
ENTER THE BIRTH DATE (XX/XX/XX): 05/10/70
ENTER THE STUDENT'S SEX: M
ENTER THE STUDENT'S GRADE: 12
ENTER THE STUDENT'S GRADE POINT: 3.2
DO YOU WANT TO ADD MORE RECORDS (Y OR N): y


ENTER THE STUDENT'S NAME: Erica Robinson
ENTER THE BIRTH DATE (XX/XX/XX): 09/29/71
ENTER THE STUDENT'S SEX: F
ENTER THE STUDENT'S GRADE: 11
ENTER THE STUDENT'S GRADE POINT: 3.4
DO YOU WANT TO ADD MORE RECORDS (Y OR N): N
```

FIGURE 13–6   PROGRAM CREATE_FILE (Cont.)

Creating Nontext Files

As previously discussed, text files can be created using the Turbo system editor. Simply type in the contents and save them on a disk. However, nontext (or typed) files cannot be created this way. They must be created using a Pascal program such as the one shown in Figure 13–6. The user is prompted to enter the data, which is then stored on disk. This process allows the data to be stored in a format that will allow it to be accessed later.

Another important difference between text and nontext files is that text files are divided into lines whereas nontext files are not. As previously mentioned, this means that the EOLN function cannot be used with nontext files. It also means that READLN and WRITELN cannot be used with a nontext file.

UPDATING A FILE

In Turbo Pascal, an existing file can be updated in two ways: by replacing an already existing file component with a new value, or by adding (appending) new components to the end of the file. It is not possible to insert a new component into the middle of a file.

First, consider how a specified file component can be updated. The user must know the position of the component to be changed. The first component in a file is in position 0, the second in position 1, and so forth. In Figure 13–1, the number 184 is in position 2, and 93 is in position 6. The component is then accessed using the SEEK procedure. For example, the statement

```
SEEK (STUDENT_FILE, 2);
```

will access the third component of file STUDENT_FILE (which is in position 2). Once the desired component is accessed, a new value can be written to it by using a WRITE statement.

To append components to the end of a file, the length of the file must be determined by using the FILESIZE function. The length of the file

STUDENT_FILE can be assigned to an integer variable SIZE by using the following statement:

```
SIZE := FILESIZE (STUDENT_FILE);
```

Then a new record can be added to the end of the file (assume that STUDENT contains a single student's record):

```
SEEK (STUDENT_FILE, SIZE);
WRITE (STUDENT_FILE, STUDENT);
```

At first thought, it may seem that the value of SIZE should have been incremented by one so the last file component was not overwritten. But, remember that file components are numbered starting with zero. Therefore, the value assigned to position SIZE is actually one past the last component of the existing file, which is at position SIZE – 1.

Examine the procedure in Figure 13–7. It demonstrates the two methods of updating a file. This procedure could be inserted in the program in Figure 13–4. Notice that the file is reset before being updated. If a REWRITE statement had been used instead, the existing file would have been erased. Using RESET allows the SEEK procedure to be used to access the file for updating.

1. In what two ways can files be updated?
2. What is the purpose of the SEEK procedure?
3. Write the statements necessary to append the integer value 14 to the end of an integer file named DIGITS.

LEARNING CHECK 13–3

```
PROCEDURE UPDATE_FILE (VAR STUDENT_FILE : STUDENTS);

{  ALLOWS THE USER TO UPDATE STUDENT_FILE BY ADDING NEW RECORDS OR
   UPDATING AN EXISTING RECORD. }

VAR
   ANSWER : INTEGER;

{* * * * * * * * * * * * * * * * * * * * * * * * * * * * * * * * * * *}

PROCEDURE  ADD_RECORD (VAR STUDENT_FILE : STUDENTS);

{  ADDS A NEW RECORD TO THE END OF STUDENT_FILE. }

VAR
   NEW_STUDENT :  STUDENT_RECORD;
   LENGTH      : INTEGER;

BEGIN    { ADD_RECORD }

   GET_DATA (NEW_STUDENT);
   LENGTH := FILESIZE (STUDENT_FILE);
   SEEK (STUDENT_FILE, LENGTH);
   WRITE (STUDENT_FILE, NEW_STUDENT);

END;    { ADD_RECORD }

{* * * * * * * * * * * * * * * * * * * * * * * * * * * * * * * * * * *}

PROCEDURE UPDATE_RECORD (VAR STUDENT_FILE : STUDENTS);

{  UPDATES AN EXISTING RECORD. }

VAR
   ALTERED_RECORD : STUDENT_RECORD;
   POSITION       : INTEGER;

BEGIN    { UPDATE_RECORD }

   GET_DATA (ALTERED_RECORD);

   WRITE ('ENTER THE POSITION OF THE RECORD TO BE UPDATED: ');
   READLN (POSITION);
   SEEK (STUDENT_FILE, POSITION);
   WRITE (STUDENT_FILE, ALTERED_RECORD);

END;    { UPDATE_RECORD }

{* * * * * * * * * * * * * * * * * * * * * * * * * * * * * * * * * * *}
```

FIGURE 13-7 PROCEDURE TO UPDATE COMPONENTS OF STUDENT_FILE

```
BEGIN   { UPDATE_FILE }

  REPEAT
    RESET (STUDENT_FILE);
    WRITELN;
    WRITELN;
    WRITELN;
    WRITELN ('1.  ADD A NEW RECORD TO THE END OF THE FILE.');
    WRITELN ('2.  UPDATE AN EXISTING RECORD.');
    WRITELN ('3.  STOP.');
    WRITELN;
    WRITE ('ENTER THE NUMBER IN FRONT OF THE TASK YOU WANT TO DO: ');
    READLN (ANSWER);
    IF ANSWER = 1
      THEN ADD_RECORD (STUDENT_FILE)
      ELSE IF ANSWER = 2
            THEN UPDATE_RECORD (STUDENT_FILE)
  UNTIL ANSWER = 3;
  CLOSE (STUDENT_FILE);

END;   { UPDATE_FILE }
```

FIGURE 13-7   PROCEDURE TO UPDATE COMPONENTS OF STUDENT_FILE (Cont.)

■■■■ SUMMARY POINTS

- A file consists of a sequence of components, all of the same data type.
- File components are stored sequentially. Files can be stored permanently on secondary storage such as a floppy diskette.
- Because files are stored externally, and not in main memory, they are not limited in size by the amount of main memory available. Therefore, files can be very large. This is a distinct advantage over arrays.
- The length of a file is the number of components it contains. The FILESIZE function returns an integer value indicating the number of components in a specified file. Each component has a position number, starting with zero.
- Files are defined in the same manner as other variables. The components of files can be of any data type.
- Pascal has one standard type of file, the text file. Each of its components is a single character value.
- The ASSIGN statement links a file variable with a disk file.
- The EOLN function is used to check for the end of a line in a text file. The EOF function is used to check for the end of a file.
- The procedure RESET prepares a file to be read, and REWRITE prepares a file to be written to.

■ READ is used to read an input file, whereas WRITE is used to write data to an output file. When a program has finished accessing a file, the CLOSE statement saves its contents permanently on disk.

■ Files can be updated by accessing and changing a specified component. The SEEK procedure is used to locate the component to be changed. Then the new component can be inserted in place of the old one.

■ New components can be appended to an already existing file by first determining the length of the file. Then the SEEK procedure can be used to locate the end of the file, and new components can be added.

▬▬ VOCABULARY LIST

File
File pointer

▬▬ CHAPTER TEST

Vocabulary

Match a term from the numbered column with the description from the lettered column that best fits the term.

1. File pointer

2. File

    a. An imaginary pointer to the file component currently being accessed.

    b. A sequence of identically typed components kept in secondary storage.

Questions

1. Where are files stored? Why is this an advantage over the way in which arrays are stored?

2. What tasks are automatically performed by the RESET procedure? What tasks are automatically performed by the REWRITE procedure?

3. Create a program segment that will declare two files of type REAL, one named DATA_IN and the other DATA_OUT. Write an appro-

priate program heading, declaration statements, ASSIGN statements, and RESET and REWRITE statements. DATA_IN should be prepared to be read from, and DATA_OUT should be prepared to be written to.

4. Explain how the EOF and EOLN functions can be used to read text files.
5. Why can the EOLN function only be used when reading text files and not when reading other types of files?
6. Name an advantage of using nontext files rather than text files.
7. Name a disadvantage of using nontext files rather than text files.
8. Explain how the FILESIZE function is used when appending values to a file.

▬▬▬ PROGRAMMING PROBLEMS

Level 1

1. Write a procedure that copies a text file named TEXT1 to a file named TEXT2. TEXT1 is single-spaced. Write the program so that TEXT2 will be double-spaced.
2. Write a program that keeps track of the number of miles a person has jogged each day for a week. The program should prompt the user to enter the miles for each day like this:

   Enter number of miles jogged on Day 1:

   This information should be written to file JOG_FILE. The file should contain the information in table form appropriately labeled. The total number of miles jogged that week should be listed below the table.

Level 2

3. An instructor teaches three sections of Computer Science 104. She already has three text files containing the names of the students in each section. Write a program that will read these three files and combine them into a single file named CS305.
4. Write a program that creates an electronic phonebook. The program should prompt the user to enter the name, address, and phone number of as many people as desired. Treat each person's name, address, and number as a record. When all the names are entered, allow the user to enter a specific name. The program should then sequentially search the file and display the appropriate record.

Level 3

5. Write a program that will allow you to create two integer files, FILE1 and FILE2, each of the same length. Then write a second program that will read an integer value from each file and display the product on the screen. This process should be repeated for all of the integers in the files. For example, if the files looked like this:

```
FILE1  1    14  10  5
FILE2  12   3   8   7
```

the following should be displayed on the screen:

```
 1 × 12 = 12
14 ×  3 = 42
10 ×  8 = 80
 5 ×  7 = 35
```

6. Karl Kutz is the director of the library at the high school. Many people donate their old books to the library. Karl has developed the following form letter to thank these people:

Dear *:

Please accept our utmost gratitude for your donation of # books. They are a much appreciated addition to our growing collection.

Sincerely,

Karl Kutz
Librarian
West High School

This form letter should be stored in the file LETTER. Write a program that will allow Karl to enter the name of the donor and the number of books donated while the program is running. The form letter should then be copied to file DONOR_LETTER with the name and number of records properly inserted.

CHAPTER 14

Graphics

OBJECTIVES

After studying this chapter, you should be able to:

- Explain the difference between graphics and text modes.
- Explain how the turtle is used in Turtlegraphics to create drawings.
- Position and turn the turtle as needed.
- Use the various Turtlegraphics statements to draw figures.
- Explain how color graphics can be created.

OUTLINE

▄▄▄▄ INTRODUCTION

This chapter will discuss using Turtlegraphics. This is one type of graphics that is included with your Turbo Pascal compiler in both Version 3 and Version 4. It is also available with Turbo Pascal for the Macintosh, Version 1. Turtlegraphics is a relatively easy-to-use graphics package that was created by a group of programmers at the Massachusetts Institute of Technology.

The monitor screen accepts two types of images: text and graphics images. So far in this book, only programs displaying output in **text mode** have been written. In text mode, characters are displayed on the screen. When **graphics mode** is used, the entire screen is divided into small blocks, called **pixels**. These blocks can be turned on and off to create images.

When using Turbo Pascal Version 4, the following USES statement must be placed after the program heading:

```
USES
    CRT, GRAPH3;
```

This statement informs the compiler that this program will be using graphics.

▄▄▄▄ MONOCHROME GRAPHICS

Monochrome graphics refers to graphics using a two-color monitor (black and white, green and black, and so forth). When using monochrome graphics, the following statement should be placed immediately after the BEGIN in the main program:

GRAPHMODE;

This places the program in monochrome graphics mode. The screen is now divided into 320 horizontal and 200 vertical pixels. The screen is divided into four sections (or quadrants) like those used in mathematics:

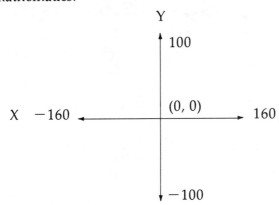

The position (0, 0) in the middle of the screen is referred to as home position. Coordinates are specified in the same way as in mathematics; for example, the coordinate (−80, −50) is in the middle of the lower left quadrant. The horizontal (or X) coordinate is stated first and then the vertical (or Y) coordinate.

Turtlegraphics uses a small figure, called a turtle (which is invisible), to draw figures on the screen. The basic idea is simple. The turtle moves across the screen dragging a pen. Therefore, as the turtle moves in different directions for different distances, lines will appear on the screen. Initially, the following statement should be used to place the turtle in "home" position:

HOME;

After this statement is executed, the turtle is in the middle of the screen (0, 0), facing upward (or North). The statement

CLEARSCREEN;

also places the turtle at home position. In addition, it clears the display screen.

DIFFERENCES FOR VERSION 3 USERS

In Version 3, the following statement should be used instead of the USES statement:

{$I GRAPH.P }

DIFFERENCES FOR MACINTOSH USERS

When using Turtlegraphics on the Macintosh, the following USES statements must be placed after the program heading:

```
USES
    MEMTYPES, QUICKDRAW, OSINTF, TOOLINTF, TURTLE;
```

Make certain that the "Turtle Folder" is on your Turbo Pascal compiler disk. This folder contains the units needed to perform Turtlegraphics. The GRAPHMODE procedure is not used on the Macintosh. The statement to clear the screen is CLEAR rather than CLEARSCREEN. In addition, remember that it is necessary to insert a READLN statement in your program so that program output will remain on the screen until the Return key is pressed. The program in Figure 14–1 could be rewritten to run on the Macintosh as follows:

```
PROGRAM CIRCLE;

{ DRAWS A CIRCLE BY CONTINUALLY TURNING THE TURTLE TWO DEGREES
  AND THEN DRAWING A LINE TWO PIXELS LONG UNTIL THE COMPLETE CIRCLE
  IS DRAWN. }

USES
    MEMTYPES, QUICKDRAW, OSINTF, TOOLINTF, TURTLE;

VAR
    POSITION : INTEGER;

BEGIN   { CIRCLE }

    SETPOSITION (-60,0);
    PENDOWN;

    FOR POSITION := 1 TO 180 DO
    BEGIN
        FORWD (2);
        TURNRIGHT (2);
    END;   { FOR }

    { DISPLAY A CAPTION. }
    GOTOXY (5, 24);
    WRITELN ('THIS PROGRAM DISPLAYS A CIRCLE.':50);
    READLN;

END. { CIRCLE }
```

▇▇▇ CONTROLLING THE TURTLE

To make the turtle draw a line by dragging its make-believe pen, the pen has to be placed down:

```
PENDOWN;
```

The following statements will cause the turtle to draw a line from its home position 10 pixels upward (North):

```
HOME;
PENDOWN;
FORWD (10);
```

The line will go North because when HOME is executed, the turtle is facing north. The FORWD statement causes the turtle to go forward the specified number of pixels.

The statement

```
BACK (10);
```

will cause the turtle to draw a line from the middle of the screen South (downward) 10 pixels. To draw a line from the center 10 pixels to the right (or East), first turn the turtle in that direction:

```
TURNRIGHT (90);
```

This statement causes the turtle to turn to the right the specified number of degrees. In order to head directly East, the turtle must turn 90 degrees (360/4). Now the turtle can be moved 10 pixels to the East:

```
FORWD (10);
```

Once the turtle is facing East, using the BACK statement

```
BACK (10);
```

makes it go West. Another possibility, however, is to turn the turtle so that it is facing West and then go forward. Assuming that it is currently facing East, it will have to turn 180 degrees:

```
TURNRIGHT (180);
```

Now, the FORWD command can be used to draw a line toward the West. It is also possible to turn the turtle toward the left by using the TURNLEFT statement. The following program segment will cause the turtle to draw a line from home 10 pixels toward the West:

```
HOME;
TURNLEFT (90);
PENDOWN;
FORWD (10);
```

To draw a line from the coordinate (10, 0) to the coordinate (20, 0), the following program segment could be used:

```
HOME;
TURNRIGHT (90);
PENUP;
FORWD (10);
PENDOWN;
FORWD (10);
```

In this program segment, the turtle starts at home and then is turned right so that it is heading East. Next, its pen is lifted up so that it will not draw a line from (0, 0) to (10, 0). Once it reaches (10, 0), the pen is put down, and a line is drawn from (10, 0) to (20, 0).

There is a simpler way of performing this task. Start the turtle at (10, 0) by using the SETPOSITION statement:

```
SETPOSITION (10,0);
PENDOWN;
TURNRIGHT (90);
FORWD (10);
```

The SETPOSITION statement places the turtle at the desired coordinate without drawing a line.

TABLE 14-1 GRAPHICS COMMANDS

Statement	Purpose
BACK (pixels)	Moves the turtle backward the specified number of pixels.
CLEARSCREEN	Clears the output screen and places the turtle at home (middle of the screen, facing North).
FORWD (pixels)	Moves the turtle forward the specified number of pixels.
GRAPHCOLOR-MODE	Places the computer in medium resolution (320 × 100) color graphics mode.
GRAPHMODE	Places the computer in medium resolution (320 × 200) monochrome graphics mode.
HOME	Puts the turtle in the middle of the screen facing North.
NOWRAP	The turtle will not "reappear" on the opposite side of the display screen when it leaves the viewing area.
PENDOWN	Places the turtle's pen down so that when it moves it will leave a "trail."
PENUP	Lifts the turtle's pen up so that when it moves it will not leave a "trail."

SETHEADING (degrees)	Turns the turtle to the specified degree.
SETPENCOLOR (color)	Selects a color for the line drawn by the turtle.
SETPOSITION (X, Y)	Moves the turtle to the specified location without drawing a line.
TEXTMODE	Places the computer in text mode so that text characters can be entered.
TURNLEFT (degrees)	Turns the turtle the specified number of degrees counterclockwise.
TURNRIGHT (degrees)	Turns the turtle the specified number of degrees clockwise.
WRAP	The turtle will "reappear" on the opposite side of the display screen when it leaves the viewing area.

1. What command tells the compiler that you will be using mono-chrome graphics?
2. Where is the turtle's home position? What command will place the turtle at home?
3. Write statements that perform the commands in parts a–c.

   a. Place the turtle at home and draw a line 20 pixels to the West.
   b. Draw a line starting at the coordinate (20, 0) and going to the coordinate (50, 0).
   c. Draw a line starting at the coordinate (0, −30) and going to the coordinate (0, 10).

LEARNING CHECK 14–1

■ DRAWING A CIRCLE

A circle can be drawn by drawing a very short line (for example, 2 pixels long) and then turning the turtle a couple of degrees and drawing another very short line. This process is continued until the turtle has drawn a complete circle. Figure 14–1 shows a program that will create such a circle. The center of the circle is at (−60, 0). A FOR loop is used to draw a short line repeatedly. Notice the loop is executed 180 times.

```
PROGRAM CIRCLE;

{ DRAWS A CIRCLE BY CONTINUALLY TURNING THE TURTLE TWO DEGREES
  AND THEN DRAWING A LINE TWO PIXELS LONG UNTIL THE COMPLETE CIRCLE
  IS DRAWN. }

USES
   CRT, GRAPH3;

VAR
   POSITION : INTEGER;

BEGIN   { CIRCLE }

   GRAPHMODE;
   SETPOSITION (-60,0);
   PENDOWN;

   FOR POSITION := 1 TO 180 DO
   BEGIN
      FORWD (2);
      TURNRIGHT (2);
   END;    { FOR }

   { DISPLAY A CAPTION. }
   GOTOXY (5, 24);
   WRITELN ('THIS PROGRAM DISPLAYS A CIRCLE.');

END.  { CIRCLE }
```

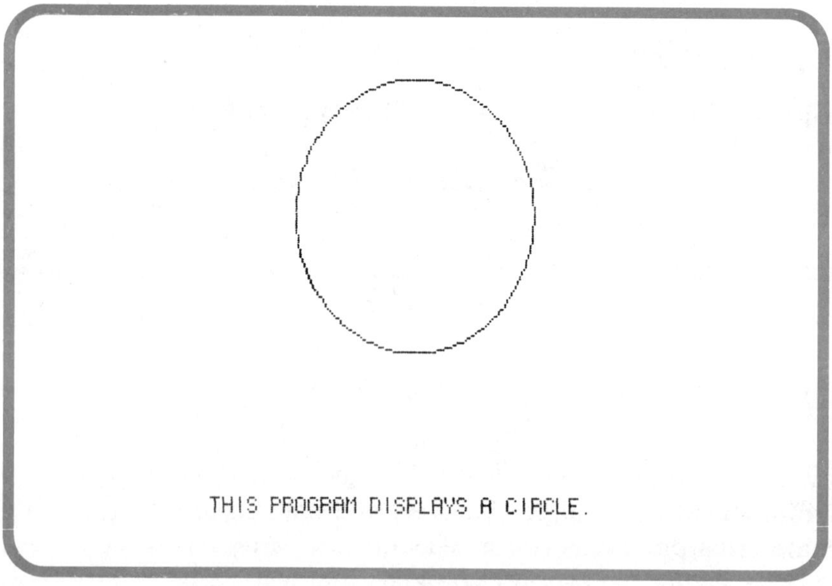

FIGURE 14-1 DRAWING A CIRCLE

Each time through the loop, the turtle is turned clockwise 2 degrees and draws a line 2 pixels long. Because the turtle is turned 2 degrees each time, after 180 times it will have made a complete circle (there are 360 degrees in a circle). It is often possible to place Turtlegraphics statements in loops to get the desired result.

A statement has been placed at the bottom of the illustration. This was done by using a WRITELN statement. Notice the GOTOXY statement:

```
GOTOXY (5, 24);
```

It is used to position the output of the WRITELN. Remember that when the GOTOXY statement is used, the coordinates are stated differently than in Turtlegraphics. The upper left corner is (0, 0). When creating text in graphics mode, the screen can only display 40 characters across and 24 lines of text vertically. This is because the text is twice as large as in regular text mode. Using the value of 24 in this WRITELN statement places the text on the lowest possible line.

DRAWING A BAR GRAPH

Bar graphs are a useful way of graphically illustrating program results. They can be made by drawing a sequence of rectangles. To illustrate graphically the number of students in each of five English classes using the following data:

Class Number	Number of Students
1	29
2	24
3	31
4	28
5	22

a horizontal rectangle will be drawn for each class. A procedure can be used to perform this task five times. Different parameters will have to be passed to the procedure to indicate the length of the rectangle depending on the size of the class. Figure 14–2 contains the program that creates this graph. In addition to a procedure that draws the rectangles, a second procedure is used to display the labels indicating the class number. For each class member, a line 4 pixels long is drawn. Therefore, if a class has 22 students, the total length of the bar will be 88 pixels. The value of BAR_NUMBER is decremented by 30 pixels at the end of the procedure so that the next bar will be placed 30 pixels below the position of the previous one.

```
PROGRAM BAR_GRAPH;

{ THIS PROGRAM CREATES A BAR GRAPH SHOWING HOW MANY STUDENTS ARE
  ENROLLED IN EACH OF FIVE ENGLISH CLASSES. }

USES
   CRT, GRAPH3;

VAR
   BAR_NUMBER, NUMBER_STUDENTS : INTEGER;

{*********************************************************************}

PROCEDURE DRAW_BAR (NUMBER_STUDENTS : INTEGER; VAR BAR_NUMBER : INTEGER);

{ DRAWS EACH BAR IN THE GRAPH THE CORRECT LENGTH. }

BEGIN   { DRAW_BAR }

   SETPOSITION (-100, BAR_NUMBER);
   TURNRIGHT (90);
   FORWD (NUMBER_STUDENTS * 4);     { DRAW TOP LINE }
   TURNRIGHT (90);
   FORWD (20);                      { DRAW RIGHT SIDE }
   TURNRIGHT (90);
   FORWD (NUMBER_STUDENTS * 4);     { DRAW BOTTOM LINE }
   TURNRIGHT (90);
   FORWD (20);                      { DRAW LEFT SIDE }
   BAR_NUMBER := BAR_NUMBER - 30;   { SET POSITION TO START NEXT BAR }

END;   { DRAW_BAR }

{*********************************************************************}

PROCEDURE DISPLAY_LABELS;

{ DISPLAYS THE CLASS NUMBER ON THE LEFT SIDE OF EACH BAR. }

VAR
   COUNT : INTEGER;

BEGIN   { DISPLAY_LABELS }

   GOTOXY (1,4);          { POSITION LABEL FOR FIRST BAR }
   WRITELN ('CLASS 1');
   FOR COUNT :=  2 TO 5 DO
   BEGIN
      GOTOXY (1, COUNT * 4);   { POSITION EACH SUBSEQUENT LABEL }
      WRITELN ('CLASS ', COUNT);
   END;   { FOR }

END;   { DISPLAY_LABELS }
```

FIGURE 14-2 CREATING A BAR GRAPH

```
{****************************************************************}

BEGIN    { MAIN }

    GRAPHMODE;
    DISPLAY_LABELS;
    BAR_NUMBER := 80;          { SET VERTICAL POSITION FOR FIRST BAR }

    { CALL PROCEDURE TO DRAW EACH BAR. }
    DRAW_BAR (29, BAR_NUMBER);
    DRAW_BAR (24, BAR_NUMBER);
    DRAW_BAR (31, BAR_NUMBER);
    DRAW_BAR (28, BAR_NUMBER);
    DRAW_BAR (22, BAR_NUMBER);

END.    { MAIN }
```

CLASS 1 ▭

CLASS 2 ▭

CLASS 3 ▭

CLASS 4 ▭

CLASS 5 ▭

FIGURE 14–2 CREATING A BAR GRAPH (Cont.)

USING WINDOWS

Ordinarily, the entire screen in which the turtle can move is seen. It is also possible to show a "window" that consists of only a subsection of the entire screen. For example, the following command will allow only the upper right quadrant of the screen to be seen:

```
TURTLEWINDOW (80, 50, 160, 100);
```

The coordinates contained within this window will now be as follows:

- (0, 0): home, center of the current window—when the entire screen was showing, the center of this window was at (80, 50).
- X coordinates can range from −80 through 80.
- Y coordinates can range from 50 through −49.

▉▉▉▉ USING COLOR

If you have a color monitor, you can display your drawings in color. To allow your program to display colored output, use the following command:

```
GRAPHCOLORMODE;
```

Four different "palettes" determine the colors that are currently available. These palettes are numbered 0 through 3. Table 14–2 shows the colors available in each palette. Notice that color 0 is always "background." You have a choice of the 16 background colors listed in Table 14–3. The following statement will select a background color of blue (number 1):

```
GRAPHBACKGROUND (1);
```

The following statement selects palette 2:

```
PALETTE (2);
```

This provides a choice of the background color (0), light green (1), light red (2), or yellow (3) for the turtle's pen color. After a palette is selected, the following statement selects a pen color:

```
SETPENCOLOR (3);
```

Anything drawn will now appear yellow. The following program segment causes a green line to be drawn on a red background:

```
GRAPHCOLORMODE;
HOME;
PENDOWN;
PALETTE (0);
GRAPHBACKGROUND (4);
SETPENCOLOR (1);
BACK (5);
```

TABLE 14–2 PALETTES AND COLORS

Color	0	1	2	3
Palette 0	Background	Green	Red	Brown
Palette 1	Background	Cyan	Magenta	Light gray
Palette 2	Background	Light green	Light red	Yellow
Palette 3	Background	Light cyan	Light magenta	White

TABLE 14–3 BACKGROUND COLORS

0	Black
1	Blue
2	Green
3	Cyan
4	Red
5	Magenta
6	Brown
7	Light gray
8	Dark gray
9	Light blue
10	Light green
11	Light cyan
12	Light red
13	Light magenta
14	Yellow
15	White

1. Write a procedure that will draw a circle whose center is at (40, 0).
2. What is the purpose of the TURTLEWINDOW statement?
3. Write the two statements that will allow the turtle's pen color to be light green.
4. Write a statement that will cause the background color of the screen to be magenta.

LEARNING CHECK 14–2

SUMMARY POINTS

- Written output is displayed in text mode whereas illustrations are displayed in graphics mode.
- The command GRAPHMODE places the computer in monochrome graphics mode. The entire screen is divided into a grid of pixels, 320 pixels wide and 200 pixels high. Coordinates are used to specify a particular pixel. The center of the screen is at (0, 0). The first coordinate is the X (horizontal) coordinate, and the second is the Y (vertical) coordinate.
- Turtlegraphics uses an imaginary turtle to create shapes. The turtle drags a pen, which draws a line. The statement PENUP lifts up the pen so no line is drawn whereas PENDOWN places the pen down so there will be a line.

■ The turtle can be placed at (0, 0), facing North, by using the HOME command. The FORWD command causes the turtle to go forward the specified number of pixels whereas BACK makes it go backward.

■ TURNLEFT turns the turtle counterclockwise the stated number of degrees; TURNRIGHT turns the turtle clockwise.

■ SETPOSITION (X, Y) places the turtle at the specified coordinates.

■ TURTLEWINDOW causes only a portion of the display screen to be visible.

■ With a color monitor, color graphics may be used by replacing the GRAPHMODE statement with GRAPHCOLORMODE.

■ One of 16 background colors can be selected by using the GRAPHBACKGROUND statement.

■ Before choosing a pen color, one of four palettes must be selected by using the PALETTE statement. The palette chosen determines the selection of pen colors currently available.

■ SETPENCOLOR allows the programmer to choose the color of the turtle's pen.

▬▬▬ VOCABULARY LIST

Graphics mode
Pixels
Text mode

▬▬▬ CHAPTER TEST

Vocabulary

Match a term from the numbered column with the description from the lettered column that best fits the term.

1. Pixel

a. The mode in which illustrations can be displayed.

2. Graphics mode

b. The mode in which text output is displayed.

3. Text mode

c. A block of light that can be turned on or off to create images.

Questions

1. What is the difference between graphics mode and text mode?
2. Write a program segment to draw a square 40 pixels in length with its center at (0, 0).
3. How does the SETPOSITION statement work?
4. How are the TURNLEFT and TURNRIGHT statements used to aim the turtle in a specified direction?
5. Refer to Figure 14–1. Why was the FOR loop in this program executed 180 times?
6. In color graphics mode, how many different background colors are possible?
7. How is a background color selected in color graphics mode?
8. In color graphics, what is the purpose of selecting a palette before selecting the color of the pen?

▬▬▬ PROGRAMMING PROBLEMS

Level 1

1. Write a program that will display your initials on the screen. Create a border around the edge of the screen. If you are using a color monitor, make the initials and the border different colors.
2. Write a program that will display the Olympics rings on the screen:

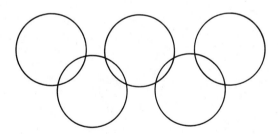

   Call a procedure to draw each of the circles.

Level 2

3. Rewrite the program in Figure 14–2 so that the bar graph is vertical rather than horizontal.
4. Write a program that will draw a smiling face.
5. Write a program that will draw a picture of a house.

APPENDIX A

Rules for Creating Identifiers

Turbo Pascal identifiers are used to name parts of a program such as variables, constants, procedures, functions, and so forth. They must follow these rules:

- They must begin with a letter (uppercase or lowercase).
- They can contain only letters or digits (0–9) or the underscore character (_).
- Uppercase and lowercase letters are seen by the compiler as being identical.
- Identifiers can have any number of characters. However, only the first 63 characters are significant.

APPENDIX B

Syntax Diagrams

Syntax Diagram Symbols

indicates a Pascal reserved identifier

indicates a Pascal operator or punctuation

indicates a Pascal element that is defined
by yet another syntax diagram

Program

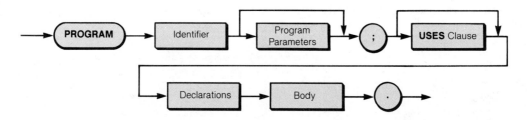

Identifier

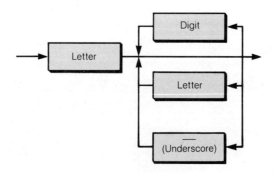

USES Clause

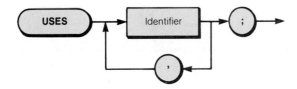

Program Parameters

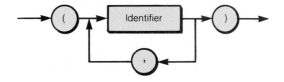

Constant Definition

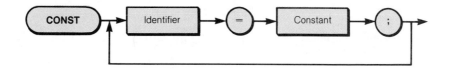

Type Definition

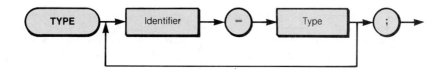

Variable Declaration

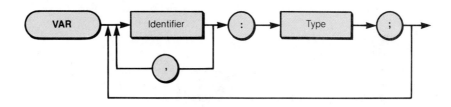

Procedure Definition

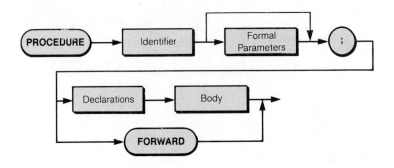

Function Definition

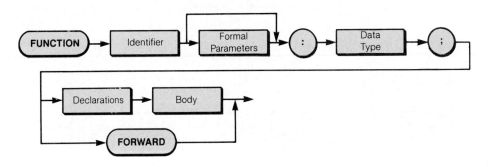

Formal Parameter List

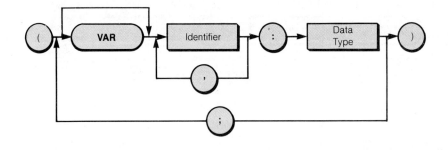

Body

Statements

Assignment Statement

Compound Statement

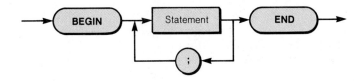

Single-Alternative Decision Statement

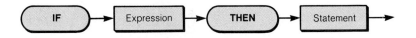

Double-Alternative Decision Statement

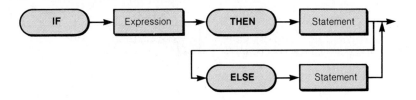

WHILE/DO Statement

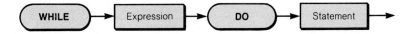

CASE Statement

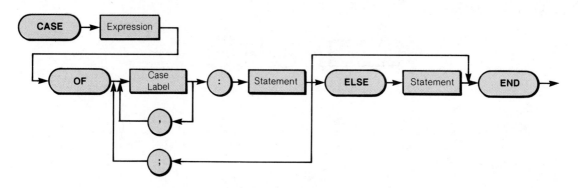

REPEAT/UNTIL Statement

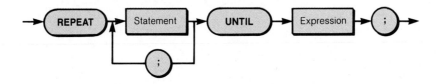

FOR Statement

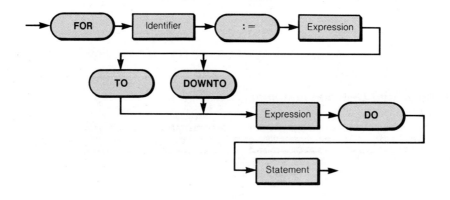

Procedure Call Statement

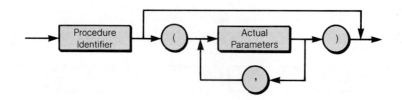

GOTO Statement

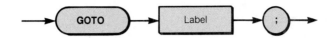

WITH Statement

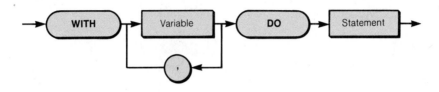

Actual Parameter

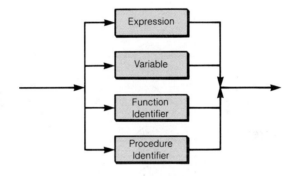

Expression

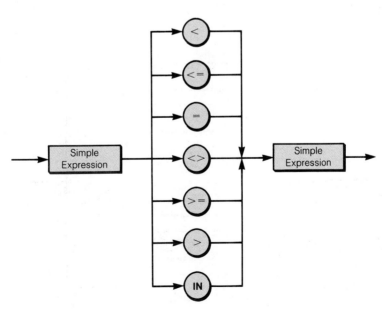

Simple Expression

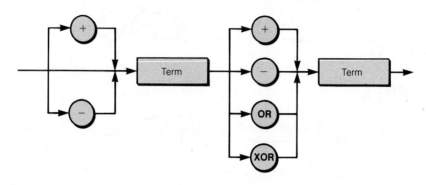

Term

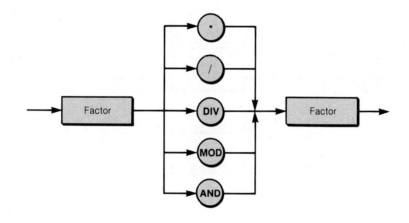

Factor

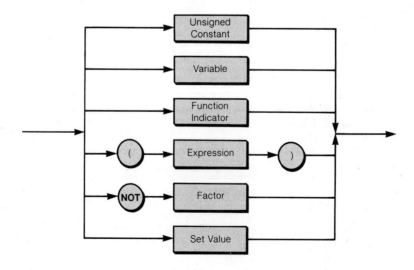

Set Value

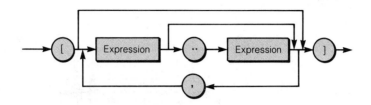

Type

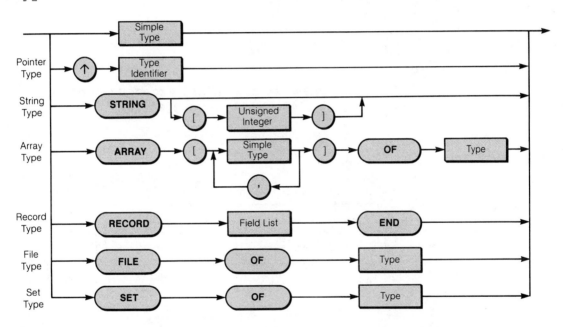

Simple Type

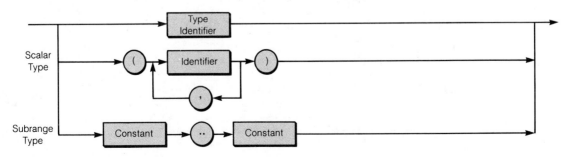

Simple Types

INTEGER

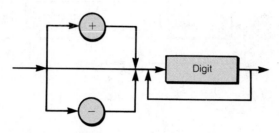

Note: The data type INTEGER can contain values from −32768 through 32767.

LONGINT

Note: LONGINT is the same as INTEGER except it can contain values from −2147483648 through 2147483647.

REAL

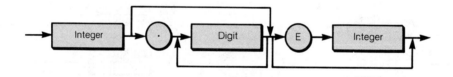

BOOLEAN

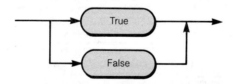

CHAR

STRING

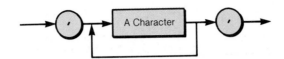

Field List

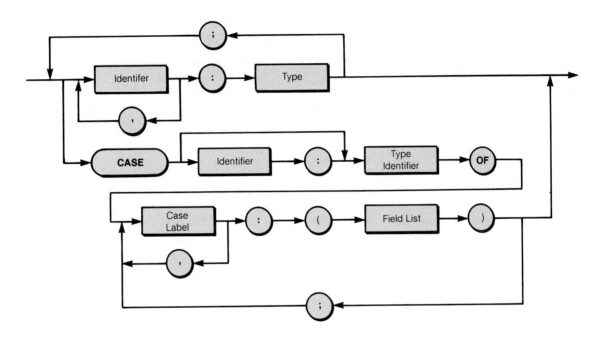

Case Label

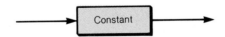

Constant

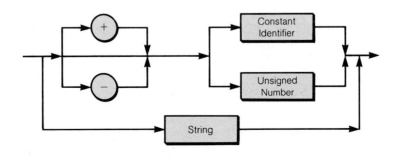

Variable

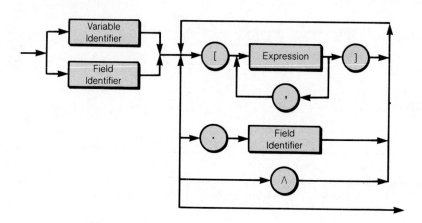

Turbo Pascal Reserved Words

ABSOLUTE	IF	REPEAT
AND	*IMPLEMENTATION	SET
ARRAY	IN	SHL
BEGIN	INLINE	SHR
CASE	*INTERFACE	STRING
CONST	*INTERRUPT	THEN
DIV	LABEL	TO
DO	MOD	TYPE
DOWNTO	NIL	*UNIT
ELSE	NOT	UNTIL
END	OF	*USES
EXTERNAL	OR	VAR
FILE	**OVERLAY	WHILE
FOR	PACKED	WITH
FORWARD	PROCEDURE	XOR
FUNCTION	PROGRAM	
GOTO	RECORD	

*Not a reserved word in Version 3.
**Not a reserved word in Version 4.
Note: Reserved words can be any combination of uppercase and lower-
     case letters.

Turbo Pascal Operators

Assignment

:=

Arithmetic

+	(addition)
—	(subtraction)
*	(multiplication)
/	(division)
div	(integer division)
mod	(remainder of integer division)

Relational

=	(equal to)
<>	(not equal to)
<	(less than)
<=	(less than or equal to)
>	(greater than)
>=	(greater than or equal to)
IN	(is a member of)

Logical (BOOLEAN)

NOT
AND
OR
XOR

Set

+   (union)
−   (difference)
*   (intersection)

STRING

+   (concatentation)

ASCII (American Standard Code for Information Interchange) Table

Commonly used ASCII characters are listed in the following table.

	CHAR		CHAR		CHAR
32	SPC	59	;	86	V
33	!	60	<	87	W
34	"	61	=	88	X
35	#	62	>	89	Y
36	$	63	?	90	Z
37	%	64	@	91	[
38	&	65	A	92	\
39	'	66	B	93	]
40	(	67	C	94	∧
41	)	68	D	95	—
42	*	69	E	96	'
43	+	70	F	97	a
44	,	71	G	98	b
45	-	72	H	99	c
46	.	73	I	100	d
47	/	74	J	101	e
48	0	75	K	102	f
49	1	76	L	103	g
50	2	77	M	104	h
51	3	78	N	105	i
52	4	79	O	106	j
53	5	80	P	107	k
54	6	81	Q	108	l
55	7	82	R	109	m
56	8	83	S	110	n
57	9	84	T	111	o
58	:	85	U	112	p

	CHAR		CHAR		CHAR		CHAR
113	q	149	ò	185	╣	221	▌
114	r	150	û	186	║	222	▐
115	s	151	ù	187	╗	223	▀
116	t	152	ÿ	188	╝	224	α
117	u	153	Ö	189	╜	225	β
118	v	154	Ü	190	╛	226	Γ
119	w	155	¢	191	┐	227	π
120	x	156	£	192	└	228	Σ
121	y	157	¥	193	┴	229	σ
122	z	158	Pt	194	┬	230	μ
123	{	159	ƒ	195	├	231	τ
124	|	160	á	196	─	232	Φ
125	}	161	í	197	┼	233	θ
126	~	162	ó	198	╞	234	Ω
127	DEL	163	ú	199	╟	235	δ
128	Ç	164	ñ	200	╚	236	∞
129	ü	165	Ñ	201	╔	237	Ø
130	é	166	ª	202	╩	238	ϵ
131	â	167	º	203	╦	239	∩
132	ä	168	¿	204	╠	240	≡
133	à	169	⌐	205	═	241	±
134	å	170	¬	206	╬	242	≥
135	ç	171	½	207	╧	243	≤
136	ê	172	¼	208	╨	244	⌠
137	ë	173	¡	209	╤	245	⌡
138	è	174	«	210	╥	246	÷
139	ï	175	»	211	╙	247	≈
140	î	176	░	212	╘	248	°
141	ì	177	▒	213	╒	249	•
142	Ä	178	▓	214	╓	250	·
143	Å	179	│	215	╫	251	√
144	É	180	┤	216	╪	252	ⁿ
145	æ	181	╡	217	┘	253	²
146	Æ	182	╢	218	┌	254	■
147	ô	183	╖	219	█	255	
148	ö	184	╕	220	▄		

Common Standard Functions in Turbo Pascal

Arithmetic Functions

NAME	DATA TYPE OF ARGUMENT	DATA TYPE OF RESULT	VALUE RETURNED
ABS (X)	INTEGER/REAL	Same as argument	Absolute value of X
ARCTAN (X)	INTEGER/REAL	REAL	Arctangent of X (X in radians)
COS (X)	INTEGER/REAL	INTEGER/REAL	Cosine of X (X in radians)
EXP (X)	INTEGER/REAL	REAL	e to the X power
FRAC (X)	REAL	REAL	Fractional part of real number
INT (X)	REAL	REAL	Integer portion of real number
LN (X)	INTEGER/REAL	REAL	Natural logarithm of X
PI	None	REAL	Value of pi
SIN (X)	INTEGER/REAL	REAL	Sine of X (X in radians)
SQR (X)	INTEGER/REAL	Same as X	Square of X
SQRT (X)	INTEGER/REAL (positive)	REAL	Square root of X

Transfer Functions

NAME	DATA TYPE OF ARGUMENT	DATA TYPE OF RESULT	VALUE RETURNED
CHR	INTEGER	CHAR	The character corresponding to the specified number.
ORD	Any ordinal value	INTEGER	The number corresponding to the specified ordinal value.

| ROUND (X) | REAL | LONGINT | Rounds X to nearest integer. |
| TRUNC (X) | REAL | LONGINT | Cuts off a real number at the decimal point. |

String Functions

NAME	PURPOSE	EXAMPLE
CONCAT	Joins together a series of strings.	ALL := CONCAT (STR1, STR2);
COPY	Returns a substring starting at a specified position and continuing for a specified length.	PART := COPY (NAME, 6, 5);
LENGTH	Returns the length of a string as an integer value.	LONG := LENGTH (STRING);
POS	Returns an integer indicating the starting location of a specified substring.	SUB := POS ('A.', NAME);

Ordinal Functions

NAME	PURPOSE	EXAMPLE
ODD (X)	Returns true if X is odd, false if X is even.	ODD (483)
PRED (X)	Returns the predecessor of the ordinal argument.	PRED (483)
SUCC (X)	Returns the successor of the ordinal argument.	SUCC (483)

Miscellaneous Functions

NAME	PURPOSE	EXAMPLE
EOF	Returns true if the end of a file is encountered, otherwise it is false.	WHILE NOT EOF DO
EOLN	Returns true if the end of a line is encountered, otherwise it is false.	WHILE NOT EOLN DO
FILESIZE	Returns the number of components in a file.	FILESIZE (STUDENT_FILE);
KEYPRESSED*	Returns a value of true if a key has been pressed, otherwise it is false.	KEYPRESSED
RANDOM	Returns a random number from zero to one.	X := RANDOM;
RANDOM (X)	Returns a random number from zero to X.	X := RANDOM (50);

| READKEY*† | Returns a single character entered at the keyboard. | LETTER := READKEY; |
| UPCASE (X) | Returns the uppercase value of a character. | UPCASE ('v') |

*These functions are contained in the CRT unit.
†READKEY is not available in Version 3. Macintosh Turbo Pascal uses READCHAR.

APPENDIX G

Common Standard Procedures in Turbo Pascal

Input and Output Procedures

NAME	PURPOSE	EXAMPLE
READ	Reads data from keyboard or file.	READ (NUM1);
READLN	Reads data from keyboard or file; includes a carriage return.	READLN (NUM1);
WRITE	Outputs values to monitor screen or disk file.	WRITE ('HI');
WRITELN	Outputs values to monitor screen or disk file; includes a carriage return.	WRITELN ('HI');

File-Handling Procedures

NAME	PURPOSE	EXAMPLE
ASSIGN	Links a file variable with a disk file.	ASSIGN (TEXT_IN, 'TEXT_IN.P');
REWRITE	Prepares a file to have data written to it.	REWRITE (TEXT_OUT);
RESET	Prepares a file to have data read from it.	RESET (TEXT_IN);
SEEK	Locates a specified file component.	SEEK (10);
CLOSE	Stores a file permanently on disk.	CLOSE (TEXT_OUT);
APPEND	Appends a component to the end of a file.	APPEND (NEXT_REC);

String Procedures

NAME	PURPOSE	EXAMPLE
DELETE	Deletes a substring from a string value starting at a specified position for a specified length.	DELETE (STR1, 8, 5);
INSERT	Inserts a substring into a string value starting at a specified position.	INSERT ('NO ', STR1, 5);
STR	Converts a numeric value to a string value.	STR (145, NUM_STR);
VAL	Converts the string value to a numeric value.	VAL ('145', NUM);

Ordinal Procedures

NAME	PURPOSE	EXAMPLE
DEC*	Decrements a variable to the previous ordinal value.	DEC (NUMBER);
INC*	Increments a variable to the next ordinal value.	INC (NUMBER);

Miscellaneous Procedures

NAME	PURPOSE	EXAMPLE
HALT	Stops program execution and returns control to the operating system.	HALT;
RANDOMIZE	Initializes the built-in random generator with a random value.	RANDOMIZE;

*Not available in Version 3 or on the Macintosh.

Turbo Pascal for the IBM, Version 3

Version 3 of Turbo Pascal does much more than allow you to run Turbo Pascal programs. It also contains a built-in editor that allows you to enter your programs at the keyboard. In addition, a file manager keeps track of the Turbo files you have stored on disk and retrieves and stores these files when instructed to do so. We will discuss these features in the following sections.

The Main Menu

To start the Turbo system, insert the Turbo disk in the A drive (the left-hand drive) of your computer and turn the computer on. For the purposes of this discussion, we will assume that you are using a computer with two floppy disk drives. Once the system prompt sign appears (in the case of the IBM the A> is the prompt), enter the word Turbo and press Return. The disk drive will whir for a minute and then a message similar to the following will appear:

```
------------------------------------------
TURBO Pascal system        Version 3.01A
                                   PC-DOS

Copyright (C) 1983,84,85    BORLAND Inc.
------------------------------------------

Default display mode

Include error messages (Y/N)?
```

Note the colored rectangle that appears after the last line on the screen:

```
Include error messages (Y/N)?
```

This rectangle is called the *cursor*. It is used to indicate where something entered at the keyboard will appear on the screen. The system is now waiting for you to respond to the prompt shown above. If you enter a Y, the system will read, or *load*, the error message file that is stored on the disk into memory. (This will take a few moments.) Now the system will be able to print an appropriate message if you attempt to execute a program that contains an error. If you respond to this prompt with an N, the error messages will not be loaded and therefore cannot be displayed when appropriate. Even though these error messages take up part of the main memory of the computer, it is a good idea to use them because it makes the debugging process easier, especially for the beginning programmer.

After responding to the error message prompt (note that you did not have to press Return after entering the letter), the Turbo main menu will appear. It will look similar to the following:

```
Logged drive: A
Active directory: \

Work file:
Main file:

Edit        Compile  Run    Save

Dir         Quit  compiler Options

Text:       0 bytes
Free: 62024 bytes


>
```

This menu lists the various commands that are available. To cause a specific command to be executed, simply enter the highlighted capital letter. For example, to execute the Quit command, simply enter a Q (a lowercase q will also work). We will discuss each of these commands in the following sections.

The first line on the screen is:

```
Logged drive: A
```

This indicates that the drive currently being *accessed*, or used, is drive A. (The Turbo disk is in this drive.) If the logged drive were B, it would be necessary to place the Turbo disk into that drive so that it could be accessed. If you are using a system with a hard drive, the Turbo system will probably be on the C drive. To change the logged drive, simply type L and the prompt shown below will appear:

```
New drive:
```

It is possible to enter any letter from A through P in response to this prompt; in reality, if you are using a system with two floppy disk drives, you will want to enter either A or B. Then press the Return key.

The Work File Command

The Work File command allows you to select the name of the file you wish to access. When the W is pressed, the following prompt appears:

`Work file name:`

At this point you can enter the name of the work file. In Turbo Pascal, a file name can have a maximum of eight characters. In addition, if desired, this name can be followed by a period and an extension indicating a file type. The following are all valid file names:

```
SAVINGS
HELLO.PAS
FINDSUM.EXA
```

If the file entered has been stored on disk previously, the system will load it (that is, read it from the disk and place it in the work file so that you can work with it). If no file with this name exists, a new file will be created. If you want the file to be loaded from a disk other than the Turbo Pascal disk, this disk should be placed in the B drive (assuming the Turbo disk is in the A drive). Then the file name should indicate the drive as shown below:

`B:SAVINGS`

The system will now determine if the file SAVINGS has previously been stored on the disk in the B drive. If it is present, it will be loaded; otherwise a new file will be created. Later on, when you save the file, it will be saved automatically on the disk in the B drive.

The Edit Command

The Edit command allows you to type in your program. The built-in Turbo editor is similar to the word processing package WordStar. It is a full-screen editor, meaning that you can edit anything that appears on the screen by moving the cursor to the desired location. When you press the letter E, the file to be edited appears on the screen. If a new file is being created, the screen will be blank except for the status line that appears at the top:

`Line 5    Col 12   Insert     Indent   A:HELLO.P`

We will briefly discuss each entry in the status line. The *Line* entry indicates the number of the line that currently contains the cursor. The *Col* entry indicates the number of the column (starting from the left edge) currently containing the cursor. *Insert* indicates that anything entered at the keyboard will be inserted at the position containing the cursor. The other alternative instead of *Insert* is *Overwrite*. This would indicate that anything entered would "overwrite" the old text, erasing it. On the IBM PC, the insert key will toggle between *Insert* and *Overwrite*. *Indent* causes a statement to be indented to the same column as the preceding statement. The last entry in the status line is the name of the program currently being edited, in this case HELLO.P. Note that the name of the program is preceded by the letter of the current disk drive, A: in this example.

Now we will practice entering a Pascal program. It isn't necessary to understand the program, only to be a careful typist. The program looks like this:

```
program Greeting;
begin
   writeln ('HI THERE!');
end.
```

Make certain that your status line indicates *Insert*; then start typing this program exactly as it appears above. When you get to the end of a line, press the Return key. If you realize you've made a typing mistake immediately after pressing a key, simply backspace and type the correct letter. Once the entire program is entered, carefully proofread it. If there are any errors, use the cursor movement commands described below in the Editing Commands box to move the cursor to the desired location and correct the error. If your computer has directional arrows (such as the arrows on the right side of the IBM Personal Computer's keyboard), these can be used instead of the cursor movement commands to move the cursor to the desired location. Let's experiment with the cursor movement commands. Try holding down the Control key and the D key (<Ctrl> <D>) at the same time. As indicated in the Editing Commands box, this will move the cursor one position to the right. <Ctrl> <S>, on the other hand, will move the cursor one position to the left. <Ctrl> <E> moves the cursor up one line; <Ctrl> <X> moves it down one line. Note the position of each of these keys on the keyboard. Their position indicates the direction in which they will cause the cursor to move. For example, S is to the left and moves the cursor to the left, while D is to the right and moves the cursor in that direction.

In addition to the cursor movement commands, the Editing Commands box contains several other types of commands. The insert and delete commands allow for easy manipulation of entire words, lines, and so forth. The block commands allow you to "mark" (that is, highlight) portions of text and then move, copy, or delete these sections. Practice using these editing commands until you understand how each one works.

Once you have determined that there are no errors in the program you have entered, you will want to terminate the editing session. This is accomplished by pressing both the K and D keys while holding down the Control key (<Ctrl> <K> <D>).

EDITING COMMANDS

Cursor Movement Commands

<Ctrl> <S>	Moves cursor one space to the left
<Ctrl> <D>	Moves cursor one space to the right
<Ctrl> <E>	Moves cursor one line up
<Ctrl> <X>	Moves cursor one line down
<Ctrl> <A>	Moves cursor to the beginning of the first word to the left
<Ctrl> <F>	Moves cursor to the beginning of the first word to the right
<Ctrl> <R>	Moves cursor up one page
<Ctrl> <C>	Moves cursor down one page
<Ctrl> <W>	Scrolls the file upward (toward the beginning)
<Ctrl> <Z>	Scrolls the file downward (toward the end)

Insert and Delete Commands

<Ctrl> <T>	Deletes the word to the right of the cursor
<Ctrl> <N>	Inserts a line break at the cursor position
<Ctrl> <Y>	Deletes the line containing the cursor
<Ctrl> <Q><Y>	Deletes all text between the current cursor position and the end of the line

Commands to Manipulate Blocks of Text

<Ctrl><K><B>	Marks the beginning of a block of text to be manipulated.
<Ctrl> <K><K>	Marks the end of a block of text to be manipulated
<Ctrl> <K><T>	Marks a single word as a block (used instead of the two commands listed above when only a single word needs to be manipulated)
<Ctrl> <K><C>	Copies a previously marked block, inserting it at the current cursor position
<Ctrl> <K><V>	Moves a previously marked block from its original position to the current cursor position
<Ctrl> <K><Y>	Deletes a currently marked block

Additional Editing Commands

<Ctrl> <K><D>	Ends the editing session, returning to main menu. This command does not save the file; the Save command must be used to store the file on disk.
<Ctrl> <Q><L>	This is known as the "regret" command. It allows you to undo a previous editing command as long as you have not left the line on which the editing was performed.

The Save Command

To save your program on your disk, press the S key. It will be saved under the name you entered in response to the Work File command.

The Compile Command

Your program can be compiled (translated into machine language) by using the Compile command. After you type the letter C, the system will compile your work file. Your screen will now look similar to the following:

```
Compiling
   5 lines

Code:        0004 paragraphs (     64 bytes), 0D24 paragraphs free
Data:        0002 paragraphs (     32 bytes), 0FDA paragraphs free
Stack/Heap: 890E paragraphs (561376 bytes)

>
```

The Run Command

By pressing R, you cause the previously compiled program to be executed. If no program has been compiled, the current work file will be both compiled and executed. Therefore, it is not necessary to use the Compile command; the Run command will compile and run your program. We can now execute the program that we just entered. After typing R, your screen should look like this:

```
Running
HI THERE!
```

The program output consists of the message HI THERE! You have now entered and executed a simple Pascal program. The Turbo system has many additional features and commands that help in entering and executing programs. You may wish to refer to the documentation that came with your Turbo Pascal compiler for explanations of additional features.

The Dir and Quit Commands

The Dir (for Directory) command displays a list of the files stored on the disk in the drive currently being accessed. When D is pressed, the following prompt appears:

`Dir mask:`

Simply press Return to get the file listing. To switch drives, enter the letter of the designated drive and a colon. For example, the response

`Dir mask:` B

will cause the files on the disk in drive B to be listed. The Quit command allows you to exit the Turbo system.

Turbo Pascal for the IBM, Version 5

Fortunately, the basic commands used in editing and running a program using Version 5 of Turbo Pascal are virtually the same as in Version 4. Therefore, refer to Chapter 2 for instructions on entering and executing programs. In this appendix, we will discuss several extensions provided by Version 5.

An important difference between Version 5 and Version 4 is the manner in which output is displayed. After a WRITELN statement is executed using Version 4, the output is displayed on the screen. The user can then press any key to return to the Edit window. However, in Version 5, the output simply "flashes" on the screen for a second before control is returned to the Edit window. To avoid this problem, insert a READLN statement after the final WRITELN statement. For example, the program from Figure 4 in Chapter 8 could be altered as follows:

```
PROGRAM FACTORIAL;

{ THIS PROGRAM CALCULATES THE FACTORIAL OF A
  POSITIVE INTEGER. }

VAR
   NUMBER, TEMP : INTEGER;
   FACT         : LONGINT;

BEGIN    { FACTORIAL }

   WRITE ('WHAT IS THE INTEGER? ');
   READLN (NUMBER);
   TEMP := NUMBER;

   { IF NUMBER = 1, FACTORIAL = 1. }
   IF NUMBER = 1
      THEN FACT := 1
      ELSE
      { LOOP TO CALCULATE FACTORIAL. }
      BEGIN
```

```
       FACT := NUMBER;
       REPEAT
          NUMBER := NUMBER - 1;
          FACT := FACT * NUMBER
       UNTIL NUMBER = 1;
    END;    { ELSE }

  WRITELN (TEMP, '! = ', FACT);
  READLN;

END.    { FACTORIAL }
```

A READLN statement has been added before the final END. Now, after the program output is displayed, the user must press <Enter> to return to the Edit window.

To access the compiler when using Version 5, place the compiler disk in drive A and enter the command:

```
A>TURBO
```

If you are using a hard disk, use the change directory (CD) command to access the directory containing the compiler and enter the following:

```
C>TURBO
```

The screen appears as follows:

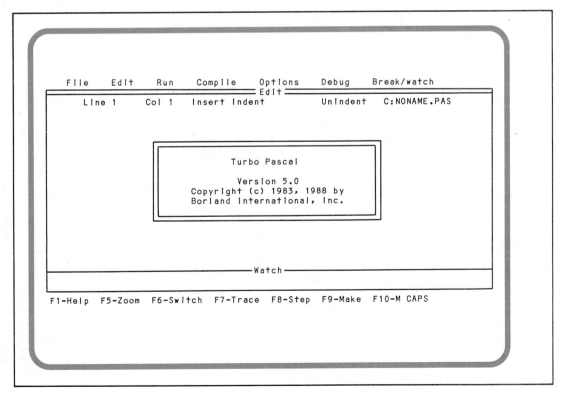

```
 File     Edit     Run     Compile     Options     Debug     Break/watch
                                    = Edit =
    Line 1        Col 1     Insert Indent            UnIndent     C:NONAME.PAS



                             Turbo Pascal

                             Version 5.0
                        Copyright (c) 1983, 1988 by
                        Borland International, Inc.




                              = Watch =

 F1-Help  F5-Zoom  F6-Switch  F7-Trace  F8-Step  F9-Make  F10-M CAPS
```

Press <Enter> to remove the box containing information on the compiler. The first five menu selections (File, Edit, Run, Compile, and Options) are the same as in Version 4 and are discussed in Chapter 2. However, the last two, Debug and Break/watch, are new. These two selections are used with the integrated debugger provided with Version 5. This debugger is very helpful when tracing through a program to locate errors. It allows the programmer to stop program execution at desired points and display the values of specified variables. The programmer can pinpoint where the program is obtaining incorrect results.

Let's use the factorial program in Chapter 8, Figure 4, to demonstrate how the integrated debugger works. Type in this program as shown below:

```
{$D+,L+}

PROGRAM FACTORIAL;

{ THIS PROGRAM CALCULATES THE FACTORIAL OF A
  POSITIVE INTEGER. }

VAR
   NUMBER, TEMP : INTEGER;
   FACT         : LONGINT;

BEGIN   { FACTORIAL }

   WRITE ('WHAT IS THE INTEGER? ');
   READLN (NUMBER);
   TEMP := NUMBER;

   { IF NUMBER = 1, FACTORIAL = 1. }
   IF NUMBER = 1
      THEN FACT := 1
      ELSE
      { LOOP TO CALCULATE FACTORIAL. }
      BEGIN
         FACT := NUMBER;
         REPEAT
            NUMBER := NUMBER - 1;
            FACT := FACT * NUMBER
         UNTIL NUMBER = 1;
      END;   { ELSE }

   WRITELN (TEMP, '! = ', FACT);
   READLN;

END.    { FACTORIAL }
```

Notice the two compiler directives at the top of the program:

`{$D+,L+}`

These directives tell the compiler that we are using the integrated debugger. Now, press the <F7> key. The statement "BEGIN {FACTORIAL}" will be highlighted. This highlighting indicates that every statement *above* the BEGIN has been executed. Press <F7> again, and the WRITE statement is highlighted. Continue pressing <F7> until the statement "TEMP := NUMBER;" is highlighted. At this point you are prompted to enter the number. You may wonder why this prompt didn't appear when the READLN was highlighted. Remember that the highlighting indicates the *next* statement to be executed, not the current one. Type in the number 6 and press <Enter>. Control will return to the Edit window. Continue pressing <F7>. Notice that the REPEAT/UNTIL loop is repeated 6 times. Finally, execution continues to the WRITELN statement, and the output is displayed. Press <Enter> to return to the Edit window.

Now, let's practice tracing the values of the two variables, NUMBER and FACT, while stepping through this program. First, we must indicate to the compiler that we want to trace these variables. Move the cursor so that it is below the variable NUMBER in the declaration section and press <Ctrl><F7>. The screen appears as follows:

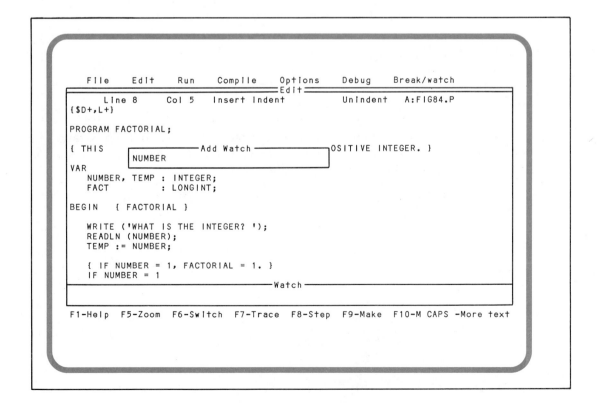

The Add Watch window allows you to specify the variables to be traced. Press <Enter> to indicate that you wish to trace NUMBER. Place the cursor below FACT and press <Ctrl><F7> again. Notice that FACT now appears in the Add Watch window. After pressing <Enter>, you are ready to step through the program. The values of NUMBER and FACT will be displayed in the Watch window at the bottom of the screen. Press <F7> to highlight BEGIN. No values have yet been assigned to NUMBER and FACT; therefore, the values displayed in the Watch window depend on any previous values assigned to those storage locations. After the statement READLN (NUMBER) is executed, the value entered for NUMBER appears below. Enter a 6 for the value of NUMBER. Continue pressing <F7> to step through the program. After the first repetition of the REPEAT/UNTIL loop, the Watch window looks like this:

```
┌──────────────────────────Watch──────────────────────────┐
│ ┌──────────────────────────────────────────────────────┐ │
│ │ FACT: 30                                             │ │
│ │  NUMBER: 5                                           │ │
│ └──────────────────────────────────────────────────────┘ │
└──────────────────────────────────────────────────────────┘
```

```
┌──────────────────────────Watch──────────────────────────┐
│ ┌──────────────────────────────────────────────────────┐ │
│ │ FACT: 720                                            │ │
│ │  NUMBER: 1                                           │ │
│ └──────────────────────────────────────────────────────┘ │
└──────────────────────────────────────────────────────────┘
```

As you can see, the integrated debugger is extremely useful in determining the values of variables at specified points in the program. The programmer can compare the actual values to the expected values and quickly pinpoint logic errors in a program.

APPENDIX J

Turbo Pascal for the Macintosh

In this appendix, we will assume you are using a Macintosh with two floppy disk drives. Place the system disk in one drive and turn on the computer. Place the Turbo Pascal disk in the other drive. The Turbo Pascal window contains an "icon" of a hand waving a checkered flag. This icon represents the Turbo Pascal compiler. Use the mouse to move the pointer so that it is on the icon and "double click" (click twice rapidly) the mouse button. The screen now looks like this:

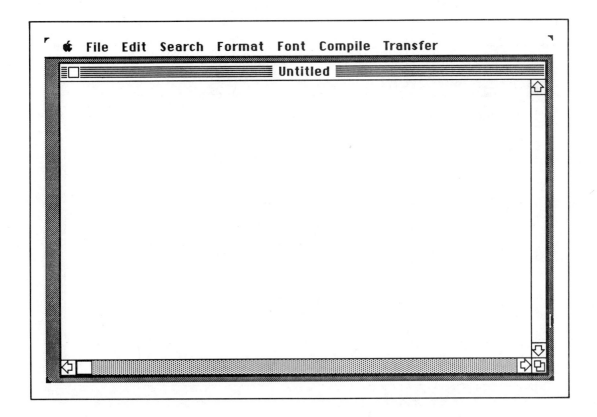

The blinking vertical line near the top of the screen is the cursor and indicates where typing will appear. Practice typing in the following program:

```
PROGRAM GREETING;

BEGIN
    WRITELN ('HI THERE!');
    READLN;
END.
```

Press the Return key at the end of each line. If you enter an incorrect letter, use the Backspace key to delete your mistake. If you wish to alter a previous line, use the mouse to move the cursor to the desired location.

After the program is entered, it can be executed. Use the mouse to select the Compile menu. Hold the mouse button down to display the menu:

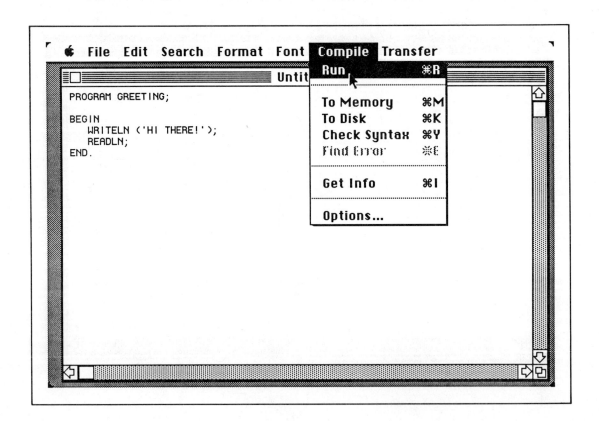

Move the pointer down to Run, and release the mouse button. The output of the program will be displayed:

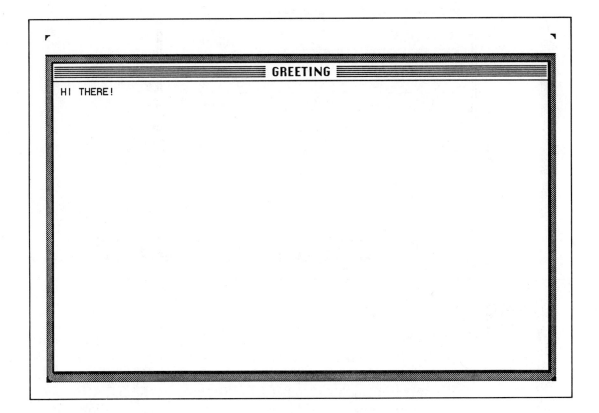

The READLN statement makes it necessary to press the Return key to return to the main menu. Try running this program without the READLN statement; the output will flash on the screen for a second before the system returns to the main menu. This is one difference between Macintosh Turbo Pascal and the IBM Version. Therefore, when running the programs in this book, you will need to remember to insert a READLN statement after program output.

To save a program on disk, select the File menu and choose the Save option. The following appears:

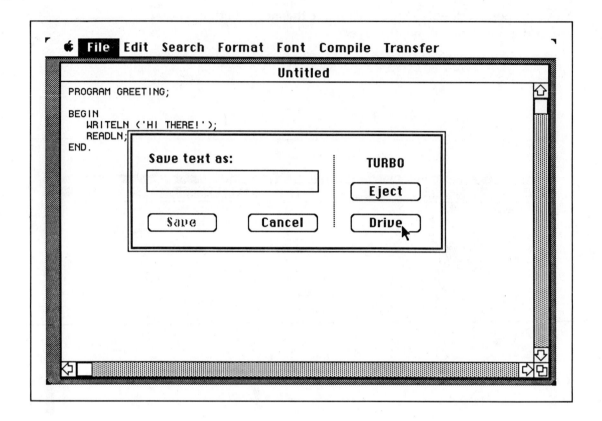

The heading on the right side indicates the disk that is currently being accessed. If you wish to save the file on the disk in the other drive, click on the Drive option. Next, enter the name under which you want the program saved. In this example, name the program FIRST. After pressing the Return key, you will hear the disk drive whir, indicating that the program is being saved on disk.

To load a program into main memory, select the Open option under the File menu. A list of files stored on the accessed disk will appear. Double click on the program that you want opened, and it will appear on the screen.

When you are done using the Turbo system, select the Quit option under the File menu. Control will be returned to the main menu. Notice that the new program named FIRST is saved as a document icon (it looks like a piece of paper) with a checkered flag on it. The checkered flag indicates that this document contains a Pascal program.

Additional information on the Macintosh Turbo Pascal compiler can be obtained by referring to the documentation that came with it.

APPENDIX K

Answers to Learning Checks

Answers to Learning Check 1-1

1. A computer program is a list of instructions that a computer can use to solve a specific problem.
2. The three basic types of tasks that computers can perform are arithmetic, making comparisons, and storage and retrieval operations.
3. The three parts of the computer system are the central processing unit, main memory, and peripheral devices.
4. The arithmetic/logic unit can perform arithmetic and make comparisons.

Answers to Learning Check 1-2

1. Peripheral devices are devices attached to the computer such as printers and disk drives.
2. Another name for secondary storage is auxiliary storage.
3. Soft copy is displayed on the screen whereas hard copy is printed in permanent form such as on paper. Soft copy is quick and easy to obtain but is not permanent. The main advantages of hard copy are that it is permanent and can be referred to anywhere.
4. Main memory is contained within the computer itself whereas secondary storage, such as floppy disks, is not a part of the computer system. When it is necessary to access a program, data, or so forth that is kept in secondary storage, it must be loaded into the computer's main memory before it can be manipulated.

Answers to Learning Check 1-3

1. Machine
2. High-level languages use English-like words in their instructions. They generally can be run on different types of computers, unlike machine language, which is specific to each type of computer. Programs in high-level languages must be translated into machine language before the computer can execute them.

3. A compiler translates an entire source program into machine language. The resulting program is called an object program, which can then be executed.

4. Pascal was a seventeenth-century mathematician and philosopher.

Answers to Learning Check 2-1

1. Developing a programming problem solution involves the following steps:

   a. Understand the problem.
   b. Develop a solution to the problem.
   c. Write the program.
   d. Type the program into a computer and run it.
   e. Correct any errors in the program.
   f. Test the program.

2. In order to understand the problem, the programmer must have a clear idea of what the output should be and what input is needed to get that output.

3. An algorithm is a sequence of steps that can be used to solve a problem.

4. Making a bed involves the following steps:

   a. Straighten the sheets.
   b. Pull up and straighten the blankets.
   c. Fluff the pillows.
   d. Place the pillows at the top of the bed.
   e. Arrange the bedspread over the blankets and pillows.

Answers to Learning Check 2-2

1. Structured programming languages allow programs to be easily divided into subsections (subprograms) and allow the programmer to efficiently control the order in which statements are executed.

2. A flowchart graphically depicts a solution to a programming problem whereas pseudocode uses a narrative description to explain the logic.

3.

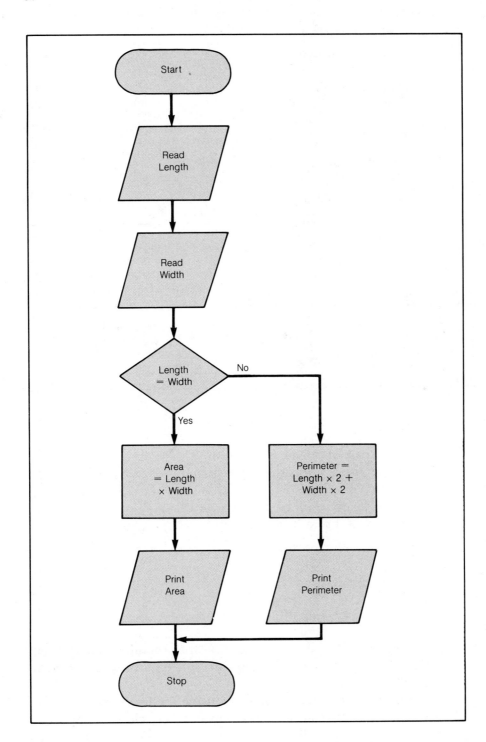

4. Top-down design could be used to depict writing a term paper by dividing the job into smaller subtasks. The list could look like this:

   a. Choose topic.
   b. Do basic research.
   c. Create general outline.
   d. Do more detailed research.
   e. Write detailed outline.
   f. Write paper.
   g. Type paper in final form.

The structure chart might look like this:

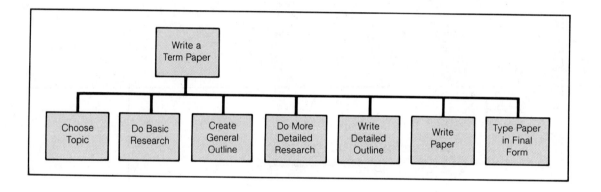

5. a. Subtract cost of movie, $3.50, from $20.00.
   b. Subtract cost of popcorn from remainder of part a.
   c. Cost of books equals $4.50 × 2.
   d. Add 6% tax to result of part c.
   e. Subtract result of d from result of b.

Answers to Learning Check 2–3

1. The purpose of the File menu is to allow the programmer to manipulate files, such as loading them from disk into main memory or creating a new file.
2. A program can be saved on disk by using the function key F2. An alternate way is to select the File menu and then select the Save command. The system will then prompt you to enter the name under which the file should be saved.

```
3. PROGRAM GREETING;

   BEGIN

       WRITELN ('MATTHEW HEINZ');

   END.
```

Answers to Learning Check 3-1

1. A variable is similar to a post office box because both consist of storage locations, each of which has a label to distinguish it from other boxes. However, a post office box can contain many pieces of mail, but a storage location can only contain a single value at a time.

2. a. Yes   f. No
   b. No   g. No
   c. Yes   h. No
   d. Yes   i. Yes
   e. No   j. Yes

3. TOP_10   Top_10   tOP_10   toP_10   ToP_10

4. The value of a variable may change during program execution whereas the value of a constant may not.

Answers to Learning Check 3-2

1. a. BOOLEAN   g. STRING
   b. REAL   h. STRING
   c. INTEGER   i. BOOLEAN
   d. CHAR   j. CHAR
   e. STRING   k. INTEGER
   f. REAL

2. a. Yes   d. Yes
   b. No   e. No
   c. Yes   f. No

3. The data type STRING can contain many character values whereas CHAR can contain only one character value.

Answers to Learning Check 3-3

1. a. Yes   d. No
   b. No   e. Yes
   c. No   f. No

```
2. VAR
      GALLON, DISTANCE, TIME : REAL;
      COUNT : INTEGER;
```

3. a. Incorrect
   b. Incorrect
   c. Correct (STRING)
   d. Correct (BOOLEAN)

Answers to Learning Check 3-4

1. Comments are used to explain a program to humans.
2. Comments can be indicated by braces { like this } or parentheses and asterisks (* like this *).
3. Semicolons are used to separate statements. Because BEGIN is not a statement, it is not followed by a semicolon.

Answers to Learning Check 4-1

1. The WRITE and WRITELN statements are commonly used to display prompts and program results.
2. The purpose of using a prompt is to indicate to the user that data is to be entered at the keyboard. It should tell the user the type of data that the program needs.
3. A literal is a value that represents only itself.

   Integer literal: 104
   Real number literal: 104.54
   Character string literal: 'Iowa City'

4. JON BAUMANN
   AGE : 15GRADE : 9SCHOOL : CITY HIGH

Answers to Learning Check 4-2

1. The READ and READLN statements allow data to be entered to a program. The READLN causes the cursor to advance to the beginning of the next line whereas the READ statement does not.
2. A prompt is always followed by a READ or READLN statement because one of these statements is needed to read the value entered by the user.

3. a. X = 44, Y = 60, Z = 99
   b. X = 44, Y = 60, Z = 13

c. X = 44, Y = 13, Z = 87
d. X = 44, Y = 13, Z = 94

Answers to Learning Check 4-3

1. a. −28.4
   b. −28.38
   c. ¢¢¢−28.38
   d. −283765
2. WRITELN (I1:6, I2:6, I3:6, I4:6, I5:6, I6:6, I7:6, I8:6);
3. When output is right justified, the last value displayed is placed in the last position of the output field. Any blanks in the output field are on the left side.

Answers to Learning Check 5-1

1. a. Invalid
   b. Valid
   c. Valid
   d. Invalid

2. The statement PLANT := 'TREE' will assign the character string TREE to the variable plant whereas the statement PLANT :=TREE assigns the current value of the variable TREE (which is MAPLE) to PLANT.
3. SCORE = 6, NUM = 22, TOTAL = 28, and GRADE = 'A'

Answers to Learning Check 5-2

1. a. NUM1 := (B−A) * 2; The value of number will be −24.0.
   b. NUM2 := (C/B) / 2; The value of NUM2 will be 4.5.
   c. A := (A+C) / B; The value of A will be 14.
   d. NUM1 := (C−B) * (C−B); The value of NUM1 will be 576.

2. a. 1   d. 240
   b. 10.7   e. 19.5
   c. 22   f. 1.75

Answers to Learning Check 5-3

1. a. False   d. True   g. False
   b. True   e. True
   c. True   f. False

2. In an IF/THEN statement, the THEN portion is executed if the condition is true, otherwise nothing is done. In an IF/THEN/ELSE statement, the THEN portion is executed if the condition is true, otherwise the ELSE portion is executed.

```
IF NUMBER > 0
   THEN WRITELN (NUMBER);

IF NUMBER > 0
   THEN WRITELN (NUMBER)
   ELSE WRITELN ('INVALID ENTRY.');
```

3. a. KEEP LOOKING
   b. (Nothing will be output.)
   c. THERE ARE ENOUGH.

Answers to Learning Check 6-1

```
1. PROGRAM SEWING;

   { THIS PROGRAM TELLS HOME ECONOMICS STUDENTS HOW MUCH FABRIC
     THEY WILL NEED FOR THEIR SEWING PROJECT.  THE PROJECTS TAKE:
          1.   APRON - 2.0 YARDS
          2.   VEST  - 3.25 YARDS
          3.   PANTS - 3.75 YARDS  }

   VAR
      ITEM  : STRING;
      YARDS : REAL;

   BEGIN   { SEWING }

      WRITE ('WHICH PROJECT ARE YOU MAKING, AN APRON, A VEST,
      OR PANTS? ');
      READLN (ITEM);

      { CALCULATE AMOUNT OF FABRIC NEEDED FOR THE ITEM. }
      IF ITEM = 'APRON'
         THEN
         BEGIN
            YARDS := 2.0;
            WRITELN ('YOU WILL NEED ', YARDS:7:2,
               ' YARDS OF FABRIC FOR YOUR APRON.');
         END
```

```
ELSE IF ITEM = 'VEST'
        THEN
        BEGIN
            YARDS := 3.25;
            WRITELN ('YOU WILL NEED ', YARDS:7:2,
                        ' YARDS OF FABRIC FOR YOUR VEST.');
        END    { ELSE }
        ELSE
        BEGIN
            YARDS := 3.75;
            WRITELN ('YOU WILL NEED ', YARDS:7:2,
                        ' YARDS OF FABRIC FOR YOUR PANTS.');
        END;

END.   { SEWING }
```

2. The compiler recognizes compound statements because they start with a BEGIN and conclude with an END.

3. Nesting IF/THEN/ELSE statements allows the programmer to check for multiple conditions.

4.
```
IF LETTER = 'A'
    THEN
    BEGIN
        VOWELS := VOWELS + 1;
        CONT := TRUE;
        WRITELN ('THIS LETTER IS A VOWEL.');
    END;   { THEN }
```

Answers to Learning Check 6-2

1. A BOOLEAN operator is an operator that is used with BOOLEAN expressions. The resulting expression evaluates as true or false. The BOOLEAN operators are NOT, AND, OR, and XOR.

2. An infinite loop is a loop that never stops executing (that is, it continues executing until the computer's resources are used up).

3. a. False
   b. True
   c. True

4.
```
COUNT := 5;
WHILE COUNT <= 100 DO
BEGIN
    WRITE (COUNT :3);
    COUNT := COUNT + 5;
END;   { WHILE }
```

Answers to Learning Check 7-1

1. WRITELN, READLN, VAL, and STR are a few examples of standard procedures.
2. PR_TABLE (14, 2.80, 0.04, TOTAL_COST);
   PR_TABLE (QUANTITY, 14.50, TAX, 100.00);
   PR_TABLE (10+6, 1.00, 0.06, 250.00);
3. a. Valid
   b. Valid
   c. Invalid
   d. Invalid
4. The value entered can be read to a character variable. Then the VAL procedure can convert it to an integer value so that it can be used in arithmetic operations.

Answers to Learning Check 7-2

1. A variable parameter is indicated by placing the reserved identifier VAR in front of that parameter in the formal parameter list.
2. HIGH, LOW, AVERAGE—global
   SCORE, COUNT, TOTAL—PROCEDURE READ_AND_-CALCULATE
   The scope of procedure READ_AND_CALCULATE is the main program.
3. R1 = 66.0, R2 = 86.73, I1 = 66, I2 = 0

Answers to Learning Check 8-1

1. Three ways of controlling a loop are (1) creating a counting loop in which a loop control variable is incremented a set amount for each repetition, (2) using a sentinel value in the input data to indicate when the loop should stop, and (3) using a BOOLEAN flag to indicate when repetition should stop.
2. A sentinel value is a value that would not occur naturally in a given set of input data. It is used to indicate the end of the input data. When it is read, the loop stops executing.
3. A BOOLEAN flag is used to control this loop.

Answers to Learning Check 8-2

1. The REPEAT/UNTIL loop executes until a specified condition becomes true. The condition is placed at the end of the loop.

2. The loop control variable is set to the starting value, incremented (or decremented) during each repetition, and compared to the stopping value. When it exceeds the stopping value, execution is terminated.

3.
```
FOR I := 100 DOWNTO 1 DO
    WRITE (I:3);
WRITELN;
```

4. The loop will execute nine times. The value of I at the end of each loop repetition will be 2, 3, 4, 5, 6, 7, 8, 9, and 10.

Answers to Learning Check 8–3

1. The CASE selector is compared to each of the labels. If it matches a label, the statement following that label is executed.

2.
```
IF CODE = 'E'
    THEN WRITELN ('ELLIPTICAL')
    ELSE IF COST = 'I'
            THEN WRITELN ('IRREGULAR')
            ELSE IF CODE = 'S'
                    THEN IF BAR = 'B'
                            THEN WRITELN ('BARRED SPIRAL')
                            ELSE WRITELN ('NORMAL SPIRAL');
```

3.
```
CASE CODE OF
    'R' : COLOR := 'Red';
    'G' : COLOR := 'Green';
    'B' : COLOR := 'Brown';
    'O' : COLOR := 'Orange';
    'W' : COLOR := 'White';
    'P' : COLOR := 'Purple';
    'Y' : COLOR := 'Yellow';
END;    { CASE }
```

Answers to Learning Check 9–1

1. Good program style consists of features such as indentation, documentation, and spacing that make a program more readable for humans.
2. Programs with good style are well documented; use blank spaces, indentation, and so forth to make them more readable; and use descriptive identifiers.
3. Control statements are indented so they stand out from the rest of the program, making them more readable.

Answers to Learning Check 9-2

1. It contains a syntax error.
2. The variable STR_CODE was declared to be of type CHAR so that the user's input could be read to it and the program would not crash if a noninteger value was entered. Then STR_CODE was converted to an integer value.
3. Stubs are used to represent those procedures not yet implemented. The main program is written, and procedures are gradually added and tested. This allows the program to be expanded in a controlled fashion.
4. Desk checking is the process of manually tracing through a program checking for syntax and logic errors. The programmer is "playing computer."

Answers to Learning Check 10-1

1. A procedure is designed to perform a specific task and can return any number of values to the calling program by using variable parameters. A function, on the other hand, is designed to determine and return a single value.

2. a. 250   c. 250
   b. 250   d. 156
                               e. 4

3. a. Function
   b. Function
   c. Procedure
   d. Procedure

4. a. 'X'   c. 109
   b. 14   d. 31
                               e. 'D'

Answers to Learning Check 10-2

1. a. 11   c. 1
   b. BOZEMANMONTANA   d. 0
                                 e. EM

2.
```
FUNCTION FIND_AREA (BASE, HEIGHT : REAL) : REAL;
   { RETURNS THE AREA OF A TRIANGLE. }

   BEGIN    { FIND_AREA }
      FIND_AREA := 0.5 * (BASE * HEIGHT);
   END;     { FIND_AREA }
```

3. A function heading must state the data type of the function whereas a procedure has no data type.

4. The COPY function returns a substring starting at the position indicated by the first integer value and continuing for the length specified by the second integer value.

Answers to Learning Check 11-1

1. An array is an ordered set of related data items, all of the same data type. The entire set is represented by a single variable name.

2. a. NUM_STUDENTS
   b. INTEGER
   c. A subrange of the type CHAR—'G' through 'P'
   d. 10 elements

3.

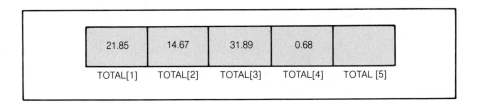

| 21.85 | 14.67 | 31.89 | 0.68 | |
| TOTAL[1] | TOTAL[2] | TOTAL[3] | TOTAL[4] | TOTAL [5] |

Answers to Learning Check 11-2

1. FOR loops are useful when reading data to arrays because the loop control variable can often double as the array subscript.

2.
```
FOR LETTER := 'B' TO 'F' DO
    READ (CODE[LETTER]);

FOR LETTER := 'B' TO 'F' DO
    WRITE (CODE[LETTER]:3);
```

3. The loop control variable POSITION must be of type CHAR or a subrange of type CHAR. The FOR loop should be stated

   FOR POSITION := 'D' TO 'G' DO

   The statement

   READ (VALUE_TYPE[POSITION]);

   should be

   READ (VALUES[POSITION]);

Answers to Learning Check 11-3

1. In a two-dimensional array, the first subscript refers to the row and the second subscript refers to the column.

2. a. 11   c. 45
   b. 36   d. 40

3. The statement

   IF CITY[POSITION]>CITY[POSITION+1]

   would need to be changed to

   IF CITY[POSITION]<CITY[POSITION+1]

Answers to Learning Check 12-1

1. A record is a structured data type that contains a group of related data items, not necessarily of the same data type.

2.
```
PLAYER = RECORD
            NAME     : STRING;
            AGE      : INTEGER;
            BAT_AVE  : REAL;
            POSITION : STRING;
         END;   { PLAYER }
```

3. a.
```
PLAYER_ARRAY : ARRAY[1..6] OF PLAYER;
```

   b.
```
FOR I := 1 TO 6 DO
  BEGIN
     WRITE ('ENTER THE NEXT NAME: ');
     READLN (PLAYER_ARRAY[I].NAME);
  END;   { FOR }
```


Answers to Learning Check 12-2

1. A set is a structured data type that is made up of a collection of values that are of the same data type and are classed together.

2. a.
```
VAR
    WEEKDAYS : DAYS;

BEGIN
    WEEKDAYS := [1, 2, 3, 4, 5];
```

   b.
```
VAR
    ODD : WHOLE;
```

```
    BEGIN
        ODD := [1, 3, 5, 7, 9, 11, 13, 15, 17, 19];

  c. VAR
        MULTTWO : WHOLE;

    BEGIN
        MULTTWO := [2, 4, 6, 8, 10, 12, 14, 16, 18, 20];
```

3. a. COMBINE = ['A', 'E','I', 'O', 'U', 'W', 'Y']
   b. TOGETHER = ['A', 'E']
   c. DIFF = ['F', 'G']
   d. FINAL = ['B', 'C']

4.
```
  TYPE
      LETTER_TYPE = SET OF 'A'..'Z';

  VAR
      VOWELS : LETTER_TYPE;
      LETTER : CHAR;

  BEGIN
      VOWELS := ['A','E','I','O','U','Y','W'];
      REPEAT
          WRITE ('ENTER A VOWEL: ');
          READLN (LETTER);
      UNTIL LETTER IN VOWELS;
```

Answers to Learning Check 13-1

1. A file is a sequence of components that are all of the same data type. Files are kept in secondary storage.
2. One disadvantage of using files is that file components take longer to access than data stored in the computer's main memory.
3. Files are unlimited in size because it is easy to expand the amount of secondary storage needed. They can be permanently saved and accessed again by a different (or the same) program. In addition, they use only the amount of secondary storage that they currently need.
4. The length of a file is the number of components that it contains.

Answers to Learning Check 13-2

1. A text file is a file in which each component consists of a single character value.

2. VAR
```
    CITIES : TEXT;

BEGIN
    ASSIGN (CITIES, 'CITIES.P');
    RESET (CITIES);
```
3. One file cannot be copied to another file by using a single assignment statement. They must be copied a component at a time.
4. The EOLN function checks for the end of an input line. When it is encountered, EOLN becomes true, otherwise it is false.

Answers to Learning Check 13-3

1. Files can be updated by appending new values to the end of the file or by updating an already existing component.
2. The SEEK procedure is used to access a particular file component so that it can be updated.
3. LENGTH := FILESIZE (DIGITS);
   SEEK # (DIGITS, # LENGTH);
   WRITE (DIGITS, 14);

Answers to Learning Check 14-1

1. GRAPHMODE
2. The turtle's home position is at the center of the screen (0, 0), facing North. The HOME or CLEARSCREEN statements will place the turtle here.
3. a. HOME;
```
       TURNLEFT (90);
       FORWD (20);
```
   b. SETPOSITION (20,0);
```
       TURNRIGHT (90);
       FORWD (30);
```
   c. SETPOSITION (0,-30);
```
       FORWD (40);
```

Answers to Learning Check 14-2

1. PROCEDURE DRAW_CIRCLE;
   { THIS PROCEDURE DRAWS A CIRCLE WHOSE CENTER IS AT (40,0);

   ```
   VAR
       POSITION : INTEGER;

   BEGIN    { DRAW_CIRCLE }

       SETPOSITION (40,0);
       PENDOWN;

       FOR POSITION := 1 TO 180 DO
       BEGIN
           FORWD (2);
           TURNRIGHT (2);
       END;    { FOR }

   END;    { DRAW_CIRCLE }
   ```

2. The TURTLEWINDOW statement allows the programmer to specify that only a portion of the output window should be displayed.

3. PALETTE (2);
   SETPENCOLOR(1);

4. GRAPHBACKGROUND (5);

Glossary

Actual parameter A value that is passed to a procedure when it is called, and is manipulated by that procedure. It is substituted for its corresponding formal parameter.

Algorithm A sequence of steps used to solve a problem.

Argument See **Actual parameter.**

Arithmetic/logic unit (ALU) The part of the CPU that performs arithmetic and logic operations.

Arithmetic operator A symbol that stands for an arithmetic process, such as addition or subtraction.

Array An ordered set of related data items, all of the same data type.

Assignment statement A statement that allows a value to be stored in a variable.

Auxiliary storage See **Secondary storage.**

BOOLEAN operator An operator used with BOOLEAN expressions; the resulting BOOLEAN expression evaluates as either true or false. In Turbo Pascal, the BOOLEAN operators are NOT, AND, OR, and XOR.

Built-in procedure See **Standard procedure.**

Central processing unit (CPU) The part of the computer that does the work. The CPU also directs the order in which operations are performed. It consists of two components: the control unit and the arithmetic/logic unit.

Character string A group of characters placed within single quotation marks. A character string can contain any character (including letters, digits, special characters, blanks, and so forth) that the computer system can represent.

Collating sequence The internal ordering that the computer assigns to the characters it is able to recognize. This ordering allows the computer to make comparisons between different character values.

Comment Statements in a program that explain to humans what is being done in the program. They are enclosed { like this } or (* like this *).

Compiler A program that translates an entire source program into machine language. The resulting program is the object program.

Compound statement A statement contained within a BEGIN-END pair; it consists of a number of statements.

Computer programmer A person who writes instructions for the computer to use to solve a problem.

Constant A value that does not change during program execution. Identifiers are used to name constants so that the programmer can refer to them by name.

Control statement A statement that allows the programmer to determine whether a statement (or a group of statements) will be executed and how many times.

Control unit The part of the CPU that determines the order in which computer operations will be performed.

Counting loop A loop executed a stated number of times. The number of repetitions to be executed must be determined before the loop is entered.

Data Facts that the computer uses to obtain results.

Decimal notation A method of representing a real number in which the whole part of the number is placed before the decimal point and the fractional part after the decimal point; for example, −45.67.

Decision statement A statement that determines whether a specified portion of a program will be executed depending on whether a stated condition evaluates as true.

Decision step A step in solving a problem in which a comparison is made. The action that will be taken next depends on the result of that comparison.

Desk check To trace through a program by hand in an attempt to locate any errors.

Double-alternative decision step A decision step in which an action is taken only if the comparison in the decision step is true. A different action is taken if the comparison is false.

Driver program A program whose primary purpose is to call procedures.

Element An individual value in an array. An array element is accessed by using the array name with a subscript.

Enumerated data type An ordinal data type defined by the programmer. Every possible value of that type must be listed in the definition.

Exponential notation A method of representing a real number by using powers of 10. For example, 63410.0 would be represented in exponential notation as 6.3410000000E+04.

Expression Any valid combination of variables, constants, operators, and parentheses.

Field A data item that is part of a record. Fields may be of any data type.

Field width parameter An integer value used to determine the size of the field in which output will be placed.

File A sequence of components, all of the same data type, kept in secondary storage.

File pointer An imaginary pointer indicating which file component is currently being accessed.

Flag A BOOLEAN variable used to indicate whether a loop should be repeated.

Flowchart A method of visually representing the steps in solving a problem.

Formal parameter An identifier listed in a procedure heading that represents a value to be passed to the procedure by the calling program through an actual parameter.

Function A subprogram used to determine and return a single value to the calling program.

Function designator An expression that includes the function's name and actual parameters; it is used to call a function.

Global variable A variable that is declared in the declaration section of a main program. It may be referred to anywhere in that program.

Graphic mode A mode in which illustrations can be displayed on the screen. The screen is divided into a grid of pixels that can be turned off and on.

Hard copy Output that is printed on paper.

Hardware The physical components of the computer system.

High-level language Any programming language using English-like statements that must be translated into machine language before execution.

Identifier A name chosen by the programmer to name an object in the program. Identifiers must start with a letter and may contain any combination of letters, numbers, or the underscore.

Infinite loop A loop that will execute indefinitely. This occurs because the condition controlling loop execution never reaches the state necessary for the loop to stop executing.

Information Data that is processed so that it is meaningful to the user.

Input Data that is submitted to the computer so that the computer can process it.

Input variable A variable whose value is entered into the computer and used to obtain the needed results.

Integer A positive or negative whole number.

Literal An expression consisting of numbers, letters, and other characters or any combination of the three; it represents only those characters and is not a symbol for any other value.

Local variable   A variable that is declared in a procedure. It is undefined outside of that procedure.

Logic error   A flaw in a program's algorithm.

Loop   A structure that allows a given section of a program to be executed as many times as necessary.

Loop control variable (lcv)   A variable used to control how many times a loop will be executed. It is incremented (or decremented) each time the loop is executed.

Machine language   The only type of instructions that the computer can execute directly. It consists of series of 1s and 0s that represent on and off electrical states. Machine language is different for each type of central processing unit.

Main memory   The storage area where the computer keeps programs, data, and processing results.

Module   See **Subprogram.**

Nested statement   A control statement placed inside another control statement.

Object program   The program that results when a compiler translates a source program into machine language.

Operand   A value on which an operation is performed.

Operator   A symbol that stands for a process such as multiplication or assigning a value to a variable.

Order of operations   The rules that determine the order in which arithmetic operations will be performed.

Ordinal data type   A data type in which each possible value (except the first) has a unique predecessor, and each possible value (except the last) has a unique successor.

Output   Results the computer obtains after processing input.

Output variable   A variable that contains the results of processing.

Peripheral device   A device, such as a monitor screen or a printer, that is attached to the computer. Many peripheral devices are used to input and output programs, data, and program results.

Pixel   A block of light that can be turned on or off to create images. When in graphics mode, the entire screen is divided into a grid of pixels.

Priming read   A READ statement used to initialize the loop control variable before entering a loop.

Procedure   A subprogram that is used to perform a specific task. Procedures allow programs to be divided into subparts.

Procedure call   A statement that causes a procedure to be executed.

Program   A list of instructions written by a programmer that the computer can use to solve a specific problem.

Program documentation   Comments placed in a program that explain it to humans.

Program style   A way of writing a program to make it easier for humans to understand.

Program tracing   The process of printing the values of variables at various points in a program in order to locate program errors.

Programmer   See **Computer programmer.**

Programming language   A language that can be used to give instructions to a computer.

Prompt   A message displayed to the user indicating the type and quantity of data that should be entered to the program.

Pseudocode   Statements written in English, not in a programming language, that give a narrative description of the solution to a programming problem.

Real number   A number with a decimal portion.

Record   A structured data type containing a group of related data items (fields) not necessarily of the same data type, but combined in a single unit.

Relational operator   An operator that compares one operand with another.

Reserved word   A word that has a specific meaning to the compiler and cannot be used as an identifier.

Right justified   A process in which output is placed so the last character is at the right margin of the output field. If necessary, blanks are placed on the left so that the field will be filled.

Run-time error An error that causes abnormal program behavior during execution.

Scope block That portion of a program in which a specific identifier is defined.

Secondary storage Storage such as floppy diskettes or magnetic tape that is not a part of main memory. Programs and data can be kept on secondary storage and then copied into main memory when they are needed.

Sentinel value A special data value used to mark the end of input data.

Sequential search The process of locating a target item within a list of items starting at the beginning of the list and examining each item until the target is found or the end of the list is reached.

Set A structured data type consisting of a collection of values classed together. All the values must be of the same type.

Single-alternative decision step A decision step in which a subsequent action is taken only if the comparison made in the decision step is true. If the comparison is false, nothing is done.

Soft copy Output displayed on the monitor screen.

Software A computer program.

Sort To organize data items in a particular order such as arranging a list of numbers from smallest to largest.

Source program The program that is submitted to a compiler to be translated into machine language so that the computer is able to execute it.

Standard procedure A procedure that is "built in" to the Turbo Pascal compiler. To use the procedure, the programmer simply includes its name in a procedure call.

Structured data type A data type composed of many components. The entire data type may be referred to as a single unit. The structured data types are arrays, records, sets, and files.

Structured programming language A programming language that allows a large problem to be methodically divided into smaller subparts. It also allows the programmer to efficiently control the order in which program statements are executed.

Stub A procedure declaration that contains only a heading, a BEGIN-END pair, and possibly a WRITELN statement indicating that the procedure was called. It is used to test the calling program.

Subprogram A part of a larger program that performs a specific task.

Subrange data type A data type defined by the programmer and containing a portion of an ordinal data type.

Subscript A value enclosed in brackets used to refer to a particular array element; for example, NAME[3].

Syntax error A violation of the grammatical rules of a language.

Syntax rules Rules that explain how the parts of a language should be put together.

Text mode The mode in which text is displayed on the screen.

Top-down design A method of designing computer programs in which a large problem is broken down into smaller and smaller subparts that are easier to solve than the one large problem.

User-defined procedure A procedure that the programmer writes to perform a specific task.

User-friendly A characteristic of a program that is written in a way that makes it as easy and enjoyable as possible for people to use.

Value parameter A parameter whose value is passed to the procedure, but any changes made to the parameter are not passed back to the calling program.

Variable A storage location the value of which may change during program execution. Identifiers are used to name variables so that the programmer can refer to them by this name.

Variable parameter A parameter whose value is passed to a procedure and is also passed back to the calling program. It must be preceded by the reserved identifier VAR in the formal parameter list.

Index